RADICAL TRADITIONS

THEOLOGY IN A POSTCRITICAL KEY

SERIES EDITORS

*Stanley M. Hauerwas, Duke University,
and Peter Ochs, University of Virginia*

RADICAL TRADITIONS cuts new lines of inquiry across a confused array of debates concerning the place of theology in modernity and, more generally, the status and role of scriptural faith in contemporary life. Charged with a rejuvenated confidence, spawned in part by the rediscovery of reason as inescapably tradition constituted, a new generation of theologians and religious scholars is returning to scriptural traditions with the hope of retrieving resources long ignored, depreciated, and in many cases ideologically suppressed by modern habits of thought. RADICAL TRADITIONS assembles a promising matrix of strategies, disciplines, and lines of thought that invites Jewish, Christian, and Islamic theologians back to the word, recovering and articulating modes of scriptural reasoning as that which always underlies modernist reasoning and therefore has the capacity — and authority — to correct it.

Far from despairing over modernity's failings, postcritical theologies rediscover resources for renewal and self-correction within the disciplines of academic study themselves. Postcritical theologies open up the possibility of participating once again in the living relationship that binds together God, text, and community of interpretation. RADICAL TRADITIONS thus advocates a "return to the text," which means a commitment to displaying the richness and wisdom of traditions that are at once text based, hermeneutical, and oriented to communal practice.

Books in this series offer the opportunity to speak openly with practitioners of other faiths or even with those who profess no (or limited) faith, both academics and nonacademics, about the ways religious traditions address pivotal issues of the day. Unfettered by foundationalist preoccupations, these books represent a call for new paradigms of reason — a thinking and rationality that are more responsive than originative. By embracing a postcritical posture, they are able to speak unapologetically out of scriptural traditions manifest in the practices of believing communities (Jewish, Christian, and others); articulate those practices through disciplines of philosophic, textual, and cultural criticism; and engage intellectual, social, and political practices that for too long have been insulated from theological evaluation. RADICAL TRADITIONS is radical not only in its confidence in non-apologetic theological speech but also in how the practice of such speech challenges the current social and political arrangements of modernity.

RADICAL TRADITIONS

Published Volumes

James J. Buckley and George A. Lindbeck, eds.,
The Church in a Postliberal Age

Jason Byassee, *Praise Seeking Understanding:
An Augustinian Defense of Christological Reading of the Old Testament*

Peter M. Candler Jr.,
*Theology, Rhetoric, Manuduction,
or Reading Scripture Together on the Path to God*

David Weiss Halivni,
Revelation Restored: Divine Writ and Critical Responses

Stanley M. Hauerwas, *Wilderness Wanderings*

P. Travis Kroeker and Bruce K. Ward,
Remembering the End: Dostoevsky as Prophet to Modernity

David Novak, *Talking with Christians: Musings of a Jewish Theologian*

Peter Ochs and Nancy Levene, eds., *Textual Reasonings:
Jewish Philosophy and Text Study at the End of the Twentieth Century*

Randi Rashkover and Martin Kavka, eds.,
Tradition in the Public Square: A David Novak Reader

Randi Rashkover and C. C. Pecknold, eds.,
Liturgy, Time, and the Politics of Redemption

Eugene F. Rogers Jr., *After the Spirit:
A Constructive Pneumatology from Resources outside the Modern West*

J. Alexander Sider, *To See History Doxologically:
History and Holiness in John Howard Yoder's Ecclesiology*

David Toole, *Waiting for Godot in Sarajevo*

Bruce Ward, *Redeeming the Enlightenment: Christianity and the Liberal Virtues*

Michael Wyschogrod,
Abraham's Promise: Judaism and Jewish-Christian Relations

John Howard Yoder, *The Jewish-Christian Schism Revisited*

To See History Doxologically

*History and Holiness in
John Howard Yoder's Ecclesiology*

J. Alexander Sider

WILLIAM B. EERDMANS PUBLISHING COMPANY
GRAND RAPIDS, MICHIGAN / CAMBRIDGE, U.K.

© 2011 J. Alexander Sider
All rights reserved

Published 2011 by
Wm. B. Eerdmans Publishing Co.
2140 Oak Industrial Drive N.E., Grand Rapids, Michigan 49505 /
P.O. Box 163, Cambridge CB3 9PU U.K.

Printed in the United States of America

17 16 15 14 13 12 11   7 6 5 4 3 2 1

Library of Congress Cataloging-in-Publication Data

Sider, J. Alexander.
To see history doxologically: history and holiness in John Howard Yoder's ecclesiology /
J. Alexander Sider.
    p.   cm.   — (Radical traditions)
Includes bibliographical references (p.   ).
ISBN 978-0-8028-6573-1 (pbk.: alk. paper)
1. Yoder, John Howard. 2. Church. 3. Holiness — Christianity.
4. History — Religious aspects — Christianity. I. Title.

BV600.3.S54   2010
262'.72 — dc22

2010043280

www.eerdmans.com

To Carrie

Contents

ACKNOWLEDGMENTS · xi

Introduction: "Is This What the One without Spot or Wrinkle Is Really Like?" · 1

1. Salvation Is Created: Praise as Politics in Oliver O'Donovan and John Howard Yoder · 17

2. Seizing Godlikeness: Ernst Troeltsch and "Constantinian" Syntheses · 57

3. Constantinianism Before and After Nicaea: Issues in Restitutionist Historiography · 97

4. Memory in the Politics of Forgiveness · 133

5. "Love One Another": Voluntariety Transformed by Dialogical Vulnerability · 161

Conclusion: The Labor of Our Redeeming · 195

BIBLIOGRAPHY · 209

INDEX · 221

Acknowledgments

My writing records debts for which I am profoundly grateful. Reading this book, you will see many of those debts writ large. Others will be less obvious to you, but many of them are just as, if not more, important to me. In order to thank the people who made this book possible, I'd like to tell the story of how it came to be written.

    I first ran into John Howard Yoder's writing in my church's library while I was studying one evening during high school. I remember I had gotten frustrated (and hence was browsing the shelves) while trying to understand scalar components in vectors, which means I was a senior in Mrs. Harvey's physics class that year. High school physics may sound a long way off from Christian theology, but Mrs. Harvey deserves special mention here and thanks because she stands foremost in my memory of teachers who taught me that learning involves hard work, frustration, and, most importantly, puzzlement. The connection with Yoder, however, is simpler. I was a high school senior in the fall of 1990 during Operation: Desert Storm. Military recruiters visited my school on almost a weekly basis, and their refrains, "Aim High! Air Force," "Be all you can be in the Army," and especially, "The few . . . The proud . . . The Marines," evoked traditions of personal honor and discipline that I found appealing, especially to my sense of responsibility. At the same time, however, I was profoundly bothered by my newly awakened sense that halfway around the world Americans and non-Americans alike were dying, in part because of my reliance on foreign oil. I do not think I would ever have considered actually joining the military, but I was disturbed enough by concepts like responsibility and courage to experience a level of confusion and psychic conflict about my Christian belief that I had not done before. And that was my state when I found the beaten green copy of *The Politics of Jesus* on the library shelf, so I sat down and began to read.

A few years later, I read *The Politics of Jesus* again, along with *What Would You Do?* and other books on war, peace, and nonviolence, including Walter Brueggeman's *Living Toward a Vision*, John Dear's *Our God Is Nonviolent*, and Hendrik Berkhof's *Christ and the Powers*. This time the context was a Messiah College class called "Theories of Peace and Justice," taught by John K. Stoner, then newly released from his duties as the executive secretary for the U.S. Peace Section of Mennonite Central Committee. In addition to introducing me to a wide variety of peace and conflict studies literature, John's class was instrumental in shaping my early thought about peace and reconciliation, because he showed again and again through example after example how difficult a set of practices peaceful living was. My early questions about responsibility and courage were not out of place. They were at the heart of any robust theology of peace.

I entered the Divinity School at Duke University in the fall of 1996 and, within a few weeks, found myself seated in Stanley Hauerwas's office, encountering that strange mix of intensity, nervous energy, and distractedness that made early visits with Dr. Hauerwas immensely intimidating and completely engrossing at the same time. At some point during my first few months in seminary, Stanley asked me if I was thinking about applying to a Ph.D. program, and, if so, what I would like to study. I muttered something about an Aristotelian account of Christian holiness, to which he replied tersely: "Well, that's what I've spent my life writing about, so we'll have to think of something else." I suppose that I did end up thinking of something else. At least Aristotle does not figure prominently in the pages of this book, but the point that I was trying to make that day in his office — that it is good therapy for parts of American Christian imaginations to think about holiness in terms of habits of mind and practices that contribute to human flourishing — remains very much a central presumption of what I have argued here. I would like to thank Stanley here both for his friendship and willingness to teach me, as well as for his commitment to *Christian* education, which I think can be encapsulated in one small anecdote.

I graduated from seminary in May of 1998, ready to begin the Ph.D. program at Duke that fall. My parents attended the Divinity School baccalaureate service, where they met Stanley for the first time. During that conversation, Stanley broke out of the puckish raconteur persona he adopts for occasions like baccalaureate services, commencements, convocations,

Acknowledgments

and graduate school receptions, looked my parents in the eyes, and said, "I can't promise when this is all said and done that we'll find Alex a job, but I can promise you that we'll keep him following Jesus." Stanley at his best could not care less whether his students are successes in the halls of academia or not. But he does care deeply about their formation as human beings, and I thank him for being that kind of teacher.

As I have already hinted, much of the material in these pages was originally written as my doctoral dissertation at Duke University. I would like to thank the faculty, students, and staff of the Graduate Program in Religion, as well as the many others at Duke who supported and taught me while I was there. They provided as stimulating an education as I could have hoped for. In addition to Stanley, I would like to thank my professors and committee members, Harry Huebner (of Canadian Mennonite University), Reinhard Hütter, David Steinmetz, and Romand Coles. I am also especially grateful for the influence and guidance of Geoffrey Wainwright and Lewis Ayres during my studies at Duke.

Both at Duke and now at Bluffton, I have been blessed with friends and colleagues in school who have left their marks on this book and in my life. In particular, I would like to thank Trevor Bechtel, Laura Brenneman, Charlie Collier, Katherine Dickson, Alex Hawkins, Randy Keeler, Kristen Kramer, Lynda Nyce, Jenny and Scott Williams, Joel Shuman, and J. D. Yoder for their support, comments, questions, and criticisms while I have worked on what at points seemed like a never-ending project.

In addition to teachers and friends, Duke provided me with the opportunity to be a Fellow of the Kenan Ethics Colloquium during the academic year 2003-2004. I am indebted to the other members of the colloquium and their keen insights as we discussed each other's work.

While I was writing this book I was also being shaped and reshaped by the community of Chapel Hill Mennonite Fellowship, in Chapel Hill, NC. Though I have been gone from that community for half a decade, worshiping at CHMF was the most profoundly transformative, embracing, and intensive church experience of my life. Going to church with people whom you like and trusting them for God's care is a rare and precious gift. So, thanks and love to Mary Jo and Tom Lehman, Sandra Vanderlinde and Steve Jolley, Katie and Isaac Villegas, Jen Peifer and Nick Plummer, Jen Graber and Stacy Vlasits, Jennifer Connerly and David Nahm, Kim and Joe Wiebe, and the many other people who participated in, and grew together as, CHMF. As a church CHMF practices what I hope this book is about.

At Duke and since, I have been graced with two friends whose im-

ACKNOWLEDGMENTS

print on me intellectually and spiritually is so deep that I have difficulty expressing it. Peter Dula and Chris Huebner have both found profound ways of expressing their gratitude to each other and to me in the acknowledgments of their own books. I am not as poetic as Peter, and I am usually more confused than Chris, but here is what I will say: their friendship is the soul of my intellectual life.

Finally, I would like to offer a word of thanks to my mother, father, and sister. Throughout my life my parents provided me with an environment in which to become myself that has been unfailingly encouraging and trustworthy. I have told this story elsewhere, but I will risk it again:

When I was in my early teens and was preparing to be baptized, my paternal grandparents returned from a life of missionary work in Zimbabwe and Zambia. My family spent a couple of Saturdays cleaning the house into which my grandparents were planning to move, and, as I was mopping the kitchen floor, my dad took the opportunity to ask me whether I had any questions about being baptized.

I said, "There's only one thing that worries me. How do I know that Christianity is true?"

I will never forget my dad's response: "Alex," he said, "I'll never be able to give you a knockdown argument for why Christianity is true. But, look at your grandparents and the lives that it's created. That's the best proof I can offer you." My parents' lives are those kind of lives as well — ones that I look at when I want to see how history as praise takes shape in people.

And to my sister, Carrie, who has taught me more about caring for others, being joyful, and living with strength in the face of adversity and pain than anyone I know: You have lived day in and out the things I have haltingly tried to say here. I dedicate this book to you.

INTRODUCTION

"Is This What the One without Spot or Wrinkle Is Really Like?"

The one who knows the mystery of the cross and the tomb, knows the reasons of things. The one who is initiated into the infinite power of the Resurrection, knows the purpose for which God knowingly created all.

Maximus the Confessor,
Centuries on Love

The key to the obedience of God's people is not their effectiveness but their patience . . . The relationship between the obedience of God's people and the triumph of God's cause is not a relationship of cause and effect but one of cross and resurrection.

John Howard Yoder,
The Politics of Jesus

The church is not holy; it is difficult.[1] At least that seems to be the sentiment of many Christians today, whose lives have led them to a painful awareness of the limits of their churches and the apparent necessity of compromise in a world all too often marked by profound brokenness. Describing the church as holy in a world like ours flies in the face of actuality. Yet I wonder whether part of the problem does not lie within this opposition between the holy and

---

1. This is to paraphrase Gillian Rose, *Mourning Becomes the Law: Philosophy and Representation* (Cambridge: Cambridge University Press, 1996), 100: "Midrash is not beautiful, it is difficult."

the difficult, within a desire to secure for ourselves a holiness ultimately unbefitting the body of the Lamb that was slain. Might not the problem lie in the difficulty of receiving the *crucified* Christ as the holy one? One need only take a quick glance at Christian art to have some sense of what I am asking. Recall, for instance, the stark difference between the crucified Christs of Matthias Grünewald and Salvador Dalí: both bodies are strangely recognizable; only one of them has been pierced with nails. Both are fictive, one escapistly so. Now ask yourself which savior you would want if you got to choose. For me, at least, it is hard to see the holy one in whom we find salvation in the twisted and gangrenous toes, the tendons of the hands agonizingly stretched to snapping, the pallid green of the corpse upon the tree, rather than in the strong body suffused with unearthly light that hangs above this world of shadows and dreams. How much harder to say that the holiness of the church might consist in its prayer to be made ugly, like the body of its crucified Lord, without that prayer becoming an empty gesture, a "but not really" under the breath? Or hardest yet, how to pray that prayer as our hope without lapsing into pieties that mask fantasies of the macabre?

These questions about the character of holiness are surprisingly old: they are not merely prompted by "a modernity where God and the world created by him seem less and less able to secure our basic practices and thoughts," as one author has recently put it.[2] Nor, to put the point slightly differently, are they prompted primarily by the horrific events of the twentieth century, as it has been incumbent upon theologians to insist for some time now.[3] Indeed, it is precisely the distance we continue to perceive between the holy and the difficult which prompted in the fifth century of this era Augustine's incredulity at the church: "Is *this* what the one without spot or wrinkle is *really* like?"[4]

---

2. Romand Coles, *Self/Power/Other: Political Theory and Dialogical Ethics* (Ithaca: Cornell University Press, 1992), vii.

3. Already in 1977 Sebastian Moore remarked on the demand to describe the twentieth century, and primarily the Shoah, in exceptional terms with a reference to Hannah Arendt: "Sin is the sealing of alienation, its total normalizing. Hannah Arendt's phrase 'the banality of evil,' fearlessly used in connection with the concentration camps which less morally perceptive people can only describe with superlatives of malevolence, is entirely apposite here. The Godlessness of man is not rebellion against God but, just what the word says, God-less-ness." *The Crucified Jesus Is No Stranger* (Minneapolis: Seabury, 1977), 112. Moore's point, I take it, is similar to my own: just as surprise is the last reaction warranted by human atrocity, so also it is the last reaction warranted by the pseudo-opposition between holiness and difficulty.

4. Augustine, *On Baptism* 5.27.38, in *Documents in Early Christian Thought*, ed. Maurice Wiles and Mark Santer (Cambridge: Cambridge University Press, 1975), 163; emphasis added.

Introduction

John Howard Yoder, the theologian with whom I am most concerned in this book, probed deeply into the wound left in the contemporary Christian conscience by the opposition between holiness and difficulty. In the chapter of *The Politics of Jesus* entitled "Trial Balance," Yoder sketches a series of dualisms that seem fundamental for Christian theology and repeat the opposition between holiness and difficulty. Among the dualisms, Yoder contends that "[t]he systematic tradition tells us we must *choose between the political and the sectarian*."[5] Since Ernst Troeltsch's study of *The Social Teachings of the Christian Churches* in the early twentieth century, the possibility that the questions for Christian social ethics might be conceived in terms other than ones dictated by this dualism is difficult to imagine. In keeping with their "Constantinian heritage," Yoder claims, Troeltsch and theologians who took their cues from him assumed that political logic is static: "Either one accepts, without serious qualification, the responsibility of politics, that is, of governing, with whatever means that takes, or one chooses a withdrawn position of either personal-monastic-vocational or sectarian character which is 'apolitical.'"[6]

Difficulty or holiness. Such an either/or is a form of ecclesial unfaithfulness, for it amounts to the confession that the holiness Jesus embodied, precisely because it is so hard and so material, is an "impossible ideal." His "way is not *really* for the here and now."[7] Yet Yoder's refusal to "choose between the political and the sectarian" points to a variety of connections important for Christian theology, including those between difficulty and holiness, ecclesiology and Christology, history and nonviolence. These chapters concern those connections, the exploration of which is part and parcel of a lived attempt, as Yoder put it, "to see history doxologically."

What that enigmatic phrase might mean will emerge more fully later. Nevertheless, some anticipatory remarks seem in order. In "Why Ecclesiology Is Social Ethics," Yoder describes doxology this way:

> When I say doxology, that means not only that the glory of God is verbally recognized but that it is celebrated. The word points not simply to an awareness or a conviction but to a spirituality and the cultivation

---

5. John Howard Yoder, *The Politics of Jesus: Vicit Agnus Noster*, 2nd ed. (Grand Rapids: Eerdmans, 1994), 105; emphasis in original. The other dualisms include the following: the choice between the Jesus of history/Jesus of dogma, prophetic witness/institutional stability, external/internal reign of God, and the individual/social (pp. 103-8).

6. Yoder, *Politics of Jesus*, 105.

7. Yoder, *Politics of Jesus*, 107n15.

of a distinctive consciousness. To celebrate and to celebrate repeatedly in memory of Jesus, the glory of God as righteous and as sovereign means to cultivate explicitly an alternative consciousness, to maintain a sense of reality running against the stream of the unquestioningly accepted commonplaces of the age.[8]

To see history doxologically is to live in the world as a sign of divine presence. Explicitly cultivating an alternative to the unquestioningly accepted commonplaces of the age requires celebration, a spirituality or way of life marked by celebration. Doxology is not a string of propositions that demand cognitive assent; neither is it the expression of personal preferences. Instead, doxology concerns the *habitus* of performing God's story in the face of, in opposition to, and perhaps in concert with, other stories that compete for plausibility in the world. Something of such a *habitus* is recalled in the poem "Manifesto: The Mad Farmer Liberation Front" by the agrarian essayist Wendell Berry. Throughout the poem, Berry describes a life that runs profoundly counter to the accepted commonplaces of middle-class America. Resist greed, he says. Loving "the quick profit, the annual raise" — these are recipes for the misery of an invariable, automated life, "a window in your head." Instead, be charitable. "Work for nothing." Love, even where love is undeserved. Do not be bent on overcoming everything, but "Praise ignorance, for what [you] have not encountered [you] have not destroyed." Lose your mind, lest your life become one that people can know without knowing you. Lastly, and in summary, Berry says, "practice resurrection."[9]

The alternative consciousness hinted at in Berry's manifesto may not sound much like Christian doctrine, but this much is clear: the life he recommends is unpredictable; its roots and springs are not secured by calculation and strategy, it "won't compute," and supremely it is lived as praise in gratitude for gifts we neither made nor claimed — "call that profit" — but rather found us.

In these respects Berry, I think, hints at the way of life Yoder thought embodied doxology. Yoder's own fullest account of what is entailed by a doxological consciousness came in his 1988 presidential address to the Annual Meeting of the Society of Christian Ethics. In that address, entitled "To Serve Our God and to Rule the World," Yoder used the early church as his

---

8. Yoder, *Royal Priesthood*, 123.
9. In *The Country of Marriage* (New York: Harcourt Brace Jovanovich, 1971), 16-17.

template to "describe the cosmos in terms dictated by the knowledge that a once slaughtered Lamb is now living."[10] The address was given to professional theologians and ethicists, many of whom were and are interested in figuring out where Christian ethics "fits" in the disciplinary structures of contemporary academic investigation. Yet for Yoder, the question of finding the right fit put the cart before the horse: Christian ethics does not operate on the presumption of a ready-made world in which we already have our bearings and can set about to take stock of the additional coordinates with which ethics provides us. As he put it, "There is no nonsectarian 'scratch' to start from, beneath or beyond particular identities, no neutral common ground which some sort of search for 'foundations' could lay bare."[11] Instead, cultivating a doxological consciousness itself orients the world — "it is a way of seeing, a grasp of which end is up, which way is forward."[12] It requires that we acknowledge that all our modes of sight, diagnostics, and critical inquiry are not autonomous, but are "embedded in a larger life process" both characterized by praise and by the confession that such a process of praise "rules the world."[13] How a community lives into that doxological vision, what kinds of stance — criticism, repentance, forgiveness, affirmation — it must adopt toward itself as well as toward its others in order to see history as praise is the subject of what follows.

Again, the issues at stake are not new. In 251 C.E., after two years of imperial persecution and one year of exile, Cyprian, bishop of Carthage, faced dissent, conflict, and division in his church over the repentance of those Christians who had succumbed to Roman pressures, either by sacrificing to pagan idols — and thus violating their baptismal vows — or by obtaining official certificates which stated, falsely, that they had performed the requisite sacrifices.[14] In Rome, the priests of the Christian church di-

---

10. Yoder, *Royal Priesthood*, 128.
11. Yoder, *Royal Priesthood*, 129.
12. Yoder, *Royal Priesthood*, 129.
13. Yoder, *Royal Priesthood*, 129.
14. The precise situation is disputed. At the very least, division seems to have come on two sides. On the one hand was the "laxist" schism led by the deposed African bishop Privatus of Lambaesis (or was it the deacon Felicissimus, who seems to have led the delegation from North Africa seeking recognition in Rome?). On the other was the "rigorist" party of Novatian, who made himself bishop of Rome in opposition to the election of Cornelius to the office. It is not clear whether *On the Unity of the Catholic Church* was written in response only to the "laxist" schism or to both schisms. The view generally held is that Novatian had appealed to Cyprian already by the early spring of 251, prior to contesting Cornelius's accession to the office, and that, therefore, Cyprian was at the very least aware of

rected those who had sacrificed, as well as those who had obtained certificates, to repent and begin a protracted process of readmission to communion, which would not end until the persecution had ceased. But in Carthage, a majority of the clergy, as well as those imprisoned for confessing Christ, decided to readmit the lapsed to communion without a lengthy process of repentance and before the end of the persecution. Such readmission was to take place on the recommendation of a letter procured by the lapsed from one of the martyrs (or their legatees among the confessors — those who suffered imprisonment for confessing Christ, but were not executed), a practice which generated a kind of "black market" in letters of recommendation.[15]

Cyprian refused to recognize the validity of such recommendations and argued that none of the lapsed could be readmitted to communion prior to the end of the persecution. After some time, he extended communion to dying penitents, which was also the practice of the church in Rome. But his relatively stringent stance on the issue provoked the dissenting confessors and clergy in Carthage to dig in their heels, arguing that Cyprian did not have the authority to overrule the recommendation of the martyrs.

Soon the "laxists" who opposed Cyprian in North Africa were complemented by a contingent of "rigorists," led in Rome by Novatian, who refused reconciliation even with dying penitents. By 252, Cyprian's authority as bishop of Carthage was being ignored by the laxists, who installed one of Cyprian's former priests, Fortunatus, as bishop over their communion, and countermanded by Novatian, who sent a presbyter named Maximus to Carthage as its bishop. The outlook was exceedingly bleak, serious enough to prompt Cyprian to write the first version of *On the Unity of the Catholic Church*, which reads, at points, rather hotly:

> It is these same men whom the Lord indicates and censures when He says: "They have forsaken me, the fountain of the water of life, and they have digged out for themselves crumbling cisterns, which cannot hold the water." Whereas there can be but the one baptism, they think they can baptize; they have abandoned the fountain of life, yet promise

---

Novatian's rigorist bent. See, e.g., Maurice Bénevot, SJ, "Introduction" to *St. Cyprian: The Lapsed and The Unity of the Catholic Church*, Ancient Christian Writers: The Works of the Fathers in Translation, ed. Johannes Quasten and Joseph Plumpe, vol. 25 (Westminster: Newman, 1957), 5-6. Cf. J. Patout Burns, *Cyprian the Bishop*, Routledge Early Church Monographs (London: Routledge, 2002), 1-11.

15. Burns, *Cyprian the Bishop*, 2.

the life and grace of the waters of salvation. It is not cleansing that men find there, but soiling; their sins are not washed away but only added to. That "new birth" does not bring forth sons unto God, but to the devil. Born of a lie, they cannot inherit what the truth has promised; begotten by the faithless, they are deprived of the grace of faith. The reward for those "in peace" can never come to men who have broken the peace of the Lord by the frenzy of dissent.[16]

Cyprian's argument with his opponents was premised on the assumption that, because the service of God is in principle indissoluble, both in the sense of worship and in the sense of discipline (which itself is both teaching and reproof), there can be but one institution that holds the catholic faith. One can leave the unity of the church, but one cannot divide it. The service, therefore, of those who were not subjects of that institution was false, null, and void. Their service was not a gift of God, and therefore it could not be rendered back to God. Thus, Cyprian contended that, no matter how earnest, in their efforts to lead a holy life and to administer baptism apart from the catholic church, they polluted themselves as well as those they led astray. The character of the church was at stake: What is its holiness like? Where is it? Does it have edges? If so, how do we talk about them?[17]

This was neither the first time questions concerning the identity and limits of the church arose in Christianity, nor, it hardly needs to be said, would it be the last. Indeed, the division and ensuing controversy lived on even after Cyprian's martyrdom in 258 C.E. The record of dissent between 251 and 258 is partially preserved in Cyprian's copious correspondence from the period, which repeatedly delineated his position in the face of objection and refutation from all quarters. Notable among that correspondence, not only for its length and cogency, but also for its role in later ecclesiastical tradition, is Epistle 73, *Ad Iubaianus,* dated from the mid- to late summer of 256.[18] The letter encapsulates Cyprian's stance on baptism,

---

16. Cyprian, *The Lapsed and The Unity of the Catholic Church,* 53-54.

17. Burns noted that Cyprian's policies for dealing with lapsed and schismatic clergy did not indicate that he considered the holiness of the church itself to be in jeopardy. Cyprian's concern lay with the lapsed: "Those contaminated in body or mind by their contact with idolatry were a danger to themselves and not to the holy church." The issue of the church's holiness was correlative to but not directly indicated by the ineffectiveness of *prima facie* Christian practices performed outside and in opposition to the unity of the church. See Burns, *Cyprian the Bishop,* 132-40. The quote is from p. 140.

18. On the dating of Ep. 73, Cyprian's 72nd epistle, addressed to Stephen, bishop of Rome, seems to have been composed for (in response to?) the council of 71 bishops referred

which he saw as a critical marker of the church's unity, but underlying the account of baptism was a deeper set of assumptions concerning the nature of the church's authority. For Cyprian the church's authority is founded in the unity of its practice:

> [A]fter the resurrection [the Lord] . . . spoke to the apostles . . . using these words: "As the Father has sent me, so send I you. When He had said this, He breathed on them and said: Receive the Holy Spirit. Whose sins you shall forgive, they will be forgiven them; whose sins you shall retain, they will be retained." From all this we perceive that only those leaders who are set in authority within the Church and have been established in accordance with the law of the gospel and the institution of the Lord have the lawful power to baptize and to grant forgiveness of sins; outside the Church there can be neither binding nor loosing, for there is nobody who has the power either to bind or to loose.[19]

For Cyprian, then, the church does the things that God in Christ has authorized it to do, and one locates the church by asking where those things are done that the church is authorized to do. Its activity must therefore be describable as a unity. Three paragraphs later Cyprian elaborates his claims with a favorite patristic analogy. "The Church," he argues, "is like Paradise." Inside its walls are trees that bear fruit, some good, some bad. The trees that bear bad fruit are cut down and cast outside into the fire. The good trees are watered and sustained by springs that flow in the garden:

> Is it possible for anyone who is not on the inside within the Church to water another. . . ? Can he give to another the health-giving and saving draughts of Paradise when he stands himself self-condemned in his wickedness, when he has been banished beyond the springs of Paradise and is dry and parched, faint with a never-ending thirst?

---

to in Epistle 73.1.2. Graeme W. Clarke placed that council in May or June 256. Furthermore, Cyprian must have written Epistle 75, to Firmillian of Cappadocia, by the time of the council in Carthage on September 1, 256. This places Epp. 73 and 74 in June, July, or August of that same year. See Clarke, "Introduction" to *The Letters of St. Cyprian of Carthage*, vol. 4, trans. and ed. G. W. Clarke, in Ancient Christian Writers: The Works of the Fathers in Translation, no. 47, gen. eds. Walter J. Burghardt and Thomas C. Lawler (Mahwah: Newman, 1989), 16.

19. Cyprian, Ep. 73.7.2. Cyprian here modulated his characteristic argument, namely, that the church is one because its keys were given to Peter (see, e.g., chapters 4 and 5 of *The Unity of the Catholic Church*).

Introduction

Cyprian continues to liken the springs to the water that flowed from Christ's side when he was pierced by the centurion's spear, and thus extends the ecclesiological imagery of the garden into baptismal and eucharistic registers:

> The Lord proclaims that whoever is thirsty should come and drink from the rivers of living water which flowed from out of His belly. And where are the thirsty to go? . . . We are the ones who, by divine privilege, water the thirsty people of God; we are the ones who guard the boundaries of her life-giving springs. . . .[20]

Cyprian's vocabulary of boundaries, guardians, and walls sounds uncannily familiar, for borders of various kinds have been at the front of many recent political imaginations. The idea of the boundary, however, exercises a more ambivalent power in the contemporary imagination than it seems to have in much patristic theology. In contrast to Cyprian, Sheldon Wolin, for instance, writes: "Both as container and as excluder, boundaries work to foster the impression of a circumscribed space in which likeness dwells, the likeness of natives, of an autochthonous people, or of a nationality, or of citizens with equal rights. Likeness is prized because it appears as the prime ingredient of unity. Unity, in turn, is thought to be the sine qua non of collective power."[21] "As container or excluder," inside or outside — the edge between the two is not habitable.[22] The importance of

---

20. Ep. 73.10-11.3. For Cyprian, not being within the church is better characterized as acting in opposition to the church. Cyprian does not rely on an account of the church abstracted from the agency of its members. For the uses of the allusion to Gen. 2:8-9 prior to Cyprian's, see, e.g., *Ad Diognetus* 12.1ff; Irenaeus, *Adversus haereses* 5.20.2; Hippolytus, *Commentary in Daniel* 1.17; Tertullian, *Adv. Marc.* 2.4.4. For Cyprian's own use of the analogy, often exegetically interwoven with *Song of Songs* 4.2, see Epp. 69.2.1 and 75.15.1. For the notion of "the sacrament of unity" (*si sacramentum unitatis agnoscimus*), cf. *De unit.* 4 and 7 and Ep. 69.6.1 (*quam sit inseparabile unitatis sacramentum*).

21. See Wolin's "Fugitive Democracy," in *Democracy and Difference: Contesting the Boundaries of the Political*, ed. Seyla Benhabib (Princeton: Princeton University Press, 1996), 32.

22. Rom Coles, drawing on Barry Lopez's imagery in *Arctic Dreams*, discussed the significance of the edge in the contemporary imagination in *Self/Power/Other*, 1-13. Coles writes: "Western civilization has a long and dark history with respect to edges; it tends to view them as indicative of an evil that lies on the other side; it constitutes them as regions to be forever thrust back and ultimately eliminated at the moment when we conquer the other. Yet it is not just specific edges that pose problems but edges per se; we are a civilization that on the whole, at least since Plato, dreams of a reality without wild edges, a world encom-

Cyprian's spatial imagery in this analogy between the church and the garden of Paradise is difficult to overvalue. Indeed, the inside/outside dynamic forms the backbone of his claim against the faithfulness of schismatic baptism. Cyprian's rhetoric was shaped by the assumption that the church can be concretely and affirmatively located, and that its location has something to do with the way it conceives of its "edges" and "walls." Cyprian's church had a site in a way that enabled one to affirm its presence here rather than there, there rather than someplace else. "Walls" secured its identity, but even as they did so they produced the threat of insecurity, the possibility that identity might be defiled. About this, two things need to be said.

In the first place, Augustine's use of Cyprianic rhetoric and imagery figures prominently in the later church's appeals to and enlistment of Cyprian's ecclesiology. In book 5 of *On Baptism*, written to refute Donatist "rigorism," Augustine asked how

> these people, whom Cyprian describes as having renounced the world in word alone and not in deed and yet being within, have got into the locked garden and the sealed fountain. If they too are there, they too must be the bride of Christ. But is this what the one without spot or wrinkle is really like? . . . She is a closed garden and a sealed fountain precisely in so far as she is a lily — namely in the persons of those righteous people who are Jews secretly by circumcision of the heart. . . . The multitude of the thorns, whether their separation be concealed or open, lies outside, beyond this number.[23]

Augustine's argument centered on the same texts as Cyprian's. Yet, where Cyprian used scripture to demand that ecclesial insideness and outsideness be concretely demonstrable, Augustine employed scriptural arguments for the concealment and suspension of the same dynamic. For many of us, this life is too difficult, or too fraught by an experience of insideness and outsideness intermingled, to be called holy.

Textbook accounts of Cyprian's and Augustine's ecclesiologies often

---

passed within one Reason. In the shadow of this dream it is little wonder that our approach to edges is obliterating and that when we are involved, edges are desolate rather than fruitful localities" (p. 2). John Howard Yoder imagines, I think, a way of conceiving of edges that does not seek to extend mastery over others.

23. Augustine, *On Baptism* 5.27.38, in Wiles and Santer, eds., *Documents in Early Christian Thought*, 163.

Introduction

locate the difference between them in the assumption that Cyprian's church is visible while Augustine's true church is invisible. There is something to be said for this, but for Cyprian the holiness of the church is not simply a matter of its visibility.[24] Instead, holiness is secured by policing the walls of the garden, by keeping the borders of the church clearly defined and delimited. Insideness and outsideness are the relevant markers, not visibility or invisibility.

In the second place, it is not as if Cyprian's analogy erects walls around the church that presume an uncontested account of its identity. It turned out to be Cyprian, with his apparently obvious, even empirical, conception of the unity of the church, who refused to follow the implications of insideness and outsideness to their seemingly logical conclusions. Instead, being inside *is* its own set of difficulties and negotiations. There was for Cyprian no clear equation, *inside = holy; outside = difficult*. Augustine, by contrast, finally has less difficulty with such an equation, for inside/outside has become part of every believer's ecclesial constitution. But Cyprian, who found himself vehemently at odds with Stephen, bishop of Rome, over the issue of the readmission of the lapsed to communion, could not bring himself to declare Stephen "outside," as his own account of the church's unity, of the way it guards its walls, might have forced him to do. The tensions that maintain insideness turn out to be much greater than a reading of Cyprian's texts would initially lead one to imagine. In this respect at least, then, it turns out to be the case that Cyprian, rather than Augustine, refuses to ameliorate the difficulties of being inside inherent in a robustly Christian conception of holiness.[25]

I am interested in how the inside/outside dynamic at play in Cyprian's ecclesiology configures contemporary thought about holiness,

---

24. One might say, adopting a Kantian phrase, that on Cyprian's view the church's visibility is the "condition of possibility" for holiness but is not itself constitutive of that holiness. The visible church might be apostate, as Cyprian's assessment of his own disagreement with Stephen indicates. In this sense, considerations of visibility/invisibility remain important. Nevertheless, the very distinction is anachronistic when applied to Cyprian; the idea that the true church might be invisible never occurred to him — he never chose one side in an argument that was already set up.

25. We need to ask at least two sets of interconnected questions here. In the first place, how does Cyprian suggest that the borders of the church should be policed and maintained? With what kind of problems in conceiving of the church does his answer to this question present him? Secondly, what kind of difference does Augustine's changing of the question's parameters from inside/outside to visible/invisible make for conceiving of holiness in the church?

and particularly in how it can be used to defuse the difficulty of talking about the church as holy *in* its difficulty. John Howard Yoder's ecclesiology has been approached before, but most often as a sample of a neo-Anabaptist obsession with pacifism. Pacifism is certainly a prominent theme in Yoder's work, but for all its prominence, it is subordinate to an attempt to think the church as a *kenotic* politics and way of being in time that destabilized the borders between church and world, nevertheless without abolishing them. For Yoder, the careful transgression of the borders between church and world was a fundamental gospel task, but so was the establishment and even development of those same borders. In the chapters that follow, I have tried to think through these ambivalences of Yoder's approach to borders.

I have approached that task by expanding a set of conversations in which Yoder's name typically arises. In the first chapter of this book, therefore, I look at the ecclesiology of a prominent Christian theologian and ethicist in conjunction with Yoder. Oliver O'Donovan places the church at the center of his account of the Christian life, and in this resonates powerfully with Yoder. Moreover, both theologians advocate blurring of the inside/outside dynamic in ways that seem to me suggestive for a reexamination of the church's holiness. For both O'Donovan and Yoder, an adequate picture of salvation involves the church in a reappraisal of creation in the light of Christ's resurrection. In the course of this investigation, however, deep differences emerge between Yoder and O'Donovan. For O'Donovan the church is ultimately superfluous to salvation because it is conceived as a focus for but not the locus of the healing of creation that Christ brings. Thus O'Donovan articulates a contemporary Christendom ecclesiology that erases the boundaries between church and world. By way of contrast, Yoder's reflections on history and theology led him to reject Christendom ecclesiologies as totalizing expatriations of outsiders into the arms of the church. In the terms in which I have been speaking, O'Donovan espouses Christendom as a way of ameliorating the difficulty of holiness.

In Chapter Two, I trace the development of one strand of Yoder's thought about the church. That development began with Ernst Troeltsch's historicism in the early part of the twentieth century, which construed the pseudo-opposition between holiness and difficulty in ways that reverberated throughout Christian theology and ethics. Troeltsch began a program for excising the church from Christian ethics and so rendered Christianity in the North Atlantic world at once individualist and inescapably idealist.

What may surprise some readers is how deeply Mennonites drank at

Introduction

Troeltsch's well in the last century, as a series of theologians grappled with the status of "sectarians" Troeltsch and Niebuhr conferred upon them.[26] Those theologians, represented by Guy F. Hershberger and, somewhat later, J. Lawrence Burkholder, attempted to see a way past Troeltsch while nevertheless accepting the epithet as sociologically accurate.[27] At roughly the same time, however, Yoder was involved with a group of Anabaptist theologians who started publishing a pamphlet called *Concern*, in which they attempted to clarify the relationship between the sociological designation "sectarian" and the church's social political witness. Yoder's first published book, *The Christian Witness to the State*, was itself a *Concern* pamphlet in its first incarnation and represents the beginning of his career-long task of relocating the church at the center of Christian ethics. He is therefore often seen as opposing Troeltsch's typological approach to Christian ethics. While he certainly did this, it is nevertheless crucial to see him as an heir to Troeltsch in another respect, namely, in trying to think through the implications of a non-reductive historicism for Christian theology. Christian ethicists have never been done grappling with Troeltsch, but Yoder shifted the terrain of the debate from typology to history in a way that has been underappreciated.

I find Troeltsch's refusal to disambiguate history deeply attractive. It seems to accord, though I recognize this as no final court of appeal, with the world I experience. Yet, I also discern in Troeltsch a refusal to ambiguate ambiguity, a failure of nerve, perhaps, or a failure of imagination in the face of so many ruptures in the ordinary course of time that fostered an inability to historicize historicism, or at the very least to acknowledge the skepticism about historicism itself that historicism might be taken to entail. It has to do with Troeltsch's reluctance to investigate his own historicity, despite the persistent attempts to do something of the sort in accounting for and historicizing how "we" (Christians, Germans, Europeans, moderns) came

---

26. Readers who are unfamiliar with the twentieth-century Mennonite theological landscape should consult Albert N. Keim, *Harold S. Bender, 1897-1962* (Scottdale: Herald Press, 1998). Bender was the dean of Mennonite theological scholarship for Yoder's generation. Perry Bush, *Two Kingdoms, Two Loyalties: Mennonite Pacifism in Modern America* (Baltimore: Johns Hopkins University Press, 1998), also offers a helpful overview of the wider (non-academic) Mennonite climate during Yoder's lifetime.

27. See especially Guy F. Hershberger, *War, Peace, and Nonresistance* (Scottdale: Herald Press, 1944) and J. Lawrence Burkholder, *The Problem of Social Responsibility from the Perspective of the Mennonite Church* (Ph.D. diss., Princeton Theological Seminary, 1958), reprinted by the Institute of Mennonite Studies, Elkhart, Indiana, 1989.

to be who "we" are. Claiming those various "we's" and the caesuras of the past that constitute them creates a space for Troeltsch in which to stand and say and yet remain hidden, and so to cultivate a relief for history's interruptions of itself — thus, to cultivate a sense in which the uncertainty that accompanies historicism can be pronounced. In other words, Troeltsch's historicism did not open *itself* to question in a way that Yoder's negotiation of our aporetic historicities required.

Part and parcel of Yoder's negotiation of historicity was a critique of the so-called Constantinian synthesis, that historically knotty set of events in the third through fifth centuries that coincided with Christianity's emergence as a civilizational religion. So, in the third chapter I take up Yoder's analysis of Constantinianism. To Yoder's mind, Constantine and the ecclesiologies for which he became the legitimating figurehead were emblematic of the church's emergent and persistent need to "make history come out right," an undertaking in which Troeltsch in some ways, and O'Donovan in others, remain invested. That project, on Yoder's account, constituted a "structured denial of the gospel," in part because it sought to reconstitute the past so as to furnish it with a more appropriate denouement, and in part because it cultivated an ecclesiology that denies that the life, ministry, death, and resurrection of Jesus are normative for Christian practice.

The first part of Chapter Three, then, is exposition in service of clarification: What did Yoder say about Constantinianism and how does it shed light on his ecclesiological agenda? Nevertheless, a number of critical issues arise around Yoder's diagnosis of Constantinian ecclesiologies, which I take up in the second half of the chapter. The issues arise from a tension between Yoder's meta-political reading of Constantinianism, on the one hand, and his commitment to restitutionist historiography, on the other. There is a sense in which Yoder's account of Constantinianism insulates him against the imperative to revisit his sources and refine the report he gives of Constantinianism's who, what, where, and why. Put differently, Yoder's own arguments against Constantinianism may themselves be methodologically Constantinian. This is because the refusal of the restitutionist task was on Yoder's own grounds also a denial of the gospel. So: How to allow the disavowal of Constantine to leave us stranded in our own historicity without strandedness itself becoming a handle on history? I do not so much offer a solution to the problem as present it in order to stand as a caution against the assumption that one could develop a straightforwardly "non-Constantinian" theology. But investigating Yoder's negotiation of Constantinianism in light of his conception of historiography as an evangelical directive also yields a positive heading in that it envisions an ecclesiology that radicalizes a politics of listening.

Chapter Three serves as a climax to the first chapters. In Chapters Four and Five I turn to the ecclesial practices that fill out what is involved in proclaiming a doxological vision of history. In Chapter Four I look specifically at how memory of the past, and particularly the memory of past suffering, presents a set of obstacles to the church's activity of praise. Emphasizing praise as the way the church participates in salvation might foster an enormous blindness to the cries for justice and mercy of oppressed people and victims everywhere. Or praise might become its own kind of palliative, an opiate for the masses that masks a mammoth complacency on Christians' part in the face of suffering. What kind of practice of praise will begin to be adequate to the history of loss that has made us who we are? Correlatively, can *we* be saved without those histories — does an adequate picture of salvation involve us being saved from our histories? Yoder argued not, but rather for painful processes of forgiveness and reconciliation that are ways of negotiating "the things we can never undo."[28] Our histories of loss are the material of our salvation, which we see displayed in the crucifixion of Jesus.

In Chapter Five, I investigate two practices of dialogical vulnerability, the rule of Paul and the fullness of Christ, that Yoder thought essential to an ecclesiology that could resist an engineering approach to ethics. If, I argue, the church is structured by practices like an open meeting and the celebration of diverse charismata, then it will also need to be forged in such a way as to display processes of peaceably negotiated intra- and extra-ecclesial conflict. If, furthermore, conflict has a potentially positive, rather than strictly negative, role in the church's life, this will in turn shape how the church thinks about its edges and borders, and particularly will inflect what it means to speak of the church as voluntary in a world obsessed with security and guarantees.

The ecclesiology that emerges thinks the church as a gathering of those committed to following Jesus' gospel as the promise of a way of engaging history patiently and dispossessively, that is, as deliberation, contention, negotiation, discernment, and repentance. Yoder thought that in institutionalizing social processes that incarnated thinking in the light of

---

28. Paul J. Wadell, CP, "Redeeming the Things We Can Never Undo: The Role of Forgiveness in Anne Tyler's *Saint Maybe,*" *New Theology Review* 8:2 (May 1995): 34-48.

time the church could learn to see its life as praise and proclaim history doxologically.

Two final introductory remarks. In the first place, some readers will be mystified by my conjuring up Yoder as an advocate of the *difficulty* of holiness: "How can you be for difficulty and reject violence unconditionally?" While I think that question is unfair, Yoder was, at many points, difficult in just this way. He seemed so certain of his pacifism, although it asked him to be patient and modest; he seemed so certain of his rejection of absolutism, which asked him to be equivocal; he seemed so certain of his capacity to read history honestly, though he knew that history is written to be used. "Mystery" should not be invoked casually, but it may be appropriate at this point, because the tensions to which Yoder's style points are very close to the heart of language about God. As Rowan Williams has stressed, such language makes "claims about the context of the whole moral universe, claims of crucial concern to the right leading of human life" and at the same time "declares itself to be uniquely 'under judgment,' and to be dealing with what supremely *resists* the urge to finish and close what it being said."[29]

Second, I have tried to "practice what I preach" throughout the following chapters. In other words, I envision these chapters as exercises in difficulty. They are not polemical: indeed, I have been deeply conscious of my desire to end each of them on a high note, so I have tried (not altogether successfully) to resist that urge. Moreover, I have attempted to engage my interlocutors patiently wherever possible, not only by producing sympathetic accounts of them, but also doing so at length, in order to allow the nuances of their positions to emerge. If their voices can genuinely tug at, answer, and question mine, then I hope to count that as an acknowledgment of their part in this conversation, from which I might continue to learn.

---

29. Rowan Williams, *On Christian Theology* (Oxford: Blackwell, 2000), 5.

CHAPTER 1

Salvation Is Created: Praise as Politics in Oliver O'Donovan and John Howard Yoder

Introduction

"Salvation is created. Salvation here on earth. O God, Alleluia." Pavel Chesnokov's Christmas hymn refers to the incarnation of Christ, but the text's theological density properly extends to the entire economy of salvation, of which the church is a part. To say that salvation is *created* is to claim at least four things.

In the first place, it says that salvation comes to us from outside the realm of our expectations, aspirations, and art. We receive salvation as an unanticipatable gift of God. Second, however, despite the unanticipatedness of the gift, "salvation is created" also says that it is something with which we can interact. If salvation comes to us from outside anything we could ask or imagine, it nevertheless comes *to us*. Here, the contrasts between transcendence and immanence, grace and nature, infinity and finitude do not quite index what is confessed. Nor does "panentheism" fit the bill. Two things are worth noting in this regard. (1) Each of the contrasts above presumes the possibility of articulating a relationship, a kind of "over-againstness" or "either/or" between the terms in question. God's creative activity, however, does not stand in this kind of relationship to creation, for God is not one object among many. (2) While "panentheism" is a neologism, the position for which this term is shorthand is not necessarily new. Theodore of Mopsuestia, for instance, in discussing the nature of God's indwelling in humanity, distinguished his own position from two alternatives, the first of which bears striking similarity to panentheism. Theodore wrote that God's indwelling is promised by God as something special for the saints or . . . for those whom he wills to devote themselves to him. What would be the point of his promise, 'I will dwell among them and will walk among them and will be their God and they shall be my people,' which implies some kind of special favor to them, if the indwelling is something enjoyed by all in the ordinary run of things?[1]

Closer, perhaps, is the language of *theosis* associated with Eastern Orthodoxy, where salvation is conceived as one theandric activity in no way separate or cut off from the humanity of God the Word.[2] But the flip side of this coin, so to speak, is precisely to say that salvation, because human, occurs within an ordered and limited material world. Augustine put the point thus: "The God who created us without us will not save us without us."[3]

Third, "salvation is created" therefore implies a rejection of forensic readings of the atonement. Atonement needs to be articulated as a re-creation of the possibility of participating freely and obediently in God's activities, which include creation.[4] Some accounts of atonement will appear to do this more readily than others, but the description of salvation I will pursue in this and subsequent chapters should not be read as an a priori rejection of atonement theologies that have characteristically been conceived along forensic lines. Indeed, many theologies of the atonement that have been seen in the last two centuries as forensic can be rehabilitated, at least to a certain extent.

Recent American Mennonite literature regarding the doctrine of the atonement has been marked by an effort to distance theological reflection

---

1. *On the Incarnation VII*, in *Documents in Early Christian Thought*, ed. Maurice Wiles and Mark Santer (New York: Cambridge University Press, 1975), 57-58.

2. See, for a helpful contemporary rendering of *theosis*, Paniottis Nellas, *Deification in Christ* (Crestwood, NY: St. Vladimir's Seminary Press, 1987). Notice that Theodore of Mopsuestia, in the book mentioned above, goes on to describe deification as God's εὐδοκία, or good pleasure, in distinction from much of the Eastern church, but nevertheless suggestively for our purposes, in that it highlights the character of salvation as gift. See *On the Incarnation VII*, in Wiles and Santer, eds., *Documents in Early Christian Thought*, 58-61.

3. Augustine, Sermon 169.11.13 (PL 38): "*Qui ergo fecit te sine te, non te iustificat sine te.*"

4. "Salvation is created" also rejects forensic accounts of holiness, because holiness depends for its intelligibility on the redemptive economy of God in Jesus Christ. As Jeremy Begbie says, it can, therefore, never be divorced from "the transformation of the disorder of creation in the history of Jesus Christ." *Voicing Creation's Praise* (Edinburgh: T&T Clark, 1991), 224-25.

from forensic accounts and conceive salvation in a more expansive fashion. I am in favor of this trend insofar as it refuses to think of atonement as a special topic in theology. This, I would say, is the major thrust of the second half of John Howard Yoder's *Preface to Theology*, which discusses Christ's work under the *munus triplex*.[5] I am less sympathetic with the attempt by J. Denny Weaver, most recently in *The Nonviolent Atonement*, to reject Anselmian accounts of atonement on two fronts, first, as abstractions from the scriptural narrative, and second, as implicating God in violence.[6] Beyond turning a deaf ear toward the theological subtleties of Anselm's text, Weaver has replaced one unsatisfactory account of atonement with another (his "historicized Christus Victor" theory), which, despite its self-consciously narrative structure, still treats atonement as a special topic. Outside recent Mennonite literature, R. R. Reno's *Redemptive Change* is a good antidote to the need to develop an account of atonement in contemporary theology.[7]

Finally, and in summary of the preceding three points, in order to say that salvation is created one must posit an analogy between what is created and what is saved: τὸ γὰρ ἀπρόσληπτον ἀθεράπευτον.[8] "What would not have been assumed would not have been healed"; so, by extension, what is created participates in what is saved.[9] But to speak of an analogy is also to ask about pictures: What does salvation look like? How is participation in God's economy to be conceived, looked at, and encountered? These are notorious questions, for if salvation is created, then creation is also new — not in the sense of a bunch of new things waiting around for us to interact with, but rather in the sense that the creation of salvation creates a new way of seeing creation. Though that new way of seeing unavoidably carries new ways of picturing, of asking how salvation is embodied, it is not yet to say that those pictures are complete. So, to describe salvation as created, as being in the world, and as revolutionary gift is to confess that our pictures

---

5. John Howard Yoder, *Preface to Theology: Christology and Theological Method* (Grand Rapids: Brazos, 2002).

6. J. Denny Weaver, *The Nonviolent Atonement* (Grand Rapids: Eerdmans, 2001).

7. R. R. Reno, *Redemptive Change: Atonement and the Christian Cure of the Soul* (Harrisburg: Trinity Press International, 2002).

8. Gregory of Nazianzus, Epistle 101.32.3, "ad Cledonium," in *Grégoire de Nazianze. Lettres théologiques*, Sources chrétiennes 208, ed. P. Gallay (Paris: Cerf, 1974). Cf. Cyril of Alexandria, *In Ioannis Evangelium* 89c; Gregory of Nyssa, *Adv. Apollinarem* 26.

9. Such an extension of Nazianzen's logic might be one way of putting what was at stake for John of Damascus and Theodore the Studite in the Iconoclast controversies.

of salvation will be broken, not broken in the sense of "unfaithful," but broken in the sense that it will be difficult to show something that demands a transformation of what we mean by showing. Put aphoristically: the analogical imagination is also the repentant imagination.

If salvation creates a new way of seeing creation, it is not because salvation is "supernatural" in that spooky and extrinsicist sense that dominates contemporary talk about religion. Nor am I saying that salvation is unnatural; picturing salvation has, rather, much more to do with the difficult process of learning to see where we went wrong in describing what is natural. The alternative I propose calls for renewed and deep engagement with the church as a picture of salvation involving both the holiness in which it is constituted by God and the quite normal, painfully frail lives of the people who gather together in God's name. That is to say, the process of redescribing creation as saved will involve an account of the church as holy in its difficulty. Put differently, the church shows itself as the analogy between creation and salvation. Two questions converge in this inquiry: the first is the question of the possibility of a political theology, and the second is the question of the location of the church. The first question, I think, is answerable only on the basis of a coherent statement of the second.

The main purpose of this chapter is to consider with Oliver O'Donovan and John Howard Yoder how best to speak of the church's holiness. O'Donovan and Yoder each develop pictures of salvation by dwelling on a series of connections between history and eschatology and on the significance of Christian eschatology for ecclesiology. In this they are remarkable, for, as Janet Williams has noted, such a concatenation of themes has been viewed with a mixture of suspicion and bewilderment in contemporary Christian discourse, despite the efforts of twentieth-century theologians like Barth, Bultmann, Moltmann, and Pannenberg "to retrieve eschatology for the center of Christian thought and praxis."[10] Yet, for O'Donovan and Yoder the church's activity of praise is its historical participation in the coming kingdom, and thus the political worship of the church is the relevant picture of salvation to pursue.

This point — that praise is politics — distinguishes what I have to say from Raymond Plant, for instance, who argued in *Politics, Theology, and History* that political theology consists in "the possibility of relating Christian beliefs in a coherent and rigorous way to the problems of social, economic

---

10. Janet Williams, "Judging Judgment: An Apophatic Approach," *Theology Today* 58:4 (January 2002): 541.

and political organization."[11] As I shall argue in the next chapter, that correlationist way of configuring theology's political nature has roots in Ernst Troeltsch's social philosophy. I take O'Donovan and Yoder to envision political theology as involving both a break with Troeltsch and, correspondingly, a somewhat more expansive task; namely, to examine the nature of the church as itself a *politeia*. Yet, it is important to notice a caveat that O'Donovan presses: political theology is "overextended when it is embraced by an appeal to theology which has no interest in political questions as such, but merely professes an ecclesial antifoundationalism, the political content reduced to the banal reminder that theology must relate to some community of discourse."[12] I do not know what counts as a political question "as such," but I agree with O'Donovan that Christian theology needs to address recognizably political issues, especially ones having to do with justice and authority, if it is to show itself as the analogy between creation and salvation.

Hebrews and the Gospel as Promise

I begin, however, with a picture of salvation from the Epistle to the Hebrews. In the letter's second chapter, the writer pauses anxiously over a picture of salvation inherited from Psalm 8. The psalmist, reflecting on the wonders of God's creation, asks, "What are human beings that you are mindful of them, or mortals that you care for them?"[13] And he answers by placing humanity within a hierarchy of created order:

---

11. Raymond Plant, *Politics, Theology and History* (Cambridge: Cambridge University Press, 2001), 1.

12. Oliver O'Donovan, *The Desire of the Nations: Rediscovering the Roots of Political Theology* (Cambridge: Cambridge University Press, 1996), 4.

13. The translation of *huios anthropou* by "mortals" should not be too easily bought. While Hebrews does not seem to know "son of man" as a messianic title, the very transition from references to humanity as a whole to references to Jesus (2:8-9) makes it clear that Christ and humanity are two things that can be compared. Thus, the resonance of the entire passage, 2:5-11, is determinatively christological (or anthropological — the point is that to say the latter in this context will be to say the former and vice versa), and we should adjust our modern critical resistance to detecting a christological timbre in "son of man" accordingly. As a witness against the assumption that patristic theology evacuated the anthropological register of "son of man," Chrysostom notes that 2:8, "You have put all things under his feet," pertains properly to Christ *even though* "these things were spoken of human nature in general." See P. E. Pusey, ed., *The Homilies of S. John Chrysostom on the Epistle of S. Paul the Apostle to the Hebrews* (Oxford: James Parker and Co., 1877), 4:2.

> You have made them a little lower than God
> and crowned them with glory and honor.
> You have given them dominion over the works of your hands;
> you have put all things under their feet. (Ps. 8:5-6)

The quotation, which the author of Hebrews takes from the Septuagint, ends, and Hebrews continues by teasing out the implied logic of the psalmist's vision: "Now in subjecting all things to them, God left nothing outside their control" (Heb. 2:8a). But then, the writer pauses, and anxiety pours in: "As it is, we do not yet see everything in subjection to them" (Heb. 2:8b). The writer's inherited picture of salvation, of God's glory manifest in humanity, simply does not match his experience of the world. It is a broken vision, and it will not be easily repaired.

We do not know precisely what causes the author of Hebrews to pause just here; the letter contains relatively few landmarks that would allow us to match it with a context about which we know something on other bases. We have, furthermore, almost no sense of the community to which Hebrews was addressed.[14] Barnabas Lindars sums up what scholars are willing to say in a statement notable chiefly for its vagueness: "Hebrews is addressed to comparatively well-educated Jewish Christians somewhere in the Mediterranean Dispersion."[15] "Somewhere," but not "anywhere." That is, the letter to the Hebrews was clearly written to a specific location with its own peculiar set of difficulties and temptations; its appeal is not *immediately* "catholic." This is an extremely important point, for if we are to gain some sense of the shape of the author's anxiety that is indexed in the pregnant pause that surrounds "As it is . . . ," we have to engage in some speculation on the nature of the community to which Hebrews was written.

Fortunately, the epistle is not entirely barren of indicators. Indeed, at least two things seem clear from the text: that the community had faced persecution in the past (Heb. 10:32-39) and that some of its members considered the possibility of abandoning faith in Christ in favor of a "return" to Judaism. Yet, even this second point is disputed. The main alternative to the

---

14. There is no scholarly consensus on this subject. For a useful overview of the literature to 1982, see John W. Thompson, *The Beginnings of Christian Philosophy: The Epistle to the Hebrews,* Catholic Biblical Quarterly Monograph Series, vol. 13 (Washington, DC: Catholic Biblical Association of America, 1982), 1-15. Dating the letter is somewhat easier than ascertaining its audience: since Hebrews is known to 1 Clement, it cannot be later than 96 C.E.

15. Barnabas Lindars, SSF, *The Theology of the Letter to the Hebrews* (Cambridge: Cambridge University Press, 1991), 19.

argument that Hebrews counsels against "going back" to Jewish practice is that the letter counsels moral rigor (the quotation marks are used here and earlier because we do not need to presuppose, and, in any event, we have little idea where to draw the lines, that those moving toward Jewish faith were Jews before they were Christians, though this seems plausible).[16]

It is reasonable to expect that the two factors are interrelated: the threat of persecution, or at least its memory, shaped and limited the Hebrews' vision of the possibilities presented by the gospel and configured the risks they were willing to take on its behalf. If, as many scholars suggest, the Jewish synagogue was the environing tradition of the readers of Hebrews, then one might surmise that this was also the context in which the Hebrews incurred the hostilities to which the text points.[17] In such circumstances one can imagine a number of possible responses: repentance, recantation, and a corresponding absorption back into the life of the synagogue; digging in the heels and a corresponding edification of the boundaries between the two communities; this latter, in turn, might take at least two forms, one triumphalistic — "a higher ministry," "a better covenant," "a great high priest" — another, agonized and attentive to the crisis this breakage with the past produced; finally, triumphalism and agonism might fund an alternating current, that is, a dialectical engagement with the past.

This last option, I suggest, is what takes shape in the Epistle to the Hebrews. The memory of persecution in the community renders its relationship to the past ambiguous. The psalmist said, "Everything in subjection to

---

16. It probably counsels both, but moral laxity is a more general threat than reversion to Jewish practices, so if, for instance, one takes the audience of Hebrews to have been particularly broad, very "Hellenistic," or heavily indebted to "Gnosticism" and/or middle Platonism, then it is likely that one will decide that Hebrews is primarily about cultivating moral rigor. Alternatively, the date of the letter might also affect its theme. If one takes Hebrews to be early (most scholars do not) then one will likely opt for the reversion to Judaism threat. If one takes the epistle to be late, one will opt for moral rigor. The deciding factor seems to be whether the Temple in Jerusalem was destroyed by the time of Hebrews' publication, on the assumption that if the Jewish sacrificial system were no longer in effect when Hebrews was written then its references to that system would be symbolic and metaphorical, not references to things that Jews actually were doing. Personally, I favor a late date and a predominantly Jewish-Christian audience, on the assumption that a set of distinctions between Jews and Christians would have to be in the process of becoming relatively clear to the readers in order for the rhetoric of Hebrews to make sense.

17. I envision a situation rather like that constructed by J. Louis Martyn in *History and Theology in the Fourth Gospel*, now in its third edition (Louisville: Westminster/John Knox, 2003). Martyn provocatively entitled the first part of his book "A Synagogue-Church Drama: Erecting the Wall of Separation."

them," "nothing outside their control," but evidently it did not feel as though he could have been right — so, again, the author's pause, which has a certain realism about it: "As it is, we do not yet see everything in subjection to them." No doubt the anxiety to which this writer gives voice is familiar, not only to readers then, but also to readers today. John Donne pronounces a similar anxiety in the seventeenth century, as he struggles to picture salvation in a way that expresses both his hopes and his fears: "I, like an usurped town, to another due, / Labor to admit you, but Oh, to no end."[18] And the psalmist cries out in another place, "How long, how long, O Lord? Will you forget me forever?" (Ps. 13:1). "Not yet," "labor," "forever": these anxieties are about time, the time it takes to see one's hopes acknowledged. In Hebrews, the writer's anxiety is not strictly personal; it is also corporate, and so the anxiety about time opened out into the spatially extended life of the community. Had the community taken a misstep, made an inaccurate prognosis, not calculated the odds correctly, erred in its judgment in following Jesus? This was an anxiety about how and, crucially, where to locate the church in the story of salvation's creation, and, like Donne and the psalmist, it was funded by a fear of failure, by a sense of foreboding that there may be no secure way, no appointed time, to make the church "fit"; that, in other words, one might not be able to cultivate an adequately habitable picture of salvation.

After the pause, when the writer's world again begins to move, the other foot falls: "But we do see Jesus, who for a little while was made lower than the angels, now crowned with glory and honor because of the suffering of death, so that by the grace of God he might taste death for everyone" (Heb. 2:9). Now, the question is, what kind of picture of salvation is this that Hebrews offers? It is, to say the least, a bizarre alternative to the psalmist's vision. Under the pressure of human limitation, our "drooping hands" and "weak knees," under precisely the sense of realism that caused the writer to stop short at the psalmist's vision, he directs our vision to Jesus, who he says is crowned with glory and honor because of the suffering of death. If the psalmist said, "Everything in subjection to them," the writer to the Hebrews replies, "No: crowned with glory and honor because he was subject to everything." Here, exaltation and subjection are not alternatives, not diametrically opposed responses to the same event.

The point is not only that acknowledging this should feel difficult. The point is also that subjection and exaltation judge our sense of time.

---

18. John Donne, Holy Sonnet 14, in *The Norton Anthology of English Literature*, 6th ed., vol. 1, ed. M. H. Abrams (New York: W. W. Norton, 1993), 1117.

Rowan Greer argued that "Hebrews contains . . . a strong double judgment concerning Christ. That is, passages in which Christ is described as the brightness of God's glory and the very stamp of His person are balanced by descriptions of the Christ who was made lower than the angels and tasted death for all."[19] Hebrews pushes its readers to this double judgment and then beyond, because it offers seeing Jesus, exalted-because-subjected, as the reason to continue to follow him. Beyond: For the author of Hebrews, what kind of church contemplates Christ as the pioneer of salvation made perfect through suffering?

At least three things need to be said in response to this question. In the first place, Hebrews calls Christ the *archegos,* the pioneer, of salvation because he was made perfect through sufferings (Heb. 2:10). He passed through suffering to perfection and in so doing blazed a trail to glory. But trails are made only to be followed. So, the picture of salvation Hebrews envisions is a summons to a task, and this determinatively orients the people of God toward the future. But more than this, Hebrews sees the ground on the basis of which this people exists as lying in the future as well. The good news is a calling, which implies an odd orientation in time. Characteristically, human experience of the past shapes the possibilities for envisioning the future. Imagined futures that claim no continuity with the past are fantastic, at best. The past is experienced as a deposit or a foundation; it constitutes the horizon out of which we act, out of which we raise our hopes and fears for what is to come. But Hebrews envisions a radical break with the past, and yet a break that itself funds a new kind of continuity in time, namely, the continuity of a promise that is itself a revolution in consciousness. For Hebrews, Jesus does not represent something to which people could look back and then go forward. Because he is the *archegos* and/as *teleiotes* of the faith made perfect through suffering, he is relevant not as past, but as future.[20] Or, to say it with Ernst Käsemann, for the writer to the Hebrews the *evangelion* is available only as *epangelia* — the gospel is to be encountered as promise.[21]

The gospel's promissory character allows it to be gospel. As a prom-

---

19. Rowan A. Greer, *The Captain of Our Salvation: A Study in the Patristic Exegesis of Hebrews* (Tübingen: J. C. B. Mohr, 1973), 6. Cf. John Chrysostom, *Homilies on the Letter to the Hebrews* 1.3.

20. The two preceding sentences paraphrase Herbert McCabe, *What Is Ethics All About?* (Washington: Corpus, 1968), 140.

21. Ernst Käsemann, *The Wandering People of God: An Investigation of the Letter to the Hebrews,* trans. Roy A. Harrisville and Irving L. Sandberg (Minneapolis: Augsburg, 1984), 19.

ise rather than a destination it may determinatively revolutionize the past. Every revolution involves a founding discontinuity with the past it claims to turn over, but as such, and only on the basis of this discontinuity, new lines of continuity with that past can be drawn. This is, in effect, to constitute a new past by creating a new relation to one's history. Consider, for instance, the epistle's opening verses, which contrast the differing ways God speaks: "Long ago God spoke to our ancestors in many and various ways by the prophets, but in these last days he has spoken to us by a Son, whom he appointed heir of all things, through whom he also created the worlds" (Heb. 1:1-3). In one sense, the break between how God spoke long ago and how God has spoken "in these last days" is complete. "But" is primarily disjunctive, yet nevertheless the disjunction has the force of positing a revolutionary continuity between the "now" and the "then."

In the second place, and building on the sense of disjunction with the past, the writer to the Hebrews conceives of the church under the sign of Israel's wandering in the wilderness. Käsemann argued that by Hebrews 3:17 wandering becomes the epistle's principal trope for understanding the church's form of existence:

> Hebrews intends to show to the Christian community the greatness of the promise given it and the seriousness of the temptation threatening it. For this reason, it sets before its eyes the picture of Israel wandering through the wilderness. From such a type the possibilities of Christian existence can be perceived. This assumes that type and antitype share a basic posture. Such a common posture does in fact exist in both, insofar as in both there is issued a λόγος τῆς ἀκοῆς which summons to wandering, and both must hold fast this Logos precisely in their wandering (4:1f.).[22]

Hebrews draws out both a typological and decidedly ateleological continuity with the past. In other words, because the break with Israel's history has been decisive — God has always spoken by prophets and angels, but in these last days God has spoken by a Son — the author's attempt to envision a new and revolutionary continuity with the past by pointing to the image of Israel wandering through the wilderness places the church of the Hebrews "in limbo" in terms of its orientation and directionality in time. In this posture, both fidelity to the gospel as promise and the threat of forsaking that promise loom as real possibilities. This, I think, gives force to

---

22. Käsemann, *Wandering People of God*, 17-18.

the author's *paraklesis* that sets the dynamic for the whole letter: "Therefore, we must pay greater attention to what we have heard, so that we do not drift away from it. For if the message declared through angels was valid, and every transgression or disobedience received a just penalty, how can we escape if we neglect so great a salvation?" (Heb. 2:1-3a).

Both fidelity and "drifting away" are envisioned as real possibilities for the church, and this leads to the third point: the gospel promise that the church bears is dispossessive, the *epangelia* is encountered as *marturia* (Heb. 11:2, 4, 39), God's people's witness by their present labor to a way into holiness.[23] For the writer to the Hebrews the connection between gospel and promise is more than that between content and form. The gospel is more than the content that fills out the otherwise empty shape of the promise. Rather, the shape of salvation requires the good news to be encountered as a promise in the lives of people who do not point to themselves but away from themselves down the trail that Christ has blazed.

The ecclesiological impact of this dynamic can be seen at the epistle's close in the contrast between the two covenants and the exhortation to go "outside the camp" (Heb. 13:13). Beginning in verse 18 of chapter 12, the writer envisions what was promised:

> You have not come to something that can be touched, a blazing fire, and darkness, and gloom, and a tempest, and the sound of a trumpet, and a voice whose words made the hearers beg that not another word be spoken to them. (For they could not endure the order that was given, "If even an animal touches the mountain, it shall be stoned to death." Indeed, so terrifying was the sight that Moses said, "I tremble with fear.") But you have come to Mount Zion and to the city of the living God, the heavenly Jerusalem, and to innumerable angels in festal gathering, and to the assembly of the firstborn who are enrolled in heaven, and to God the judge of all, and to the spirits of the righteous made perfect, and to Jesus, the mediator of a new covenant, and to the sprinkled blood that speaks a better word than the blood of Abel. (Heb. 12:18-24)

This is not exactly prolepsis, as the consistent combination of the present and aorist tenses in the perfect indicates. Rather, the Hebrews have come to Mount Zion and the heavenly Jerusalem by having come to Jesus, whose work is already complete (Heb. 10:12). The writer does not see the relation-

---

23. Käsemann, *Wandering People of God*, 15-37; cf. Heb. 10:19.

ship between eschatology and Christology as one of future and present (or past), just as the heavenly Jerusalem and Jesus are not straightforwardly different destinations: they are certainly not to be distinguished along an axis of "already/not yet." Both are present realities that have been made possible by Jesus, "the pioneer and perfecter of our faith" (Heb. 12:2).

Still, the eschatology of Hebrews needs to be distinguished from the notion of "realized eschatology" popularized in mid-twentieth-century scholarship, because having come to the heavenly Jerusalem is also to have approached the gospel as promise. The gospel, because it is a promise, cannot be possessed, owned, secured, or edified. It can only be witnessed in the life of faith, as the eleventh chapter, with its repeated "By faith . . . by faith . . . by faith," insists. Thus, although the heavenly Jerusalem *has come*, it remains appropriate for the writer to remind the Hebrews that they have "here . . . no lasting city, but . . . are looking for the city that *is to come*" (Heb. 13:14, emphasis added). Moreover, Hebrews fuses the images of city and the camp in the wilderness, with the result that the permanence of the heavenly city is associated with impermanence (or at least the transitory, changing, and nomadic nature of the camp). Walls, boundaries, ways of keeping people out (or in) mark the cities with which Hebrews is familiar, but, strikingly, the heavenly Jerusalem has no borders or walls — it is not something that can be touched, for what can be touched can be shaken.

Because the heavenly Jerusalem is given as promise, everywhere is its border. The gospel as promise is, for the author of Hebrews, continually given as an ecstatic mission that takes the shape of mutual love and hospitality (Heb. 13:1-2). Indeed, the Sabbath rest for the people of God, which operates as the object of the promise early in the letter, has by the end of the letter been transformed into a calling to go "outside the camp and bear the abuse [Jesus] endured" (Heb. 13:13). In consequence, the openness of the heavenly Jerusalem corresponds to the vulnerability of its Lord.[24]

In this sketchy foray into Hebrews' nascent ecclesiology, salvation is pictured as the promise of a gathered community that is called to follow Jesus, himself a new kind of humanity, "a priest forever, after the order of Melchizedek" (Heb. 6:20; 7:17). Yet, the author's initial use of Psalm 8 indicates that this very picture of salvation is elicited and offered in the space

---

24. Käsemann's *katapausis* thesis seems to me not to take account of this turn of the screw. Thus, despite his early emphasis on the gospel as promise and the correlative ecclesiological implications of wandering and dispossession, Käsemann's reliance on "gnosticism" allows him to posit the city as pure destination rather than also as the site of calling out.

opened up by a fear of failure, namely, that *our* humanity is, after all, old, frail, and vulnerable — not at all like Christ's. It is a fear that we are condemned to suffering and aimless wandering, to exile from a city we have never known and might never reach. In this context the good news is that frailty and vulnerability are not foreign to the author and perfecter of our faith; that, because they are not foreign to him, we might follow where he has led; that, because we might follow where he has led, the eschatological city for which we hoped no longer has to be thought merely as destination, a kind of cosmic bedroom after the travails of a hard day's night, but can now be thought also as mission that explodes its edges, borders, and walls in the hope of a sociality unmitigated by domination or exclusion. This is a hopeful vision, to be sure, but how must that explosion look if it is not to betray its nature as promise and as gospel? This is where attention to the differences between O'Donovan's and Yoder's conceptions of Christian eschatology and, correlatively, how eschatology informs ecclesiological reflection, pays off.

Oliver O'Donovan's Political Theology

Oliver O'Donovan's theological political imagination provides a rich backdrop against which to juxtapose Yoder. Here, I will position O'Donovan's political theology in terms of his theology of scripture to establish a context for a close reading of *The Desire of the Nations*, in which O'Donovan maintains that "[a] theological account of how this world is ruled . . . must proceed from and through an account of the church."[25] Following this, I develop a set of criticisms of O'Donovan's theopolitics based on the reading of the book of Hebrews I set forth above. O'Donovan, I argue, does not ultimately need the church for his picture of salvation because the vindication of the created order in the resurrection of Christ furnishes him with an account of politics that is conceptually more primitive than the creation of the church.

O'Donovan's Theology of Scripture

Christian theology is first and foremost an intensive enterprise in that it takes scripture as its primary imaginative resource. This is to say that doc-

---

25. O'Donovan, *The Desire of the Nations*, 159.

trine, while necessary, is strictly complementary and subordinate to the exegetical task. Both O'Donovan's *Resurrection and Moral Order* and *The Desire of the Nations* exhibit an extraordinary fidelity to scripture. Indeed, O'Donovan's attention to and use of scripture has attracted a large amount of attention, as reflected in the publication of *A Royal Priesthood?*, an entire volume dedicated to interrogating O'Donovan's use of the Bible "ethically and politically."[26] In the next few paragraphs I shall highlight the salient features of O'Donovan's "theology of scripture" so as to draw out two things. In the first place, I argue, one cannot attend to the place of the church in O'Donovan's political theology without seeing how that placement is structured by his reading of scripture. In the second place I shall uncover a set of risks for theology that are elicited by O'Donovan's intensive focus on scripture. Theology's exegetical task is not only a matter of how or what one reads; it is also a matter of with whom one reads, and this latter focus is not always within the purview of O'Donovan's analysis, a fact that ramifies in his ecclesiology.

How then does O'Donovan's theology of scripture affect both the shape and the placement of the church in his political theology? Three things warrant notice. (1) O'Donovan's theology of scripture highlights the internal diversity of voices in the Bible to which the church as a *politeia* must attend. (2) That diversity is a product of history and needs to be treated as such; thus, the form of the church must be historically adaptable. (3) The diversity in scripture shapes its unity as scripture. This unity is christological and therefore analogous to the unity of the church. Since, as I have said, scripture is of fundamental importance to O'Donovan's political theology, each point deserves to be fleshed out.

In the first place, although O'Donovan's rationale for his extended forays into scripture studies is quite straightforward — Craig Bartholomew noted that for O'Donovan "theology is political simply as a result of being true to the gospel" — O'Donovan does not conceive of "being true to the gospel" as at all a simple matter.[27] Rather, theology is true to the gospel when it resists reading strategies that ameliorate the difficulty of the text. One way of envisioning how O'Donovan's theology is "true to the gospel" is as a challenge to theologies of scripture that rely on "a canon

---

26. Craig Bartholomew, Jonathan Chaplin, Robert Song, and Al Wolters, eds., *A Royal Priesthood? The Use of the Bible Ethically and Politically: A Dialogue with Oliver O'Donovan*, The Scripture and Hermeneutics Series, vol. 3 (Grand Rapids: Zondervan, 2002).

27. Craig G. Bartholomew, "Introduction," in *A Royal Priesthood?* 27.

within the canon," or the idea that certain texts comprise the proper hermeneutical key for reading other texts. Scripture is for him marked by generative dissonance: the task of the theologian is not to dissolve this dissonance, not to relieve the challenge of reading the whole text of scripture.

This particular approach to scripture distinguishes O'Donovan from a wide range of theologians, Augustine and Origen included, but also Yoder. While each of these other theologians maintains the difficulty of reading scripture well in his own way (Origen and Augustine via their "hierarchical" reading strategies and Yoder through the assumption that any reading of scripture as scripture will express the consensus of the reading community), O'Donovan locates scripture's difficulty differently. In contrast to Origen and Augustine, O'Donovan keeps interpretation rooted firmly in history; the theologian's imagination is not licensed to move into "spiritual" registers, especially if that movement presupposes, as Origen and Augustine do on occasion, that scripture bears only a prima facie dissonance because our epistemic resources are inadequate for understanding the plain sense of the text. In contrast to Yoder, O'Donovan does not appear to think that the community of interpretation is the final arbiter of what the text says. Interestingly, Origen and Augustine on the one hand, and Yoder on the other, share orientations to scripture that insist on the priority of some passages to others. And, while it may be neither possible nor desirable to avoid this altogether, there is a sense in which O'Donovan's caution is proper: reading some texts through others can contract what Richard Hays called the "inexhaustible hermeneutical potential" of scripture.[28] It is not that exodus, or jubilee, or justification by faith through grace are wrong as lenses for a theology of scripture; it is that they are inadequate.[29] Every focal concept, no matter how fecund in terms of the possibilities for reading that it cultivates, also generates a set of limitations or blindnesses to the text that have political manifestations.

Consider, as grounds for these claims, O'Donovan's comments regarding neologisms in "The Concept of Publicity."[30] While not a reflection on scripture, I think the general point that every grammar carries with it a

---

28. Richard Hays, *The Moral Vision of the New Testament: Community, Cross, New Creation* (San Francisco: HarperCollins, 1996), 1. Cf. Frank Kermode, *The Genesis of Secrecy: On the Interpretation of Narrative* (Cambridge, MA: Harvard University Press, 1979).

29. O'Donovan criticizes these hermeneutical foci in *Desire of the Nations*, 12-19.

30. Oliver O'Donovan, "The Concept of Publicity," in *Studies in Christian Ethics* 13:1 (2000): 18-32.

set of risks could be extended to include focal hermeneutical concepts like "liberation" and "shalom" or, for that matter, "authority" and "rule":

> Everybody has always thought that the world began yesterday; but a cool investigation can show us that it didn't. And so neologisms are replaced with older, more durable categories derived from tradition. There thus develops a difference between unofficial language, fluid and fashion-bound, and official language, which we assume when we intend to be serious or searching. But official *sang-froid*, no less than neologism, can conceal as much as it reveals.[31]

New conceptual grammar is sometimes faddish. The point to be pressed is that O'Donovan's theology of scripture is not hermeneutically naïve; he does not say that popular contemporary foci are wrong as such, only that they make no attempt to deal with the entire scriptural picture. While Yoder assumed that every reading is unstable, limited, and subject to supplementation because it is particular, O'Donovan highlights the destabilizing potential of the text by arguing that theologically adequate readings of scripture suspend the reader in the dissonance generated by the reader's interaction with clashing currents in the text. Such dissonance could not be supplemented: scripture will be encountered as other; it will be different; it will produce cognitive dissonance — and this is all part of its character as scripture. Each new reading proves the point. But this is not to suggest that there is no right way to read the text. Rather, the theologically adequate way to read scripture lies in remaining faithful to its internal dissonance as cultivating a space in which to proclaim the gospel. O'Donovan's approach to scripture is rather like what James Alison says it means even to speak of "Holy Scripture":

> We mean that we don't question it so as to break it, but rather we allow it to get close enough to us to produce a break in us. If we can hear the parts of the text which make no sense, rather than only those parts which we use to justify ourselves and strengthen our self-image, then perhaps from within that same sense of strangeness we will hear the Other whose image we are called to recover.[32]

---

31. O'Donovan, "The Concept of Publicity," 18.
32. James Alison, *Raising Abel: The Recovery of the Eschatological Imagination* (New York: Crossroad Herder, 1996), 17.

This approach shapes what O'Donovan is willing to say (and what he is unwilling to say) regarding how one derives a normative political orientation from scripture. In other words, *The Desire of the Nations* demands to be read within the compass of this theology of scripture and not, as some theologians have argued, as implying a decidedly one-sided and establishmentarian posture. Walter Moberly, for instance, has criticized the "massive lacuna in O'Donovan's use of the OT." O'Donovan, Moberly suggests, attends to the political imagery and voice of the Psalms and the sixth-century prophets at the expense of the imagery of the Deuteronomist and the Pentateuch.[33] Thus, on Moberly's account, politically centrifugal currents in scripture, such as nomadism and diaspora, are consistently undervalued in O'Donovan's interpretation of the Bible. It is, however, more accurate to say that *The Desire of the Nations* presupposes the appeal and force of readings of the Old Testament that stress the political instability of God's people; O'Donovan manifestly does not ignore them. Rather, in the face of popular "revolutionary" readings of scripture (that emphasize "exodus," "jubilee," "shalom," or "liberation" as hermeneutical skeleton keys), O'Donovan sounds the balancing, diaphonic tones of "settlement," "monarchy," "deliberation" and "law." Being true to the gospel, for O'Donovan, is a matter of attempting to attend to all the countervailing voices in scripture in an effort to allow them to balance each other.

O'Donovan's theology of scripture is also a matter of historical consciousness, and this is the second point that demands elaboration. His principle of generative dissonance is primarily an issue of "historical diastasis." In his response to William Schweiker's and Nicholas Wolterstorff's reviews of *The Desire of the Nations*, O'Donovan clarifies what he means by historical diastasis: "The articulation of Scripture into 'Old' and 'New' implies a distance in time that must be reflected in a Christian reading of ancient Israel."[34] Christians reading the Old Testament need to beware at least three pitfalls, which "a self-conscious allowance for historical diastasis" will help them avoid. In the first place, there is the Marcionite danger of "repudiat[ing] . . . the Old in the name of the New." Second, there is the danger of "assimilat[ing] . . . Old and New to one another."

---

33. R. W. L. Moberly, "The Use of Scripture in *The Desire of the Nations*," in *A Royal Priesthood?* 53. Cf. Stanley Hauerwas and James Fodor, "Remaining in Babylon: Oliver O'Donovan's Defense of Christendom," *Studies in Christian Ethics* 11:2 (1998): 48.

34. Oliver O'Donovan, "Deliberation, History, and Reading: A Response to Schweiker and Wolterstorff," *Scottish Journal of Theology* 54:1 (2001): 127-44. The quotation is found on pp. 140-41.

And third, there is the danger of allowing the New to supersede the Old.[35] Each of these reading strategies is dangerous because, in one way or another, it alleviates the difficulty of reading scripture by detemporalizing the task.

One final suggestion regarding O'Donovan's theology of scripture needs to be made in order for the argument of *The Desire of the Nations* to be clear: the generative dissonance *of* scripture should not be taken to undermine its unity *as* scripture. O'Donovan emphasizes the point by insisting that scripture "coheres as a narrative," and that its "narrative coherence, however it may be elaborated, constitutes a decisive testimony for faith."[36] In light of the two preceding points, the claim that generative dissonance marks O'Donovan's theology of scripture should be read as an apophatic or iconoclastic set of restraints on the scriptural imagination. Yet, that dissonance is subtended by a more fundamental unity, not only of narrative coherence, but also of a christological unity that properly pertains to the dramatic character of the word of God. In Christ the narrative of scripture coheres because the resurrection "does not appear like an isolated meteor from the sky but as the climax of a history of divine rule."[37] In terms of the theology of scripture found in *The Desire of the Nations*, the christological coherence of scripture allows the theologian, as well as the church, to bear the full weight of the threat of dissolution (unceasing suspicion) generated by the diaphonic voices of scripture.

The ecclesiology appropriate to such a theology of scripture will be necessarily minimal. In reflecting on the mediation of God's kingly rule, O'Donovan draws on the narrative in Exodus regarding Moses' descent from Mt. Sinai to promulgate the law (Exod. 34:29ff.). "The shining face of Moses," O'Donovan contends, "is an image of the law itself, through which God is immediately and continually present" (p. 51). Yet Moses' face, as an image of divine immediacy, must be veiled after the law has been delivered:

> When Moses had finished speaking with them, he put a veil on his face; but whenever Moses went in before the LORD to speak with him, he would take the veil off, until he came out; and when he came out, and told the Israelites what he had been commanded, the Israelites would see the face of Moses, that the skin of his face was shining; and

---

35. O'Donovan, "Deliberation, History, and Reading," 141.
36. O'Donovan, "Deliberation, History, and Reading," 140.
37. O'Donovan, *Desire of the Nations*, 20. In the remainder of this section, page references to this book will be given parenthetically in the text.

Moses would put the veil on his face again, until he went in to speak with him. (Exod. 34:33-35)

The implication, in O'Donovan's understanding of this passage, is that just as the glory of the Lord is apparent on Moses' face, which must be veiled, the Lord's presence is hidden in the figure of the law, but this hiding is nevertheless not precisely a mediation.[38] The hiding is rather the form that God's immediacy takes. The law is therefore not a mediation or representation of God's rule; it is the presence of the divine rule, which can, after Sinai, be experienced only indirectly. God's rule is imageless because God is imageless, and not only does O'Donovan's exposition of the tensions involved in Israel's political theology derive from this presupposition, but a good deal of his theology of scripture does as well (p. 49).

The Church in The Desire of the Nations

Creation, order, history, rule, vindication: these are the focal motifs of O'Donovan's theopolitical picture of salvation in *The Desire of the Nations*. The catena of motifs is calculated to disturb. What motivates such a political theology in a time when deconstruction, contingency, and aesthetics are the buzzwords du jour? The short answer is O'Donovan's impression that interminability, undecidability, and vulnerability characterize all political discourse that eschews robustly theological inflection. But that short answer deserves elaboration: Are there not other theological registers, and substantial ones, that resist articulation in terms that seem obsessed with sovereignty? Perhaps, but political theology deals with the authority of God, and that authority goes underacknowledged in many of the most persuasive theological voices of today. In *The Desire of the Nations* O'Donovan therefore attempts to think the possibility of a political theology that could move beyond that universal suspicion that characterizes political inquiry today. Politics, O'Donovan argues, needs to provide and express the direction of a society; without such guidance a society ceases to be a politics at all (p. 10). Yet, where suspicion is total, where ethics serves a merely critical function for unmasking the interest behind various politi-

---

38. Cf. Origen, *In Exodum Homilia*, die griechischen christlichen Schriftsteller der ersten drei Jahrhunderte, 6. Bd. (Leipzig: J. C. Hinrichs, 1920), 264, where Origen says of Moses: *"facies vero eius glorificata est, sed velamine tegitur, quia sermo eius habet scientiae gloriam, sed occultam"* (12.3.26-27).

cal claims, no politics can steer society without being subject to the charge of merely legitimating its own interests (p. 11). Where, in other words, a society shares sufficiently few substantive convictions, answers to the question of the shape of the common good will invariably be seen as attempts to replace the good with one or more particular visions of specific goods, and this, O'Donovan contends, renders any discussion of a genuinely common good impossible.

Any political structure or institution, O'Donovan argues, is "historically fluid," and this means that before political ethics begins, a work of political theory or political theology is required in order to define the horizons of the discourse (p. 14).[39] The problem is that defining those horizons requires a workable account of authority, which is what contemporary Western politics lacks. A culture of total suspicion destabilizes political engagement by delegitimating authority — leaving politics in the bind of negotiating competing claims to political legitimacy without a concept of legitimacy that would enable the successful negotiation of those claims: "can democracy *avoid corruption* by mass communications? . . . Can civil rights be safeguarded *without surrendering* democratic control to arbitrarily appointed courts? . . . Can ethnic, cultural and linguistic communities assert their identities *without oppressing* individual freedoms?" (p. 18, my emphasis). In each case, one set of goods is threatened by another, yet every set of goods is interested and so equally threatened (and threatening). For O'Donovan, the way out of this deadlock is to envision a theopolitics that, because founded in "true political concepts," would recover the lost ground of authority and therefore not be vulnerable to the charge of mere legitimation (p. 15). O'Donovan's search in *The Desire of the Nations* is thus not exactly for an ecclesiology — he refuses to give a clear account of the church's institutions (for the church "appears rather underdressed politically") — but for a theology funded by (and funding) an overarching political conceptuality that could subject competing claims between rival conceptions of the good to common scrutiny (p. 25).

O'Donovan's ecclesiology in *The Desire of the Nations* correlates with his theology of scripture. Just as scripture is defined by its internal and dissonant relations, the church is also defined as a set of relations, in-

---

39. O'Donovan does not indicate how hard and fast he takes the line between political theology and political ethics to be. The main point, I take it, is that ethics requires deliberation on a particular set of contemporary circumstances, deliberation that can only proceed on the basis of some theoretical grammar.

cluding a reflexive self-relation, a relation to Israel, a relation to Christ, a relation to the eschaton, and a relation to the world. Although these relations are variously interconnected, there is a discernible hierarchy among them that follows the shape of the narrative of scripture.

For O'Donovan, the church's relation to Israel is primary for political theology. The other relations follow from this relation, and in this respect he agrees fundamentally with a host of contemporary theologians who argue that one cannot talk coherently about the church without speaking of Israel. At least part of the impetus for this claim arises out of the growing recognition in the five decades since the Holocaust that the genocidal mood that gripped Europe in the mid-twentieth century had roots in a Christian refusal to acknowledge the ongoing interplay between God and God's people, Israel.

Yet this is not to imply that the churches' refusal to acknowledge the paradigmatic role of God's people was entirely one of ignorance. As Andrew Shanks suggests:

> One ... needs to view the phenomenon of theological anti-Semitism ... as just the ugliest, and most fateful consequence of [the] ... need to neutralize the scandal of the cross. After all, the deepest level of the scandal ... lies in the way the cross confronts us with an image of *our own* potential destructiveness: its role as a symbol of the potential destructiveness of human crowds and organizations generally — including those to which we ourselves belong (the church itself as well).[40]

If Shanks is right, and anti-Semitism has been a coping mechanism that alleviates the painful reality of the gospel, then the church's long history of escalating anti-Semitic violence is not simply a problem of relations to outsiders. It is also a problem of self-relation, which we might state in Girardian terms: a social group's desire for internal coherence, unity, and peace is accomplished by the expulsion of an element falsely (or arbitrarily) held to be responsible for its disunity. O'Donovan's argument is that something like this has happened to the church and to the modern Western culture it fostered. By scapegoating the Jews the church gave rise to the crisis of authority that debilitated political engagement in the modern West.

If such a claim seems rather implausible, O'Donovan goes further.

---

40. Andrew Shanks, *Hegel's Political Theology* (Cambridge: Cambridge University Press, 1991), 11-12.

Not only has the Christian rejection of the Jews contributed to the culture of political suspicion that currently mires the North Atlantic world, but Old Testament Israel's political orientation needs to be considered regulative for "our own political analysis and deliberation" (p. 29). "The public tradition of Israel," O'Donovan says, "carries an unrealised promise for the full socialisation of God's believing people, the appearing . . . of the New Jerusalem from heaven. This means that any question about social forms and structures must be referred to a normative critical standard: do they fulfill that will of God for human society to which Israel's forms authoritatively point us?" (p. 25). In short, O'Donovan finds the basic political conceptuality for which he is looking in the unique covenant between God and Israel. That covenant he argues, demonstrates that the kind of authority implied in the confession, "Yhwh reigns," serves "as a framework for exploring the major questions about authority posed by the Western tradition" (p. 45).

O'Donovan's account of the regulative function of Israel's political forms, however, points to the major risk associated with O'Donovan's use of scripture. To put the risk in his own terms, we might say that the principle of historical diastasis should draw a large question mark after any attempt to speak straightforwardly of "the public tradition of Israel" or "Israel's official history" (p. 28). If Israel's political history is one that we must take pains to encounter as distant, then one will always have to ask whether any given reconstruction of that history is distant enough. This is surely a matter of theological judgment, but, as such, it will need to be open to an ongoing process of discernment and revision in a way to which O'Donovan's presentation does not seem particularly amenable. Rather, because O'Donovan assumes that Israel's history is a revealed history he also assumes that the history that has been revealed is non-negotiable. But the principle of historical diastasis should not only serve to safeguard Israel's history from unwarranted revision (and who decides what is unwarranted?); it should also safeguard that history from any interpretive retelling whatsoever, and this evidently will not do for a dogmatics that treats scripture as a primary resource for contemporary practice.

Consequently, historical diastasis, while an important corrective to the primitivist temptation to assume an untrammeled proximity to scriptural history, is insufficient as a hermeneutical principle. It needs to be supplemented by an account of theological judgment that enables decisions about when the sense of historical distance from scripture that the theologian cultivates is sufficient for the purposes to which scripture needs to be put. And this is never simply a matter of how one reads the text (no matter how complex the hermeneutical apparatus). It is also a matter of with whom one reads the text; that is, whose judgments about distance and proximity to the text will one trust and take as authoritative? While *The Desire of the Nations* implies a set of answers to this question (Augustine's biblical interpretation, for instance, receives only approbation from O'Donovan), it does not raise the question in a way that allows it to refract O'Donovan's reading of scripture or his account of political authority. For Yoder, by contrast, the question of with whom one reads scripture was always in the foreground of his thought about the institutional shape of the church.

O'Donovan's exposition of the political conceptuality native to the Old Testament turns on how the expression of God's rule was actualized in Israel's life. Indeed, his entire discussion of the political shape of the people of God answers the following question: How was the imageless faith of Israel reconciled to political institutions as representations or images of the Lord's kingship? (p. 53). His answer comes in the form of six theorems (or four theorems and two corollaries) that, when generalized, underwrite a coherent discussion of the role of authority in contemporary political analysis. In the following few paragraphs I outline O'Donovan's arguments concerning each of these theorems.

The first theorem, that "[p]olitical authority arises where power, the execution of right and the perpetuation of tradition are assured together in one coordinated agency" (p. 46), grows out of O'Donovan's reflection on three affirmations that Israel made about how God revealed Godself as king: "Yhwh's authority as king [was] established by the accomplishment of victorious deliverance, by the presence of judicial discrimination and by the continuity of a community-possession" (p. 36).[41] In O'Donovan's estimation, two things follow from these affirmations. In the first place, each is necessary for political power to be authoritative rather than baseless and arbitrary, but, in the second place, every political regime will have trouble sustaining itself as authoritative in its exercise of these functions because no political agency can be its own sufficient condition.

In other words, no authority is self-generating. Rather, all authority

41. A significant precursor to O'Donovan's analysis of the political conceptuality of ancient Israel exists in the opening chapter of Paul Ramsey's *Basic Christian Ethics* (New York: Charles Scribner's Sons, 1950). It would be fascinating to trace the lines of continuity from Ramsey's account of Christian love as creating and preserving community to O'Donovan's chastened account of the Christendom state as a function of Christian mission.

arises in historically contingent circumstances. Part of what it means, however, for a politics to be authoritative is to demonstrate its legitimacy by inquiring after its own basis. Every authority we encounter attempts to think its own foundations, and if those foundations are pursued on a purely immanent level, the project is bound to misfire. This baseline assumption for O'Donovan is proven in the failure of Western political thought to theorize itself comprehensively. Therefore, O'Donovan argues, a second theorem is necessary to complement the first, namely, "That any regime should actually come to hold authority, and should continue to hold it, is a work of divine providence in history, not a mere accomplishment of the human task of political service" (p. 46). When Israel confessed that God is king, it meant at least in part that God's providence underlay its own (and, by extension, any) human political authority as its first principle.

If political authority is always encountered historically, then it also has to be acknowledged where it arises. Political authority is public, and in order to be public it must be recognized as authoritative by a social group. This is not the same thing as saying that public recognition confers authority on a political agency, as, O'Donovan argues, Israel's experience of divine kingship demonstrates. God's authority is acknowledged in the praise of God's people, but it is not established by the people's praise. Without being recognized in praise, God's reign remains real: the people do not have to recognize divine authority in order for God to give victory, to judge, or to grant possession, but if God is not acknowledged as king, then God's rule is not effective for the people. Praise is the people's public demonstration of their acknowledgment of God's authority, and it is therefore the basis of their participation in God's reign. Thus, O'Donovan's third theorem: "In acknowledging political authority, society proves its political identity" (p. 47).

Israel's political identity was a mediation of God's rule in the figures of the prophet, priest, and king. O'Donovan here picks up classical reflection on the incarnation of divine authority in a threefold office. But rather than accounting for this *munus triplex* in terms of a proto-democratic doctrine of the separation of powers (where the king secures victory, prophets exercise judgment, and the priests guard the traditions of the people), the political institutions of ancient Israel functioned as a set of constraints on the absolutist claims of the monarchy to keep it from obscuring the immediacy of God's rule in the law. For Israel, the check on absolutism was the law. Thus, the rule of law and not government is the proper expression of political authority. Or, as O'Donovan puts it in a fourth theorem, "The authority of a human regime mediates divine authority in a unitary way, but is subject to the authority of law within the community, which bears independent witness to the divine command" (p. 65).

The independence of the law has corollaries at both the international and the interpersonal levels. At the international level, O'Donovan finds that Israel never entertained the prospect of world empire, in part because unity under one government amounted to a denial that God was the sovereign lord of history. Just as the prophet and priest served as constraints on the monarch's representation of God's rule, so also the plurality of the nations constituted a check on the notion that a single world power should mediate "the universal rule of Yhwh as high-god" (p. 72).

The alternative to empire was Israel's vision of the nations gathered at Zion, which allowed it to think of the binding-together of the nations under God's rule expressed in the law. So, in the first corollary to the independence of the law, law not government is the "appropriate unifying element in international order" (p. 72). Because the law is imageless, no political organization can claim to represent totally the law's authority. The primacy of the law in international relations therefore reminds political bodies that humanity is fragmented, that those fragments are expressed in competing and overlapping accounts of collective identity, and that humanity is not "a reality that we can command politically" (p. 73). For O'Donovan, Israel's experience among the nations, as well as its correlative sense of mission to the poor and the stranger, is envisioned as a model for the nations, and thus for international order. "There are always 'others,' those not of our fold whom we must respect and encounter," O'Donovan says (p. 73).

On the interpersonal level, O'Donovan argues that the individual member of the community "finds his or her significance" in "the prior and original fact" of "the holy community" (p. 78). This is not to say that the individual was absorbed into the community of Israel, but rather that he or she came to serve as a storehouse for Israel's political experience in three related ways, namely, in the "isolation of the sufferer" exemplified by Job, in the gift of wisdom to the "counsellor to those who bear official responsibility," and in the isolation of the prophet as the one who "expresses the anger of Yhwh against the people" and "the misery and despair of the people under the blow of Yhwh's anger" (pp. 74-80). Each of these functions of the individual both grows out of and addresses the fracturing of the nation: the sufferer by pointing to the lapse in the institutional mediation of God's rule that allowed his or her grievances to go unaddressed, the counselor by embodying God's sovereignty in a context where it went unacknowledged, and the prophet by anticipating in his judgment a time when he would cease to mediate God's rule because all the people would acknowledge God's authority "in the heart" (p. 80; cf. Jer. 31:31ff.; Rom. 2:29).

The role of the individual in Israel's political life thus extends the independent testimony of the law and creates the prospect for understanding how individual authority sustains and renews the community's life. This, O'Donovan thinks, is a hopeful alternative to the radically individualist conscience of the West, for it binds the individual's authority to the collective self-understanding of the community rather than ascribing to him or her a set of pre-political rights that must be defended against competing claims. Thus, O'Donovan's second corollary to the independence of God's law is that "the conscience of the individual members of a community is a repository of the moral understanding which shaped it, and may serve to perpetuate it in a crisis of collapsing morale or institution" (p. 80).

O'Donovan maintains that these four theorems and their corollaries "provide an outline of what theology may need to put in the place traditionally held by a notion of political authority" (p. 81). There is, however, a specifically ecclesiological risk that comes with extracting general political theorems from scripture, namely, that the movement from the narrative of God's self-revelation to comprehensive statements about political authority will outpace the specific proclamation of divine rule among the people of Israel and in the church. In other words, once one has a set of true political concepts gleaned from the story of ancient Israel, it is not clear why one needs the church. Any political agency that can understand itself in terms of these six theorems will be capable of overcoming the modern impasse of suspicion that characterizes politics today.[42]

O'Donovan sees this risk and addresses it by formulating the "doctrine of the two," which stands out in singular importance amid the dizzying array of schemata in *The Desire of the Nations*.[43] The narrative of Israel's political institutions reached its climax in Jesus' ministry and

---

42. Yoder might also say that the church plays no essential role in politics — that a secular society founded on political principles like the ones O'Donovan envisions is entirely conceivable. Rather, the church's founding and continued existence is a matter of historical contingency: because it just so happens that no secular society we know of in fact operates with the political concepts O'Donovan has formulated, the church has a continuing task, function, and legitimacy, namely, to witness to the possibility of a truly political life together.

43. The doctrine of the two is notable for at least three reasons: (1) it provides a bridge between Israel, Jesus, and the church; (2) it admits of historical variation and adaptability; (3) it correlates the eschatological imagination with politics.

mission, and particularly in his announcement of the kingdom, which divided history into two ages, the old and the new. This division helps O'Donovan maintain the intensive priority of God's sanctifying activity to its translation into extensive theorems. The doctrine of the two thus moves into two of the other relations that define the church in O'Donovan's political theology, namely, its relationship to Christ and to the eschaton.

In O'Donovan's estimation Jesus' proclamation of the kingdom, of "the fulfilling of the time," opens political theological reflection to an eschatological register. In proclaiming the kingdom, Jesus transformed a basically spatial duality in Israel's political thought into a horizon in time. That duality was the fruit of Israel's experience of exile in Babylon, which "became the paradigm for Jewish existence thereafter, even with the resettlement of Judah and the rebuilding of Jerusalem" (p. 83). On the one hand, Israel found itself in a situation where it could not but acknowledge the authority of the pagan rule to which it was subjected, while, on the other hand, it continued under that subjection to witness to the rule of God.

The doctrine of the two was encountered not only as agency (that is, as an answer to the question, who is exercising rule?) but also in society (who acknowledges being ruled?). Two societies, two cities, meant two rulers. Israel could coexist with Babylon, the societies could live together indefinitely, but the same could not be said for the two rules. God's rule never paralleled that of the emperor; that would have been to concede the emperor's self-description as a god competing for authority with God. Eventually the "foreign domination of the Holy Land" (p. 84) would give way to God's own rule, and this expectation shaped Israel's nascent eschatological imagination.[44]

---

44. Israel's eschatological imagination made history the arena in which the duality of authority was to be played out. There are other possibilities for distinguishing the two rules, most notably, perhaps, a sphere of influence approach where pagan rule is acknowledged as "political" and God's rule as "spiritual." While this would not necessarily dehistoricize the duality, it would have the effect of softening the urgency of Israel's eschatological hope. To this O'Donovan adds that the problem with a political/spiritual solution to dual authority is that it treats both categories as "known quantities," when the real challenge that confronts political theology is knowing in what the alternatives consist. There is at least the problem of an excluded middle here, that is, of discovering the hidden third common term that makes political and spiritual recognizable as alternatives within a spectrum of authority. And, that discovery might show that political and spiritual are not nearly as distinct as we imagined. It is a commonplace by now to observe that ancient emperors had "spiritual" as well as "political" aspirations, as both the *divus imperator* cults of Rome during the time of the early church and the rule of Antiochus IV Epiphanes during the time of the Maccabees demonstrate. The impor-

So, Israel conceived of the doctrine of the two as a provisional arrangement to be overcome in time. When, therefore, Jesus announced the kingdom of God, it was from within the horizon of Israel's eschatological imagination — the time was fulfilled in which dual authority would no longer be Israel's experience of how this world is ruled, when God's own rule would be vindicated as sovereign by its possession in Christ's judgment. Thus, according to O'Donovan, "the duality inherited from Israel's past underwent a transformation. The Two Cities, with their concomitant Two Rules expressing Israel's alienation from its calling, gave way to the Two Eras. The coming era of God's rule held the passing era in suspension" (p. 93).

For O'Donovan the church is the "social and political presence of the future age" made possible because God's rule was vindicated in the resurrection of Jesus (p. 158). That social presence is, however, not fully disclosed to us. The church, on the one hand, is the society whose particular mission it is to show how the rule of God is realized within it, to show through its sacramental life that, because Christ has been raised from the dead and is seated at the right hand of the Father, all other authorities are called into question. Yet, on the other hand, because the "final universal presence of Christ" is not "fully apparent," so too the church is not the definitive presence of the kingdom of God on earth but awaits its own fleshing out in the time when Christ will be all in all (p. 146).

Because the church's presence on earth is qualified by an eschatological reservation, O'Donovan argues that a space is opened up for "an account of secular authority which presumes neither that the Christ-event never occurred nor that the sovereignty of Christ is now transparent and uncontested." In the time between the times, as it were, when the chthonic powers are in the process of withering before the newness of God's activity in Christ, secular authority is granted this role to play: it is authorized to enable the church to draw "men and women of every nation . . . into the governed community of God's Kingdom" (p. 146). For its part, the church's mission is to anticipate, as it gathers in praise and worship, as it suffers under the last vain flailings of the conquered powers, and it reminds those authorities of Christ's victory, "the final state in which mankind as totality will gladly be subject to the rule of God" (p. 175).

---

tance in observing that commonplace lies in recognizing that the "spiritual" aspects of imperial rule were regarded as a proper part of what emperors do. It is probably not wrong to say that Israel, and then the church, stood alone in challenging that presumption, but this is not because either of them thought that God's rule and human rule could never conflict politically.

O'Donovan argues that "the hidden and undisclosed status of the rule" that constitutes the church translates into an indeterminacy in its social structure, that is, in how it instantiates God's rule in history (p. 159). On the one hand this is a straightforward Anglican acknowledgment that church order must be, in the phrasing of the Chicago-Lambeth Quadrilateral, "locally adapted in the methods of its administration to the varying needs of the nations and peoples called of God into the unity of His Church."[45] On the other hand, the dialectic between the church's assertion of its political nature and its underdeveloped social structure plays a serious role in O'Donovan's picture of salvation. In both *Desire of the Nations* and an earlier essay, O'Donovan reads John of Patmos's polysemous view of the eschatological city — "the primal form of human society" — in the book of Revelation as hauntingly authoritative on this point (p. 155).[46] Although John deploys a rich panoply of political imagery to depict the eschatological triumph of the church, O'Donovan argues that his pictures of the church as it actually exists involve ambiguous faithfulness, in which "[t]he faithful are as scattered, isolated witnesses before the massive solidity of the idolatrous empire" (p. 155). Yet, this puzzling attenuation of the church's social existence in the seer's vision of human history serves the purpose of exploding its boundaries in a final revelation of the civic life of God's people. The church is not finally the primary eschatological reality on O'Donovan's reading of Revelation. Rather,

> Three political communities, ancient Israel, the pagan empire and the eschatological church, are being drawn together in a startling identification. In fact there is only one city, which is at once the Holy City trampled on by the Gentiles and the Great City where Christ was crucified. The community in which God and the Lamb have set their throne is one and the same with the community where Satan and the beast have set their throne. The reason why John of Patmos will not allow the church a distinct social presence is that its witnesses claim back the Great City to become the Holy City. (p. 156)

We can reflect on this picture of salvation by thinking about how it conceptualizes its borders in contrast to the reading of Hebrews I outlined above. For O'Donovan the promise of this picture of salvation lies in its

---

45. *The Book of Common Prayer* (New York: Church Hymnal Corporation, 1979), 877.
46. Cf. O'Donovan, "The Political Thought of the Book of Revelation," *Tyndale Bulletin* 37 (1986): 61-94, esp. 91-92.

erasure of outsideness in the reconstitution of the "aboriginal unity of the human community."[47] According to O'Donovan, this aboriginal unity is both universal — "It *is* restored humanity, and 'outside' it there is nothing but rejection" — and a vision of the election of the people of God, "whose destiny it is to shed God's light into the whole world."[48] In O'Donovan's view John does not mediate universality and election. He juxtaposes them so as not to deny the full weight of one or the other. Moreover, O'Donovan contends that "To ask him to do more than set these two images . . . alongside one another, is to ask him to be more theoretical than his vision allows him to be."[49]

My reflections on Hebrews above lead me to worry about this juxtaposition. For, despite the fact that there are two images, universality and election, the seer's vision is one vision. That is to say, juxtaposition is a way to sublate the dialectic between universality and election, allowing them to be framed in a single reference, however one proposes to manage the difficult balancing act. Here, then, the doctrine of the two is overcome, not by being mediated by a third, but by being ameliorated in the totality of a fourth, namely, the heavenly Jerusalem.

This heavenly Jerusalem too has no walls, just as the heavenly Jerusalem of Hebrews had none. But there is a crucial difference between the eschatological imagination that I sketched above and O'Donovan's reading of the political conceptuality of Revelation, and indeed, the role of eschatology in his political theology generally: O'Donovan's eschatology is governed by the tension between the "already" and the "not yet." His account of the Epistle to the Hebrews, which he assimilates to his understanding of Revelation — John of Patmos "follow[s] the lead of the author to the Hebrews"[50] — confirms this view.

In *Resurrection and Moral Order* O'Donovan notes that the writer to the Hebrews "appears to dismiss, almost abruptly, the great vision of Psalm 8, the vision of man set in authority over the rest of creation, lacking a very little of God, crowned with glory and honor."[51] That vision concerns the created order, the economy of God's governance of the world

---

47. O'Donovan, "The Political Thought of the Book of Revelation," 92.
48. O'Donovan, "The Political Thought of the Book of Revelation," 93.
49. O'Donovan, "The Political Thought of the Book of Revelation," 93.
50. O'Donovan, "The Political Thought of the Book of Revelation," 93; cf. O'Donovan, *Desire of the Nations*, 155.
51. Oliver O'Donovan, *Resurrection and Moral Order: An Outline for Evangelical Ethics* (Grand Rapids: Eerdmans, 1986), 53.

through the stewardship of human beings. Yet, what the psalmist presents as straightforwardly descriptive of the way things are, the writer to the Hebrews says pertains to the world which is to come: the psalmist's vision is "not realized — yet." Instead, O'Donovan says, the writer to the Hebrews "sees in Christ, and in the order of the world to come, the vindication and perfect manifestation of the created order which was always there but never fully expressed."[52]

I am not convinced that the idea of "always there but never fully expressed" makes sense; however, the more important thing to see is that O'Donovan's creation-fulfillment schema fosters an eschatological singularity of vision that conceiving the gospel as promise calls into question. On O'Donovan's account, there are no borders to the heavenly Jerusalem because there remains nothing but the city. The alternative, which I think squares with the Epistle to the Hebrews, is that there are no borders to the heavenly Jerusalem because the question of what remains is left open. Thinking with Yoder about the relationship between ecclesiology and eschatology helps to flesh out the relevance of this difference for how the church thinks of itself and the holiness it is called to embody.

Yoder's Alternative

Readers of Yoder will recognize many resonances between O'Donovan's theology and Yoder's. Indeed, from my perspective, the sheer bulk of their similarity in fundamental orientation makes the differences between them all the more important. Some of the similarities that have emerged include the insistence that the Gospel is by its very nature political; the common criticism of the modern split between "politics" and "religion," especially insofar as that split suggests that there exists a morally neutral discourse to mediate between the realms of politics and Christianity; the focus on praise as the people of God's participation in God's salvific economy; the conviction that a Christian ethic or political theology must be evangelical; and, finally, the emphasis on history as the arena in which the drama of salvation is enacted. So, it is important in juxtaposing O'Donovan to Yoder not to overstate the differences between them. They share a basic vocabulary, as the following comment by Yoder, which O'Donovan could easily have written, establishes:

52. O'Donovan, *Resurrection and Moral Order*, 53.

It is not the world, culture, civilization, which is the definitional category, which the church comes along to join up with, approve, and embellish with some corrections and complements. The Rule of God is the basic category. The rebellious but already (in principle) defeated cosmos is being brought to its knees by the Lamb.[53]

Yet, there are fundamental disagreements between O'Donovan and Yoder, the precise nature of which has often been obscured by one theologian's caricature of the other's position. As Travis Kroeker argued, "O'Donovan's dismissal of Yoder's 'free' church voluntariety as a form of 'neo-liberalism' is misplaced," while Yoder's own reduction of "all Christendom political theologies to a rather crude typological depiction of . . . the fall of the church from its calling as servant into the libidinous desire for historical mastery and political domination" does not map neatly onto O'Donovan's theopolitics, at least not as I have sketched it above.[54] In the remainder of this chapter, I want to "home in" on eschatology in Yoder's thought as a way to gain a more precise account of why O'Donovan and Yoder's ecclesiologies differ in the ways that they do.

Whereas O'Donovan's primary picture of salvation is the vindication of the created order, Yoder envisions salvation fundamentally as the community-building event of people's response to the promise of a way that leads where Christ has led.[55] The consequence of this view is that in-

---

53. John Howard Yoder, *The Priestly Kingdom: Social Ethics as Gospel* (Notre Dame: University of Notre Dame Press, 1984), 54.

54. Travis Kroeker, "Why O'Donovan's Christendom Is Not Constantinian and Yoder's Voluntariety Is Not Hobbesian: A Debate in Theological Politics Re-defined," *Annual of the Society of Christian Ethics* 20 (2000): 41-64. The quotation is from p. 41. I deal with Yoder's account of Constantinianism in Chapter Three and develop his understanding of voluntariety in Chapter Five of this book.

55. For Yoder it would also be true to say that salvation is the vindication of the created order, but with this difference: that the vindication in question is the creation of the church: "The ultimate meaning of history is to be found in the work of the church." Yoder, *The Royal Priesthood: Essays Ecclesiological and Ecumenical*, ed. Michael G. Cartwright (Grand Rapids: Eerdmans, 1994), 151. Not so for O'Donovan, who might be closer to Barth than Yoder was here. In *Church Dogmatics* IV.3.2 Barth wrote: "It cannot be said that . . . the world is referred absolutely and inescapably to the existence of the community. . . . We may thus venture three statements: 1. the world would be lost without Jesus Christ and his Word and work; 2. the world would not necessarily be lost if there were no church; and 3. the Church would be lost if it had no counterpart in the world" (p. 826). Perhaps a criticism of O'Donovan's theopolitics as implicitly Constantinian needs to begin at this point. In anatomizing the Constantinian temptation, Yoder wrote, "This is then what is really important;

sofar as one can speak of the church's holiness one needs to recognize that it resides in the disciples' imitation of Christ's suffering servanthood "for us and our salvation." And here he follows the vision of the writer to the Hebrews, whose view of the church also resists the notion that suffering is but a stepping stone to exaltation. The implication is that when God shows up, God suffers.

For Yoder, Jesus' authority for us resides in his imitability. That is a christological claim of first-order importance for thinking about eschatology, ecclesiology, and holiness. The contrast with O'Donovan is quite stark. O'Donovan locates Jesus' authority in his representation of the divine rule, manifested in his incarnation and recapitulation of the politico-theological history of Israel. As he puts it in *The Desire of the Nations,* "The Christ, when he appeared, must be a representative of the total rule of God in the hearts of his people."[56] Clearly Yoder agrees with O'Donovan that Jesus recapitulated Israel's history; Christ had to do at least that in order to be recognizable as a fulfillment of Israel's hopes. However, Yoder emphasizes Jesus' discontinuity with Israel's expectations more strongly than O'Donovan. Yoder claims, for instance, that "Jesus' contemporaries were awaiting a new age, a bringing to fulfillment of God's plan; but they expected it to confirm and to vindicate all their national hopes, prides, and solidarities. Thus Christ's claims and His kingdom were to them scandalous."[57] For O'Donovan, then, the accent fell on how Christ's authority *re*capitulated Israel's political life — it took its fundamental shape in continuity with God's revelation in Israel.[58] For Yoder, by contrast, Jesus' authority is also a re*capit*ulation of Israel's life, another heading and a new directionality that breaks the old lines of expectation that might have been taken to account for his continuity with Israel's hope. The way of life Christ proclaimed, incarnated, and inaugurated among his followers was continuous with Israel's hopes, but revolutionarily so.

---

the true meaning of history, the true locus of salvation, is in the cosmos and not in the church. What God is really doing is being done primarily through the framework of society as a whole and not in the Christian community." Yoder, *Royal Priesthood,* 198.

56. O'Donovan, *Desire of the Nations,* 115.

57. Yoder, *Royal Priesthood,* 146. Cf. Yoder, *The Original Revolution: Essays on Christian Pacifism* (Scottdale: Herald Press, 1971), 58.

58. O'Donovan also acknowledges that Christ's rule must be "a decisive step forward from anything that the political history of Israel had known." *Desire of the Nations,* 115. Cf. Robert W. Jenson, *Systematic Theology,* vol. 1: *The Triune God* (New York: Oxford, 1997), 43-45.

Indeed, Yoder's emphasis on Jesus' imitability marked a decisive break with the bulk of modern Christian ethics, including those figures with whom he is often most closely associated. Paul Ramsey, for instance, in a claim echoed by Stanley Hauerwas, notes that "in 'imitating Christ' one thing the Christian never attempts: he never imitates the fact that Jesus had no Christ to imitate."[59] In his response to *In Defense of Creation*, Hauerwas glosses Ramsey's claim as follows and at the same time slightly skews Yoder's Christology:

> Ramsey is right when he says that the difference between advocates of just war and pacifists is Christological. But when compared to the Christology of *In Defense of Creation*, that difference seems small indeed. We both [Hauerwas and Ramsey] take the life and teachings of Jesus with utmost seriousness, but I suspect the crucial difference between us lies in our understanding of Christ's work. Certainly neither Yoder nor I believe that Jesus simply exemplifies a way of life for us to follow. On the contrary, without the ontological change occasioned through Christ's resurrection, there would be no possibility of living as he did. Ramsey is quite right that there is forever a decisive distance between us and Jesus, insofar as Jesus and Jesus alone is the singular faithful Son that makes God's kingdom present. Our obedience to his life is possible only because of the Father's vindication of Jesus' obedience through the resurrection.[60]

I will not argue with Hauerwas whether obedience to Christ's life is possible only because Jesus was raised. If, as Robert Jenson claimed, "God is whoever raised Jesus from the dead, having before raised Israel from Egypt," then the resurrection is at least partly constitutive of the identity of the God to whom Jesus prayed, and the faithful imitation of Christ's life will certainly involve reference to this same God.[61] The point to be pressed

---

59. Ramsey, *Basic Christian Ethics*, 24.
60. Stanley Hauerwas, "On Being a Church Capable of Addressing a World at War: A Pacifist Response to the United Methodist Bishops' Pastoral *In Defense of Creation*," in *The Hauerwas Reader*, ed. John Berkman and Michael Cartwright (Durham, NC: Duke University Press, 2001), 427-58. The quotation is from p. 440. Cf. Hauerwas's epilogue to Paul Ramsey, *Speak Up for Just War or Pacifism: A Critique of the United Methodist Bishops' Pastoral Letter* In Defense of Creation: The Nuclear Crisis and a Just Peace (University Park: Pennsylvania State University Press, 1988), 149-82. In this quotation Hauerwas is commenting on Yoder's analysis of the limitations of the police function of the state for Christian ethics.
61. Jenson, *Systematic Theology*, vol. 1, 63.

is that for Yoder Hauerwas's and Ramsey's attempts to drive a wedge between Jesus and humanity misses the point of orthodox Christology entirely. Thus, Yoder never said that the resurrection makes living like Jesus did possible. Faith in the resurrection did not mean for Yoder that we know how to steer our lives (much less the course of history or politics) now. Rather, what makes living like Jesus did possible is that "The truth has come to our side of the ditch,"[62] or, as he said elsewhere:

> The cross was not in itself a new revelation; Isaiah 53 already foresaw the path which the Servant of YHWH would have to tread. Nor was the resurrection essentially new; God's victory over evil had been affirmed, by definition one might say, from the beginning. Nor was the selection of a faithful remnant a new idea. What was centrally new about Christ was that these ideas became incarnate.[63]

In "But We Do See Jesus," Yoder analyzed a "syndrome or a deep structure" in the Epistle to the Hebrews and other sources of New Testament christological thought that shows why his account of the resurrection differs from that dominant in Christian ethics and in O'Donovan's political theology. In at least five places throughout the New Testament, "in utterly independent ways," Yoder noted that the writers became "at home in a new linguistic world," each with its own particular cosmology, above which the writer placed Jesus as Lord. Although Jesus was affirmed as higher than the categories that the wider world held ready to hand, this christological syndrome also included "a powerful concentration upon being rejected and suffering in human form . . . as that which accredits Christ for this lordship," and, crucially, a picture of human salvation that reflected the double judgment on Christ. Yoder wrote, "[I]nstead of salvation constituting our integration into a salvation system which the cosmos holds ready for us to enter into through ritual or initiation, what we are called to enter into is the self-emptying and the death — and only by that path, and by grace, the resurrection — of the Son." The New Testament writers also affirmed that Christ's victory was enabled by "what later confession called preexistence," and they argued that believers "share by faith in all that that victory means."[64]

Yoder's main point in diagnosing this syndrome was to show that "the

---

62. Yoder, *Priestly Kingdom*, 62.
63. Yoder, *Royal Priesthood*, 148-49.
64. Yoder, *Priestly Kingdom*, 53.

development of a high Christology is the natural cultural ricochet of a missionary ecclesiology when it collides as it must with whatever cosmology explains and governs the world it invades."[65] But, in this syndrome the resurrection does not prove Jesus' authority; rather, Christ's suffering and *kenosis* license his claim to be Lord. Correlatively, that same self-emptying is the condition of possibility for the church's imitation of Christ. Had Jesus not incarnated a new way of life marked by "a new way to deal with offenders — by forgiving them," "a new way to deal with violence — by suffering," "a new way to deal with money — by sharing it," "a new way to deal with problems of leadership — by drawing upon the gift of every member, even the most humble," "a new way to deal with a corrupt society — by building a new order, not smashing the old," "a new pattern of relationships between man and woman, between parent and child, between master and slave, in which was made concrete a radical new vision of what it means to be a human person," and "a new attitude toward the state and toward the 'enemy nation,'" it would be senseless to speak of imitating him at all.[66]

How then does the resurrection play a role in Yoder's ecclesiology? Not first as that which makes Christian life possible, but rather as that in the light of which the Christian life makes sense. In other words, because "the third day he rose from the dead, ascended into heaven, and is seated at the right hand of God the Father almighty, whence he shall come to judge the quick and the dead," it makes sense to say the rest of the creed: "I believe in the Holy Spirit, the holy catholic church, the communion of saints, the forgiveness of sins, the resurrection of the body, and the life everlasting." Without Christ's resurrection, the remainder is nonsense. In this respect, one might say that the resurrection itself functioned eschatologically for Yoder, that is, as "a hope that, defying present frustration, defines a present position in terms of the yet unseen goal that gives it meaning."[67]

The emphasis on hope here is all-important. Hope cannot be hope if the object for which one hopes is guaranteed. For O'Donovan, the created order has been vindicated in the resurrection, and that vindication is now in the process of unfolding its implications. O'Donovan's eschatology anticipates the completion of the unfolding of the resurrection's consequences. The difficulty is that because the resurrection vindicates creation, the social shape that eschatological anticipation takes need not be gov-

---

65. Yoder, *Priestly Kingdom*, 54.
66. Yoder, *Original Revolution*, 29.
67. Yoder, *Royal Priesthood*, 145.

erned by the cross for O'Donovan. Rather, eschatological conviction warrants an expansion on the life of discipleship in suffering servanthood because O'Donovan's vision of the totality of God's reign in the heavenly Jerusalem without walls shows the *theologia crucis* to have been but a historical moment in the movement toward the *theologia gloria.*

For Yoder, by contrast, the importance of eschatology lies solely in the sense it makes of the disciple's action now, which is not other than an imitation of Christ's self-emptying in a life that we might characterize as a *sacrificium laudis.* Thus, when Yoder looks at the biblical visions of the heavenly Jerusalem he does not focus on the city's limitlessness as an indication that there is no outside, as if what had happened was that the whole world had finally gotten around to seeing creation as Christians have always seen it. He focuses rather on the way that discipleship to a slain lamb exceeds Christians' own conceptions of the way they see creation. As he put it in "To Serve Our God and to Rule the World," "To see history doxologically demands and enables that we appropriate especially/specifically those modes of witness which explode the limits that our own systems impose on our capacity to be illuminated and led."[68] This means that even, or perhaps especially (since here the danger of triumphalism is greatest), in its vision of the heavenly Jerusalem the Christian life demands a generous and receptive engagement with otherness.[69] There are two implications here that I shall pursue by way of conclusion: the first concerns the way a political theology needs to be pursued, and the second is about the church's shape as a doxological body.

If Christ's inauguration of a new way of life — marked among other

---

68. Yoder, *Royal Priesthood,* 129.

69. Cf. Romand Coles, *Rethinking Generosity: Critical Theory and the Politics of Caritas* (Ithaca: Cornell University Press, 1997). A certain patristic parallel can be detected with Gregory of Nyssa, who conceived of the life of glory as a continuous journey into the inexhaustible difference of the Trinity. See, e.g., Jean Cardinal Daniélou's introduction to *From Glory unto Glory: Texts from Gregory of Nyssa's Mystical Writings,* trans. and ed. Herbert Musurillo (New York: Scribner, 1961). That parallel is elaborated throughout "negative theology" in medieval theology to at least Meister Eckhart. It is probably no coincidence that the most "apophatic" theologians characteristically have had the most eleemosynary conceptions of Christian social life. Cf. Denys Turner, *The Darkness of God: Negativity in Christian Mysticism* (New York: Cambridge University Press, 1995); Mark A. MacIntosh, *Mystical Theology: The Integrity of Spirituality and Theology* (Malden, MA: Blackwell, 1998). The danger with this parallel is that otherness can become a univocal concept that is projected onto and absorbed into divine plenitude and darkness; this, I think, was not the case for Yoder, who did not ground social differences in an account of divine difference.

things by missionary mobility, enemy love, the relativization of political sovereignty, forgiveness, and sharing possessions — is the creation of salvation, then political theology will not be marked by the pursuit of true political concepts. For O'Donovan, any political conceptuality is epistemically prior to that conceptuality's embodiment in a social order (that is to say that concepts do regulative work before they do descriptive work), even though the true political concepts are reachable only, as it were, through their instantiation in a political body. But this is both to accept the problem of historicism, namely, of how to speak of the universal in the particular and contingent, and to finesse an answer to that problematic in terms of an insistence on a history of divine revelation. For Yoder, who was every bit as concerned to prioritize history and divine revelation as O'Donovan is, the problem of the universal and the particular does not appear, because truths of reason or revelation are not epistemically prior to the constitution of the church. What the church has is a lifestyle and not an ideology that would, on the one hand, secure it against possible future change by finding some "solid ground beyond the ditch"[70] and, on the other, entitle it to act as chaplain to the powers that be. Moreover, skepticism or suspicion is no threat to a way of life that simply says what it is and asks for a response, whether affirming or not.[71] If the church is a distinct social presence, if its "very existence . . . is itself a deep social change," governing and directing the responses of others to that change is not at issue.[72] Moreover, the character of the church's witness to the promise of the gospel will inhibit it from using the resurrection to secure its social or political relevance. Because the church simply incarnates a way of life that it learned by watching its Lord, "What we are looking for . . . is not a way to keep dry above the waves of relativity, but a way to stay within our bark, barely afloat and sometimes awash amidst those waves, yet neither dissolving into them nor being carried only where they want to push it."[73]

70. Yoder, *Priestly Kingdom*, 59.

71. O'Donovan's idea of "total suspicion" likely says as much about his own fears of the church's being ignored in public policy discussions as it does about what others actually believe (or refuse to believe). To put the point crudely: there is no suspicion as such; there are only suspicions. Suspicion is neither absolute nor perpetual, but particular suspicions are informed, marked, and limited by the specificities of the narratives about the world in and as which they arise. People's suspicions can be addressed by encounter and dialogue; suspicion, however, is a threat that demands a quasi-transcendental solution.

72. Yoder, *Original Revolution*, 31.

73. Yoder, *Priestly Kingdom*, 58.

Second, since its creation is salvation, the church receives itself, finds itself, and shows itself in doxology. Praise is the most determinative political activity of the church. This is the case "in contrast," as Bernd Wannenwetsch has noted, "to the prevailing modern tendency to identify the political meaning of the church primarily or exclusively in respect of its relationship to the state or the influence it seeks to bring to bear on civil society."[74] But it is also the case in contrast to O'Donovan's view that the praise of the people acknowledges a rule that exists independently of the people's confession and praise. The only rule God in fact exercises is a rule *pro nobis,* and that rule cannot be genuinely "for us" unless it is received as such. The church's praise therefore enacts God's grace by making it public and accessible, by making it available in a way that it can be responded to by the outsiders of every age because the gospel "is not information which will remain true even if people in a ghetto celebrate it only for themselves; it is about a community-building story for which the world beyond the ghetto is half the reconciling event."[75] In its life of praise, the church witnesses and proclaims salvation by embodying the gospel as the promise of a new way of life. What that way of life looks like (and does not look like) is the subject of the following chapters.

---

74. Bernd Wannenwetsch, "Liturgy," in *The Blackwell Companion to Political Theology,* ed. Peter Scott and William Cavanaugh (Oxford: Blackwell, 2003), 76.

75. Yoder, *Priestly Kingdom,* 55.

CHAPTER 2

Seizing Godlikeness:
Ernst Troeltsch and "Constantinian" Syntheses

> *If any philosophy regards time as in some way mere appearance, as a "mode of perception," as something to be explained or explained away so as to attain to a supposedly supratemporal sphere in which we can withdraw into supposed security in the castle of eternity, then that philosophy must be rejected in the light of Christ's openness to the Father.*
>
> Hans Urs von Balthasar,
> *A Theology of History*

Introduction

In this chapter I sketch a genealogy of Yoder's ecclesiological thought, roots of which lie in a critical appraisal of Ernst Troeltsch's attempt to mediate Christianity to modernity. Perhaps, in light of recent studies of Yoder's theology, this claim deserves an initial defense.[1] In the first place, I do not intend this excavation of roots to be exclusive. One would also need to address Yoder's education by Barth, Baumgartner, Cullmann, Eichrodt, and Jaspers at the University of Basel (not even to mention his indebtedness to H. S. Bender). Each of those teachers, with the possible exception of Barth,

---

1. I am thinking here primarily of Mark T. Nation's essay "John H. Yoder, Ecumenical Neo-Anabaptist: A Biographical Sketch," in *The Wisdom of the Cross: Essays in Honor of John Howard Yoder*, ed. Stanley Hauerwas, Chris K. Huebner, Harry J. Huebner, and Mark Theissen Nation (Grand Rapids: Eerdmans, 1999), 1-23; and Craig A. Carter's *The Politics of the Cross: The Theology and Social Ethics of John Howard Yoder* (Grand Rapids: Brazos, 2001), neither of whom claim Troeltsch as an important *source* for Yoder's thought.

considered the question "What is the meaning of history?" crucial. So, for instance, Walther Eichrodt entitled his commentary on Isaiah 13–23 *Der Herr der Geschichte*, while Oscar Cullmann's study of the understanding of history peculiar to the New Testament was *Christ and Time*, and Karl Jaspers included among his works *The Origin and Goal of History*.[2] Too, the late 1950s saw the publication of many "theologies of history," including, among others, Rudolf Bultmann's Gifford Lectures, *History and Eschatology*, Jean Daniélou's *Essai sur le Mystère de l'Histoire*, Hendrik Berkhof's *Christ the Meaning of History*, and Hans Urs von Balthasar's *A Theology of History*.[3] I mean to suggest neither that Yoder's work can be encapsulated by the phrase "theology of history" nor that Yoder whiled away his hours reading either Daniélou or Balthasar, though he clearly read Berkhof and Bultmann. Rather, the point is twofold: (1) what it means to think theologically in the light of time was an important disciplinary question at the beginning of Yoder's theological career, and (2) no one posed that question for Yoder's teachers more insistently than Troeltsch. Moreover, in citing Barth as a possible exception to the rule Yoder's teachers followed, I am not claiming that Barth was completely uninterested in history as a thematic focus. Instead, I mean that Barth's polemical context coupled with his immersion in the language of the Bible to produce a de-historicized theology. In other words, while Barth's work has its own set of historical markers and cues, he did not work to highlight *his own* historicity.[4] Where Yoder's atten-

---

2. Walther Eichrodt, *Der Herr der Geschichte. Jesaja 13-23 und 28-39* (Stuttgart: Calwer Verlag, 1967); Oscar Cullmann, *Christus und die Zeit. Die urchristliche Zeit- und Geschichtsauffassung* (Zollikon-Zürich: Evangelischer Verlag A.G., 1946), English translation *Christ and Time: The Primitive Christian Conception of Time and History* (Philadelphia: Westminster, 1950); Karl Jaspers, *The Origin and Goal of History* (London: Routledge & Kegan Paul, 1953). Walter Baumgartner, by slight contrast, worked in an essentially historical-critical vein — thus, while he never published concerning the significance of history for contemporary life, history was always on his horizon. Baumgartner's dissertation was entitled *Kennen Amos und Hosea eine heils-eschatologie?* (Zürich: A. Schaufelberger, 1913).

3. Rudolf Bultmann, *History and Eschatology: The Gifford Lectures, 1955* (Edinburgh: Edinburgh University Press, 1957); Jean Daniélou, *Essai sur le Mystère de l'Histoire* (Paris: Editions du Seuil, 1953), English translation *The Lord of History: Reflections on the Inner Meanings of History*, trans. Nigel Abercrombie (London: Longmans, Green., 1958); Hendrik Berkhof, *Christus de zin der geschiedenis*, 4th ed. (Nijkerk: G. F. Callenbach N.V., 1962), English translation *Christ the Meaning of History*, trans. Lambertus Buurman (London: SCM, 1966); Hans Urs von Balthasar, *Theologie der Geschichte: Ein Grundriss*, 2 Aufl. (Einsiedeln: Johannes Verlag, 1950), English translation *A Theology of History* (New York: Sheed and Ward, 1963).

4. See, e.g., Karl Barth, *Church Dogmatics* III.4, ed. G. W. Bromiley and T. F. Torrance

Seizing Godlikeness

tion to history as presenting a set of methodological aporiae is concerned, then, his indebtedness to and criticism of Troeltsch cannot be overlooked in a search for roots of his thought.

Consequently, the central question of this chapter is about history. More specifically: How does an awareness of belonging to history shape the church's conception of its political faith and activity? Troeltsch, Yoder, and I share these questions with many others for whom, in the late twentieth century, the sense of our historicity became more and more pronounced, to the extent that philosophers of culture could pound their lecterns, proclaiming "a crisis of history" or, in even more apocalyptic tones, "the end of history and the last man."[5]

Today, historicism spins itself into a variety of mythoi, for instance, into the twilit realm of Nietzsche, where, to change the metaphor, "the ice on which we walk becomes ever thinner" and the very possibility of philosophical inquiry, epistemology, ethics, and politics is called deeply into question.[6] Or, it spins itself into the reactionary and morose fortresses of resistance to our "awashness" in history — witnesses to their own contingency in denying it.[7] Again, and on a more bacchanalic imagining, history is spun out in terms of power, with the differential relations between self and other the motor force behind unspeakable brutalities and ecstasies alike. This is our milieu, one in which the question of history is unavoid-

---

(Edinburgh: T&T Clark, 1961): "What we call universal history is [man's] history even though he cannot fulfil Goethe's demand to take in a sweep of at least 6000 years. Man's question concerning the history of humanity is quite natural. But here, too, his answers or historical pictures are not vitally important. What is important is again the fact that he is in history as he is what he is in his limitation" (p. 574). History as a thematic is important for Barth because it is the form of human finitude, which has both positive and negative aspects. In this we see features of Barth's indebtedness to neo-Kantian epistemology.

5. The first declamation is Ernst Troeltsch's, from the first half of *Der Historismus und Seine Probleme, Erstes Buch: Das logische Problem der Geschichtsphilosophie, Gesammelte Schriften*, Bd. 3 (Tübingen: Mohr Siebeck, 1922), 1. The second is the title of Francis Fukuyama's millenarian reflection, *The End of History and the Last Man* (New York: Free Press, 1992).

6. Friedrich Nietzsche, *Thus Spoke Zarathustra*, trans. Walter Kaufmann (New York: Penguin, 1978), 200-201. Note also the proximity of certain readings of Wittgenstein, as in Richard Rorty, *Philosophy and the Mirror of Nature* (Princeton: Princeton University Press, 1979), and Stanley Cavell, *The Claim of Reason: Wittgenstein, Skepticism, Morality and Tragedy* (Oxford: Clarendon, 1979).

7. E.g., Leo Strauss, *Jewish Philosophy and the Crisis of Modernity: Essays and Lectures in Modern Jewish Thought* (Albany: SUNY Press, 1997); George Grant, *Time as History* (Toronto: Canadian Broadcasting Corp., 1969).

able. Yet, if these various myths ring true, if historicism is in the air we breathe, and if history is the ground on which we will have to pick our way, then it seems any road we find will be profoundly rough, brittle, and dangerous by fits and turns.

Or does it? Might there not today be something incredibly commonplace, even banal, about appeals to and the purported dangers of historicism, be they exhilarating, debilitating, or both? Have we not all seen "the lessons of history" trotted out in defense of tremendous complacency? Does not the very ubiquity of our sense of history's menace suggest that it has become all too smooth a ground, a new orienting touchstone whose risks are known? And if so, how do we locate anew — how do we consciously cultivate — the transformative potential of reflection on history, the sense of dispossession that comes with a recognition, as Hans-Georg Gadamer put it, that "history does not belong to us," but that "we belong to it"?[8] These are the questions and anxieties, I suggest, that animated Troeltsch. Derivatively, then, they shaped the way Yoder engaged in reflection on the church.

Because my purpose is to limn an environment in which Yoder's thought about the church found fertile soil, I will limit my discussion of Troeltsch to the following question: How does his thought about history configure reflection on Christianity's political (ir)relevance? I begin, then, by discussing Troeltsch's historical method and conception of the absoluteness of Christianity. Essentially, I claim, Troeltsch's historicism was a methodological attempt to facilitate the equivocation (and therefore wisdom) appropriate to encountering that which is historically distant and strange.[9] But, because Troeltsch found the tension between the absolute

---

8. Gadamer, *Truth and Method*, 2nd rev. ed., trans. Joel Weinsheimer and Donald G. Marshall (New York: Continuum, 1997), 276. I reflect on the affinities between Yoder's historical practice and Gadamer's philosophical hermeneutics in Chapter Three. Gadamer, like Yoder, argued that it is inadequate to respond to the sense of our awashness in history by further methodologizing it. His alternative, which I find congenial to Yoder's evangelical revisionism, was to begin to provide resources to help us reflect on the fragmentary and reified character of the contemporary experience of history, i.e., that the character of our historicity is most obvious where there is the greatest rupture with thinking historically.

9. Cf. Gillian Rose, *Mourning Becomes the Law: Philosophy and Representation* (Cambridge: Cambridge University Press, 1996), 3: "Wisdom works with equivocation." Karl Barth, discussing Troeltsch's doctrine of sin as it appears in the *Glaubenslehre*, commented on Troeltsch's penchant for equivocation with evident frustration: "Naturally Troeltsch . . . believed that what he said was true. But only in so far as he thought that he had to say it in the light of 'present-day Christian life'. . . . And he was conscious of this limitation, much more than Schleiermacher had been. And to that extent he could keep to the general line of

and the individual insoluble, his methodological assumptions stymied his attempt to find a fitting register of equivocation, and committed him, despite his best efforts, to a necessitarian reading of history. This showed itself most clearly in his eschatology, which assumed that the concept of a final end is necessary for an ethics to be successfully executed and yet had to prescind from all material considerations about the nature of such an end. Troeltsch's historicism therefore led him to develop the link between eschatology and ethics that Yoder thought was essential to Christian ecclesiology. Nevertheless, because Troeltsch conceived of history as an

---

Neo-Protestantism, often formulating it in a much more sharp and provocative way than his predecessors, only by raising all kinds of problems and questions and attitudes which he then either left or tried to master with all kinds of wild speculations, which he accepted only as hypotheses." *Church Dogmatics* IV.1, ed. G. W. Bromiley and T. F. Torrance (Edinburgh: T&T Clark, 1954), 384. In the main, commentators since the mid-twentieth century followed Karl Barth in seeing Troeltsch as a representative of *Kulturprotestantismus*. Barth rather famously claimed that Troeltsch's resignation of his university chair in theology (at Heidelberg) in favor of a chair in philosophy at the University of Berlin was of a piece with the cultural accommodation signaled in August 1914 when "[n]inety-three German intellectuals impressed public opinion by their proclamation in support of the war policy of Wilhelm II and his counselors." The claim locates two shifts in Troeltsch's politics: (1) the shift from theology to philosophy, i.e., from the parochial to the general, and (2) the shift from Heidelberg to Berlin, i.e., from the hinterlands of the German intellectual world to the cultural central nervous system. See Barth, "Evangelical Theology in the Nineteenth Century (1956)," in *The Humanity of God* (Richmond: John Knox Press, 1960), 11-33. The quote is from p. 14. See also Benjamin A. Reist, *Toward a Theology of Involvement: The Thought of Ernst Troeltsch* (Philadelphia: Westminster, 1966); Walter Bodenstein, *Neige des Historismus*, 122-40, and Bruce L. McCormack, *Karl Barth's Critically Realistic Dialectical Theology: Its Genesis and Development 1909-1936* (Oxford: Clarendon, 1995), 215. Hans Bosse, in *Marx-Weber-Troeltsch: Religionssoziologie und marxistische Ideologiekritik* (München: Christus Kaiser Verlag, 1970), 140-44, makes a somewhat different statement. Bosse argued that, whereas Marx thought the social conditions determining economics could be reconfigured via revolutionary praxis, Troeltsch thought the same conditions were permanent features of society. He therefore succumbed to a fundamental cultural conservatism that undermined the force of his critical political analysis. Mark D. Chapman, in *Ernst Troeltsch and Liberal Theology*, claimed that the views enumerated above "entirely underestimate Troeltsch's critical distance from his own culture. . . . Troeltsch's real position is rather more complex and is not so inherently conservative, since it allows for a reshaping of the forces that constrain human action in a synthesis *for the future*: compromise and assimilation are two very different principles" (p. 10n). My position is that, with the denial of specifically Christian eschatological claims, the future became a purely formal concept for Troeltsch, which appropriately yielded a purely formal possibility for "reshaping the forces that constrain human action." On Troeltsch's terms, it became impossible to ask what the criteria would be for describing a new cultural synthesis for the future.

arena of conflicts to be mastered and overcome, or, at the very least, ameliorated and controlled, he could not "read" the church as an alternative to the history of security and dominance that funded his social ethics. He could not, in other words, see the church as a history that refused, in Yoder's pregnant phrase, "seizing Godlikeness."[10]

Ernst Troeltsch: Christian Theology without Guarantees

Fritz Ringer, in *The Decline of the German Mandarins,* painted a compelling picture of the academic milieu within which Troeltsch operated. Between 1890 and 1930 German intellectuals reacted with skeptical pessimism and unease to the rapid economic, industrial, and technological development of Germany. Because "economic and political affairs in the age of technology do have a certain anonymity," Ringer suggests, German intellectuals "suspected that their own standards of personal cultivation would come to be rejected as outmoded and irrelevant."[11] Industrialization and urbanization, moreover, threatened the delicate balance of power in late Wilhelmine Germany that favored academics.[12] Specifically, the economic boom that brought Germany hurtling into the modern world in the last decades of the nineteenth century also brought with it the rise of new social classes, including an entrepreneurial middle class and an industrial working class, that challenged the cultural cachet of the intellectual elite.[13] The resulting atmosphere of turmoil among intellectuals led them to speak in terms of a "crisis of culture" so pervasive that Ringer described

---

10. Yoder, *The Priestly Kingdom: Social Ethics as Gospel* (Notre Dame: University of Notre Dame Press, 1985), 145.

11. Fritz K. Ringer, *The Decline of the German Mandarins: The German Academic Community, 1890-1933* (Hanover, NH: Wesleyan University Press, 1990), 1-2.

12. Ringer, in *Decline of the German Mandarins,* argued that the "mandarin type" "can achieve a predominant role within their society only under certain specific conditions. Above all, they can become and remain a functional ruling class only during a particular phase within the material development of their country. They thrive between the primarily agrarian level of economic organization and full industrialization. At that intermediate stage, the ownership of significant amounts of liquid capital has not yet become either widespread or widely accepted as a qualification for social status, and hereditary titles based on landholding, while still relevant, are no longer absolute prerequisites. In this situation, educational background and professional status may well become the only important bases for claims upon social standing that can rival the traditional prestige of the aristocracy" (p. 7).

13. Ringer, *Decline of the German Mandarins,* 12.

it as a tormenting preoccupation: "[T]he German academics reacted to the dislocation with such desperate intensity that the specter of a 'soulless' modern age came to haunt everything they said and wrote, no matter what the subject."[14] Later in the book, Ringer elaborates:

> Sometime around 1890, German academics began to express misgivings about the current condition of German learning and of German cultural life more generally. They spoke of a decline in the vitality of their intellectual traditions, a loss of meaning and relevance. They wondered whether they themselves were partly to blame for the shallowness of the age, the apparent separation of geist [sic] from politics, and the violence of the new social conflicts. They began to suspect that the universities had been neglecting their proper function of spiritual leadership, that mandarin culture had been forsaken by its guardians as well as by the rest of German society. These doubts continued to trouble the German academic community from the 1890s to the 1930s, reaching their greatest intensity during the early years of the Weimar period. By the 1920s, no German professor doubted that a profound "crisis of culture" was at hand.[15]

These politics shaped Troeltsch's career, both as a systematic theologian at the University of Heidelberg and then, later, as a philosopher of culture and history in Berlin. Ringer showed that academics such as Troeltsch found a position of relative cultural importance in late Wilhelmine Germany, which they then sought, unsuccessfully, to maintain in the face of German modernization. Once they lost their toehold as the purveyors of *Bildung*, they began to lament the degeneration of German society, to diagnose a chaotic ateleology unleashed within and by technological society, and to prescribe, in increasingly shrill tones, remedies for the spiritual downfall of German culture.

It should come as no shock, then, to find Fritz Stern, in his study of Germany between 1850 and World War II, noting that, after the November revolution of 1918, Germans in general looked to a "religious" movement to bring unity to the Republic and reground Germany's political and cultural hegemony in Europe.[16] Troeltsch was no exception. Already in 1903 a

---

14. Ringer, *Decline of the German Mandarins*, 3.
15. Ringer, *Decline of the German Mandarins*, 252–53.
16. Fritz Stern, *The Politics of Cultural Despair: A Study in the Rise of the Germanic Ideology* (Berkeley: University of California Press, 1961), 87.

purely secular German society had become inadequate for him, as was the case for a critical mass of German intellectuals in the years surrounding the First World War. Of this unrest Troeltsch wrote, "The great religious movement of modern times, the reawakened need for religions, develops outside the churches, and by and large outside theology as well."[17] For Troeltsch this was at once a sign of great hope and the cause of considerable unease.

Troeltsch's authorship was a difficult one, marked by dissatisfaction both with the shortcomings of his own work and with what he perceived as the collusion of Christian historiography with an essentially conservative politics in the Germany of his day. His theology and ethics indexed an anxiety and a sense of urgency for legitimating Christianity in the face of distinctively modern challenges, some of which he identified in 1912 in strikingly contemporary terms:

> [The] social problem is vast and complicated. It includes the problem of the capitalist economic period and of the industrial proletariat created by it; and of the growth of militaristic and bureaucratic giant states; of the enormous increase in population, which affects colonial and world policy, of the mechanical technique, which produces enormous masses of material and links up and mobilizes the whole world for purposes of trade, but which also treats men and labour like machines.[18]

---

17. Troeltsch was noting the immense popular influence of Paul de Lagarde. See Troeltsch, "Die theologische und religiöse Lage der Gegenwart," *Gesammelte Schriften*, vol. 2: *Zur religiösen Lage, Religionsphilosophie und Ethik* (Tübingen, 1913), 20-21. Quoted in Stern, *Politics of Cultural Despair*, 88.

18. *The Social Teaching of the Christian Churches*, vol. 2., trans. Olive Wyon (Louisville: Westminster/John Knox, 1992), 1010. The contemporaneity of Troeltsch's assessment is all the more pronounced if one compares it with another, in equally apocalyptic registers, from the turn of the twenty-first century: "Empire is materializing before our very eyes. . . . Many argue that the globalization of capitalist production and exchange means that economic relations have become more autonomous from political controls, and consequently that political sovereignty has declined. . . . Even the most dominant nation-states should no longer be thought of as supreme and sovereign authorities, either outside or even within their own borders. *The decline in sovereignty of nation-states, however, does not mean that sovereignty as such has declined.* Throughout the contemporary transformations, political controls, state functions, and regulatory mechanisms have continued to rule the realm of economic and social production and exchange. . . . [S]overeignty has taken a new form, composed of a series of national and supranational organisms united under a single logic of rule. This new global form of sovereignty is what we call Empire." Michael Hardt and Antonio Negri, *Empire* (Cambridge, MA: Harvard University Press, 2000), xi-xii. One could also

Capitalism, industrialism, militarism, bureaucracy, colonialism, the technological imperative, and globalism: these are just some of the forces that conspired to challenge the vision of the world held by Christians in Troeltsch's day. Consequently, if one question animated Troeltsch throughout his career, and if one question has continued to stimulate his heirs, it was how to make Christianity credible under the conditions of modernity. Not that it is easy to speak plausibly of Troeltsch's "heirs." There is no direct lineage to which one could refer, in part because the final years of Troeltsch's career coincided with the rise of "dialectical theology," which tremendously altered the theological landscape. The questions with which Troeltsch busied himself seemed outmoded in the light of Barth or Bultmann (although with hindsight it is easy to see how Bultmann continued many of Troeltsch's habits). Troeltsch's questions ceased to "grab" theologians in the way they had grabbed him and had to await a time in which their grip could again be felt. This theme resounds through many treatments of Troeltsch during the last decades of the twentieth century. For instance, Peter Hodgson noted that although Troeltsch was "[n]eglected for nearly sixty years after his death in 1923," he "has recently been rediscovered and recognized as a thinker of the first importance for a 'revisionist' theology."[19] So also, Troeltsch's biographer Hans-Georg Drescher remarks:

---

point, in finding parallels to Hardt and Negri in particular, to the effect of Troeltsch's conception of relativism on his views about money. In an encyclopedia article on eschatology, he wrote: "But the relativism that is thus introduced into every sphere of life by science is also at the same time produced and encouraged by life itself. By a process of simultaneous differentiation and interrelation, society, too, is transformed into a pure relational system, based not on firm foundations of its own but on an increasingly refined exchange of goods that simply expresses the interchangeableness of all values. Even the seemingly fixed standard of interchangeableness, money, is only the symbol of the relational character of things in general, which leads from one thing to another and conditions one by the other; and the inclination to look upon money (which constitutes, after all, no more than the possibility of exchange and interchangeableness) as in itself a possession is, accordingly symbolic of every inclination to regard mere means to the establishment of relations as last things." See "Eschatology," in *Religion in History,* trans. and ed. James Luther Adams and Walter F. Bense (Minneapolis: Fortress, 1991), 148. Despite extraordinary diagnostic similarities, Troeltsch's fears about modernity are part and parcel of what Hardt and Negri, following Gilles Deleuze, celebrate. In "Das Wesen des modernen Geistes," for instance, he argued that the modern ethos relies on a *problematic* "metaphysics of immanence." See *Religion in History,* 237-72. The quote is from p. 257.

    19. Peter C. Hodgson, *God in History: Shapes of Freedom* (Nashville: Abingdon, 1989), 130.

A variety of circumstances led to his name and his work almost being forgotten in the generation after him, and his significance was recognized only in the narrower circle of professionals interested in the history of religion and theology. Beyond doubt one reason for this is that with his interests and approaches, Troeltsch, as a prominent representative of so-called liberal theology, seemed out of date to the next generation of leading theologians.[20]

H. Richard Niebuhr's recommendation of Troeltsch in his introduction to the 1960 English edition of *The Social Teaching of the Christian Churches* in some senses heralded the arrival of the time of Troeltsch's renaissance, and it is from Niebuhr's work that, at least in English-speaking theology, we can begin to talk of Troeltsch's heirs.[21] But it might be best to speak of at least two Troeltschian legacies to Christian ethics: one, by far in the minority, represented by Yoder; the dominant other embodied by Niebuhr.[22]

There are two large points to be made in an effort to see Troeltsch as a source for Yoder's thought. In the first place, Troeltsch's "favorite book," *The Social Teaching,* needs to be placed in the context of his thought about history and historical thinking (as opposed to being read in an isolationist way that focuses on the significance of typologies for Christian ethics). Po-

---

20. Hans-Georg Drescher, *Ernst Troeltsch: His Life and Work* (Minneapolis: Fortress, 1993), xvi. Remarkably, Drescher continues: "The lack of more wide-ranging and ongoing discussion of Troeltsch's work may have been a contributory factor to his early death. No real school formed around him." Cf. the assessments of, among many others, Wolfhart Pannenberg, "The Basis of Ethics in the Thought of Ernst Troeltsch," in *Ethics,* trans. Keith Crim (Philadelphia: Westminster, 1981), 87; Robert Morgan and Michael Pye, "Preface," in *Ernst Troeltsch: Writings on Theology and Religion,* ed. Robert Morgan and Michael Pye (Atlanta: John Knox, 1977), vii; and Toshimasa Yasukata, *Ernst Troeltsch: Systematic Theologian of Radical Historicality* (Atlanta: Scholars Press, 1986), xiii.

21. See H. R. Niebuhr, "Introduction" to Troeltsch, *The Social Teaching,* 11. Cf. Yasukata, *Ernst Troeltsch,* xiii, and James Luther Adams, "Foreword" to *The Social Teaching of the Christian Churches,* ix. Adams cites Niebuhr's "Ernst Troeltsch's Philosophy of Religion" (Ph.D. diss., Yale University, 1924) as a "harbinger" of the Troeltsch revival.

22. At least two legacies. Perhaps there is a third, whose contours have been sketched by Peter Hodgson, *God in History,* who wrote: "Troeltsch has recently been rediscovered and recognized as a thinker of first importance for a 'revisionist' theology — a theology that is attempting to revision Christian faith in response to the cognitive and cultural challenges of postmodernism, as opposed to avoiding these challenges or simply capitulating to them" (p. 130). This, I take it, would be neither a Christian realist nor a postliberal engagement with Troeltsch.

sitioning *The Social Teaching* in this way allows Yoder's concern with thinking historically to take precedence over his refusal of "the social problem" as Troeltsch understood it. In the second place, Troeltsch's nuanced historicism renders his authorship aporetic and thus pertinent to the study of Yoder's theology. The first point can be demonstrated by considering Troeltsch's own understanding of how his work hung together. The second point requires significantly more elaboration, especially if it is to have the leavening effect on critical readings of Troeltsch it needs to if we are appropriately to appreciate Yoder's ecclesiology.

To the first point: in "My Books" Troeltsch described the problematic of *The Social Teaching* in a way that illustrates its continuity with his thought about historicism and its problems. Reflecting back on *The Absoluteness of Christianity*, Troeltsch wrote, "At this point [1902] I had to come to grips with *the relationships of the historically relative and the substantively absolute;* that is, with the key issue in all philosophy of history as I had learned to understand it through exposure to critical historiography."[23] As Troeltsch familiarized himself with Marxist theory through the influence of Max Weber, he rephrased the problematic that drives his thought: "To what extent are the appearance, the development, the modification, and the modern impasse of Christianity sociologically conditioned, and to what extent is Christianity itself an actively formative sociological principle?"[24] The result of asking that question was *The Social Teaching*, which he described as having "shortcomings and gaps" that made him feel "rather uneasy."[25] When he moved to the University of Berlin, Troeltsch took up problems in the philosophy of history. He noted how far the implications of his work on the history of Christian social doctrine reached:

> The attempt actually to trace the historical development of religion in a select period brought me right to the center of all sociological problems; and in thus moving beyond religion to civilization as a whole, I, like Schleiermacher, found myself obliged to bring philosophy of history and ethics closer. From all these considerations there grew up in me, as basic to my present situation, concern for the theoretical and philosophical aspects of history — its relation to empirical profes-

---

23. Troeltsch, "My Books," trans. Franklin H. Littell, from "Meine Bücher" (1922), in *Gesammelte Schriften*, 4:3-18; English translation in *Religion in History*, 365-78. The quote is from p. 370 (emphasis added).
24. Troeltsch, "My Books," 372.
25. Troeltsch, "My Books," 373.

sional research on the one hand, and to a theory of cultural values, or of ethics, on the other.[26]

The fruit of this problematic was the first volume of *Historicism and Its Problems,* which asked "how the way to valid cultural values is to be found when one starts with the historically relative," and thus took up on broader horizons the fundamental question broached in *The Absoluteness of Christianity.*[27] Throughout a period of twenty years, over three large books and numerous shorter studies, Troeltsch cycled around the same set of issues regarding the relationship between history and ethics. As he did so, he set in tension a drive to systematize, on the one hand, and a drive to individuate and relativize, on the other, a dualism Troeltsch refused to resolve, as his remarks, again in "My Books," on the nature of his "system" indicate:

> All my works up to now have only resolved specific issues, very concrete particular questions, that had to be settled before the system itself could emerge. After the first youthful dreams of a system, I committed myself to a way of thinking that proceeds from positive knowledge and that is saturated with reality. Such a way of thinking must first settle many concrete questions of detail. . . . To be sure, such work can only have philosophical meaning and significance when it is undertaken with the conscious aim of clarifying or substantiating an important part of the system. In short, it requires a systematic philosophical foundation that will dictate what kinds of questions are asked and in what direction the results will be pointed. But on the other hand, the systematic foundation itself will also be greatly advanced and influenced by this progressive clarification of individual issues and presuppositions. To be sure, a system that keeps on reforming itself will not be quickly finished, and it will suffer from a certain liability; and it is bound to strive for precision, sharpness of outline, and universality. . . . Of course, such a view of the role of the system rests on a certain view of the nature of thought and its relations to life, matters about which there has been, and continues to be, much dispute. But such a fundamental view of theoretical thinking is itself a vital part of the system and it can only arise out of extensive personal engagement in the problems of the various positive disciplines.[28]

26. Troeltsch, "My Books," 374.
27. Troeltsch, "My Books," 374.
28. Troeltsch, "My Books," 376.

With this, we are already at the threshold of the second large point to be made about Troeltsch. One might ask what it means to speak of a *system* that is always reforming itself; that is, one might justifiably wonder whether Troeltsch's thrust toward reformation does not undermine the intelligibility of his claim to systematicity. Troeltsch's explicit recourse, in the paragraph cited above, is to methodology, to a sense of guiding questions that shape historical inquiry and are themselves revised over the course of investigations but never radically revolutionized. This sits in perfect harmony with his conception of a final end to history that exercises a teleological pull over events and thus describes the historian's task as one of discerning "an outline and general direction" in history.[29] So, to Troeltsch's mind, the problem with writing history is not revisability or fallibilism. Nor is the problem constructivism, the historian's imposition of a constructed system upon "reality." Rather, the danger is always that the historian will impose a false and prematurely final unity on history, that the unity a historian finds will fail to correspond to reality. There are always further questions to be asked.

But Troeltsch does not consider the tension between large, systemic, or programmatic questions, on the one hand, and questions of detail, exactitude, and painstaking historical inquiry, on the other, to be one that needs overcoming. With that in mind, how do we evaluate both the place of *The Social Teaching* in Troeltsch's work and his conception of historical thinking in general? We need to begin, I suggest, with a look at the argument of *The Social Teaching*, painted in broad strokes.

Placing *The Social Teaching of the Christian Churches* in Troeltsch's View of History

While Troeltsch's reflections in *The Social Teaching* on the shape of a new and modern cultural synthesis were abortive, placing this text within his life's work helps clarify his argument, which is a microcosm of his more general account of history and historicism. Troeltsch viewed *The Social Teaching* as an investigation into the specificities of Christian history and

---

29. Troeltsch, *The Absoluteness of Christianity and the History of Religions*, trans. David Reid (Richmond: John Knox Press, 1971), 100. For the German text, see now Ernst Troeltsch, *Die Absolutheit des Christentums und die Religionsgeschichte (1902/1912): mit den Thesen von 1901 und den handschriftlichen Zusätzen*, Kritische Gesamtausgabe, Bd. 5, hrsg. Trutz Rendtorff und Stefan Pautler (Berlin: De Gruyter, 1998), 170.

as an attempt to answer a series of related questions, each of which took the following general form: How have Christians addressed particular social questions in varying times?[30] The stakes of that question were twofold. At the primary level of investigation, the point was to present a picture of Christian history that was oriented toward social ethics, as distinct, say, from the development of doctrine approach undertaken by Harnack. But Troeltsch's eye was always trained on another objective, namely, how to render that set of historical pictures useful for the contemporary task of addressing specifically modern social questions. Troeltsch's general thesis was that Christianity developed and adapted its institutional form throughout history so as to orient itself to the individual nature of social problems as they arose. In other words, Troeltsch thought two things motivated *The Social Teaching*: (1) Christian theologians throughout history engaged the culture in which they found themselves with a view toward creating a synthesis between the institutions of historic Christianity and the social challenges that presented themselves in that day, whatever they happened to be; and (2) the contemporary social and political situation was sufficiently threatening that a new cultural synthesis was required. That is to say, he thought the institutional form of Protestantism in Germany had become inadequate to the modern cultural crisis.

Many interpretations of *The Social Teaching* fail to locate this interplay between past social/institutional configurations of Christianity and the early twentieth-century crisis of culture as central to Troeltsch's argument. They tend instead to maintain that Troeltsch sets up, in straightforwardly "dialectical" fashion, a perpetual tension between church and sect. The argument proceeds along the following lines: Troeltsch considers the sect a vital component of Christianity because it provides the impetus for social change and progression within the dialectic, but the church mediates this raw and relatively uninstitutionalized passion, making it livable for the masses.

What is correct about, and important to notice in, this interpretation is that both horns of the dialectic could be genuinely Christian, because for Troeltsch the gospel was by definition apolitical: Jesus of Nazareth did not leave the church with a political agenda to be enacted in secular society.[31]

---

30. While Troeltsch claimed that the social question was always historical and particular, he also assumed that the social question was enduring; that is, that there was an aspect of "sameness" to it that persisted throughout history. See Troeltsch, *Social Teaching*, 1:xx, 28.

31. See Troeltsch, *Social Teaching*, 1:51-53, 58-61. Lying behind this dynamic is also the "eternal" tension within Christianity between individualism and equality.

So, for instance, Troeltsch could say, "It is . . . clear that the message of Jesus is not a programme of social reform." He continues:

> It is rather the summons to prepare for the coming of the Kingdom of God; this preparation, however, is to take place quietly within the framework of the present world order, in a purely religious fellowship of love, with an earnest endeavor to conquer self and cultivate the Christian virtues. Even the Kingdom of God itself is not (for its part at least) the new social order founded by God. It creates a new order upon earth, but it is an order which is not concerned with the State, with Society, or with the family at all. How this will work out in detail is God's affair; man's duty is simply to prepare for it.[32]

Troeltsch therefore thought that any Christian social witness has to occur at a remove from the "purely religious" sphere; at best it can interpret the gospel, but social theology and the cultural synthesis it enacted can never on Troeltsch's grounds be the gospel itself. Because of this Troeltsch's dialectic between church and sect had essentially conservative political implications. If radical sectarian politics must be mediated (diluted, compromised) in order to be received by the rest of society, then, almost by sheer inertia, the church-type would come to set the standard for Christian social action. At best, sectarian impulses would be assimilated into the universalizing vernacular of the church, such that, for instance, the politics constitutive of the radical wing of the reformations were transformed into a set of abstract values, like freedom and egalitarianism.

But while Troeltsch enforces the distinction between church and sect as necessarily irreconcilable elements in any Christian sociology, he never argues for the unmitigated superiority of the church-type to sects, at least in part because he fears that neither church nor sect offers a viable social program for Christians in the modern world. Indeed, for Troeltsch, church and sect properly pertained to the sociological development of Christianity in the Middle Ages. "The Church," Troeltsch said, "only reached her full development . . . when, in the days of Constantine, she became a State Church." And continuing, he writes:

---

32. Troeltsch, *Social Teaching*, 1:61. Interestingly, Troeltsch identified preparation for the kingdom of God with the gospel. Moreover, Jesus' preaching of the kingdom is the *kerygma*. But because the kingdom is future (hence, unknown) the shape of preparation must be radically open-ended, rather, one imagines, like asking a sous chef to prepare dinner without telling her what is on the menu.

Only then was it possible for her to realize her universal and absolute unity and supremacy, which, during the time of the Holy Roman Empire, then enabled her to subdue the State itself to the unity which had been gained with the help of the State; this meant that the Church was also able to assert her authority over the whole of the non-religious civilization as well. Since, however, it was only the Middle Ages which thus created a Christian unity of civilization, so also it was only the Middle Ages which produced definitely and clearly the complementary movement of the sect.[33]

The Protestantism of Luther's reformation thus appeared to Troeltsch as a new sociological type, a cultural synthesis that emerged in response to the failure of the Catholic conception of the church (and the sect-structure concomitant upon it) to address the changing sociology of sixteenth-century Europe. Troeltsch, however, noted that Luther was essentially a medieval figure, a product of monasticism and the nominalist reaction to Thomist scholasticism. The reformation of Christianity he led could therefore never have been truly revolutionary. Indeed, Troeltsch claims, "Beneath the thought of the Protestant Reformation there lay the fact of the medieval expansion of Christianity."[34] In other words, on Troeltsch's account Luther's reformation, his reframing of the doctrine of grace, his individualism, his consequent subjectifying of salvation, and his rejection of natural law via an appeal to the authority of scripture were all consequent upon the medieval subsumption of the secular to the church.

Because Troeltsch viewed Luther and his reformation as fundamentally medieval, he could argue that "from the very outset" the "whole intellectual outlook [of Protestantism] belongs, essentially, to the Church-type."[35] This, moreover, "is what Luther intended."[36] And, while Troeltsch continued at length to analyze the Protestant ethic, the upshot of his reading of Luther, and Protestantism in general, as it shaped the argument of *The Social Teaching* was twofold. First, Protestantism was, from its incep-

---

33. Troeltsch, *Social Teaching*, 2:463. The notion of the church's realization of "her universal and absolute unity and supremacy" encodes a progressivist presumption, which can easily give the impression that Troeltsch regarded the church-type as superior to the sect. Receiving that impression, however, would be wrong: universality, unity, and supremacy are characteristics that pertain only to the church. To suggest that these characteristics make the church superior to the sect is like comparing apples and oranges.
34. Troeltsch, *Social Teaching*, 2:476-77.
35. Troeltsch, *Social Teaching*, 2:477.
36. Troeltsch, *Social Teaching*, 2:477.

tion, consummately unmodern. Even if Protestantism was a genuinely new sociological type, the tensive relation between church and sect continued to pertain to it, although in an altered and historically appropriate form — or so Troeltsch maintained, even though he never clarified precisely what was different (historically appropriate for Protestantism). Consequently, and this is the second factor, Protestantism was an ill-conceived experiment in that it was supposed to provide an answer to but instead adopted the institutional forms of Catholicism, which had caused the social problems of the Renaissance and prompted the reformations in the first place. Indeed, Protestantism only restated the problems.[37] And this was the role, in *The Social Teaching*, of Calvinism for Troeltsch: Calvinism appeared as the primary and conclusive example of Protestantism's inability to do anything other than restate its (inherited) social problems.

Troeltsch ended *The Social Teaching* on a note of perplexity regarding the contemporary social and political situation of Christianity, observing that social theory can now be only partly determined by the church. So, Troeltsch predicted, "Christian social philosophy will bring to the [contemporary] task both its common sense and its metaphysical individualism; but it will have to share the labour with other builders, and like them it will be restricted by the peculiarities of the ground and of the material." He continued:

> Under these conditions it is impossible to give a description of the present situation, and to deduce from it principles for the future. Even if the undertaking were restricted to a mere description of the different Christian endeavors, schemes and associations of the present day, the whole situation is so complicated that the subject would have to be treated in a separate work.[38]

In summary: while finding a Christian ethic adequate to the conditions of modernity remained Troeltsch's task,[39] he also found that modern life made it "still less possible to find an unchangeable and absolute point in the Christian ethic, since this also means the mastery of an existing situation, which is determined pre-eminently by social conditions and the establishment of an ideal which corresponds to this situation."[40]

---

37. Troeltsch, *Social Teaching*, 2:511-15.
38. Troeltsch, *Social Teaching*, 2:992.
39. Troeltsch, *Social Teaching*, 2:1002.
40. Troeltsch, *Social Teaching*, 2:1003.

"Mastery" is a key concept when considering Troeltsch's influence on Yoder, especially as Troeltsch came to see that "mastery of an existing situation" could not be had under the conditions of modernity. Although his historicism led him to recognize Christianity's dominance as a matter of contingent fact, the need to ensure Christianity's relevance to modernity led Troeltsch to argue throughout his career for Christianity's cultural durability. In *The Social Teaching* that tension between contingency and durability manifested itself as a question: Is it possible to hammer out a modern synthesis between church-type organizational structure and individual autonomy?[41] Troeltsch tried to hold that question open for the rest of his life. Arguably, however, in *Der Historismus und seine Probleme,* as well as in *Christian Thought,* the tension dissolved into a formal hope in a better future that motivated the present search for practical answers to sociopolitical problems.[42] In other words, for Troeltsch the question of developing an ethic adequate to the relativities and contingencies of modern social life (that is, of crafting a historicist ethic) was linked to eschatology. Yoder developed that link without succumbing to Troeltsch's assumption that ethics had social stabilization as its first task.

Nevertheless, certain aspects of Troeltsch's historicist mindset remained important for Yoder. Is it possible to plumb the depths of Troeltsch's understanding of history in a way that leads to a reassessment of Troeltsch's constructive thought, one sensitive to the ambiguities Troeltsch thought inhered in his own historical work? Is it possible, moreover, to see in Yoder's rejection of an engineering approach to Christian

---

41. The metaphor of "hammering out" may be strained. I use it because Troeltsch always stressed the active role of the historian in shaping political vision. He assumed the task to which he was committed was hard and painstaking work. But I wonder whether the better metaphor for the question of cultural synthesis is that of a crucible rather than a forge. The metaphor that involves hammering and hard work certainly gets at the complexity of Troeltsch's sense of the social situation of Christianity in his day. But Troeltsch also seemed to think that the problem of speaking credibly as Christian in the face of modernity was insoluble. The question of the possibility of a contemporary cultural synthesis functions in Troeltsch's texts not so much as one to be answered comprehensively as it is an instrument employed to purify the issues at stake. Cultural synthesis is not the calcinate, but the crucible itself; the idea of cultural synthesis is not the product of historical inquiry, but the tool Troeltsch used to get a handle on history.

42. *Christian Thought: Its History and Application,* ed. Baron F. von Hügel (London: University of London Press, 1923; reissued New York: Meridian, 1957); German text published as *Der Historismus und Seine Überwindung. Fünf Vorträge von Ernst Troeltsch* (Berlin: Rolf Heise, 1924).

ethics a reflection and refraction of Troeltsch's problematic? These are the questions I address in the remaining sections of this chapter.

Troeltsch sensed, and in a way that changed through the course of his authorship, the challenge historicism posed to Christian faith. Perhaps the most important change through Troeltsch's authorship was that he found it increasingly necessary to adopt an ironic style, in large part because the problems he encountered in the historical method made his ethical and political interests and stakes aporetic.[43] Something of this can be seen, I think, in the frustration with which many of Troeltsch's students and colleagues encountered him in the later stages of his professorate, a frustration given voice by Baron Friedrich von Hügel in his introduction to *Christian Thought*:

> Midas died of hunger from his fatal gift of turning all he touched into gold; so also Troeltsch, *qua* vehement individualist, finds himself incapable of deriving spiritual force and food from those entrancing historical perspectives which everywhere arise under his magical touch. Since each such scene is utterly unique, we are left without common standard, or common ideal — the entire collection, however intellectually interesting, can afford no aid towards the establishment of an act and habit of faith. A sheer *salto mortale,* clear outside of and above all these fertile scenes, a leap into what is visible indeed after the dread leap. But even then visible to the leaper alone: this is indeed a disconcertingly jejune ending to such historical researches so eagerly pursued.[44]

Troeltsch did not advocate historicism for historicism's sake.[45] History, historical consciousness, and historical investigation always served, in his

---

43. This use of "irony" and "aporia" comes from Gillian Rose. The ironic is a mode of expression that places differences in juxtaposition in order to accentuate what might otherwise (or may nevertheless) remain unnoticed. Moreover, irony also depends on an expectation that what is accentuated will likely not be noticed, or, if it is, will be noticed in an ultimately unsettling way, because the juxtaposition of differences highlights their insolvency. Because the ironic functions to unsettle, it leads naturally into an aporetic (*aporia*, not porous; hence, thick, impenetrable, difficult) register, one in which differences are not ameliorated, either by synthetic sublation or by diremption — the latter of which is another of Rose's key terms — but require "looking the negative in the face, and tarrying with it," as Hegel put it. I return to Rose and difficulty in the conclusion of this book. See Gillian Rose, *The Broken Middle: Out of Our Ancient Society* (Oxford: Blackwell, 1992), 75. See also G. W. F. Hegel, *Phenomenology of Spirit*, trans. A. V. Miller (Oxford: Oxford University Press, 1977), 19.

44. Troeltsch, *Christian Thought*, 24.

45. See, e.g., Troeltsch's question in *Christian Thought*: "Is it, then, possible, and may

mind, the synthesis of the absolute and the individual *(das Individuelle)*.⁴⁶ This is to say that, for Troeltsch, historicism was consequent upon a specific metaphysics and never an independent pursuit.⁴⁷ Because of its metaphysical backdrop Troeltsch thought he could draw normative conclusions from history. In *The Absoluteness of Christianity* Troeltsch put his philosophy of history in a nutshell:

> The scientific study of history does not exclude norms. On the contrary, its most important task is that of discerning norms and striving to see them as a unified whole. But the norms themselves, as well as the way they are conceptually unified, remain individual and temporally conditioned entities throughout every moment of their existence. They always represent a situationally informed striving toward a future goal, a goal that is not yet completely realized and has not yet become absolute.⁴⁸

This passage sets up the difficulty of Troeltsch's writing. A study of history that systematically repressed norms would be partial and incomplete, amounting to a failure of nerve that shirked the full burden of the historian's responsibility and undid the anxiety of his or her task. However,

---

we expect, that the historical stream of life can be defined and shaped for us in the light of those ideas which follow from the formal nature of moral obligation? ... It cannot be denied that the relation of these mental structures to actual history presents a difficult problem" (pp. 84-85). Moreover, *der Historismus* does not have the reductive connotations for Troeltsch that historicism has gained in English. Perhaps, therefore, historicism ought to be reserved as a translation of *der Historizimus*. In this vein, some commentators have argued for "historism" (as a translation of *der Historismus*) in order to signal the difference between non-reductive and reductive approaches to history. I assume both that historicism is not necessarily reductive (e.g., because the charge of reductionism is almost always question-begging), and that the multiplication of neo-logisms is unlikely to be very helpful in sorting through what Troeltsch did and did not mean by *der Historismus*. If we keep in mind that Troeltsch did not think history was exhausted by efficient causality, historicism seems to me the most appropriate description of Troeltsch's method.

46. In some texts, the historical synthesizes nature and spirit, a dualism Troeltsch consciously inherited from Kant. Indeed, it might even be said that, for Troeltsch, spirit named Kantian spontaneity.

47. See Walter Bodenstein's argument in *Neige des Historismus* (Gütersloh, 1959), 48: "Ohne de Voraussetzung einer ganz bestimmten Metaphysik bleibt Troeltschs Gedankengang unverständlich" ("Troeltsch's train of thought remains incomprehensible without the presupposition of a quite specific metaphysics"). See also H.-G. Drescher, *Ernst Troeltsch: His Life and Work* (Minneapolis: Fortress, 1993), 162.

48. Troeltsch, *Absoluteness of Christianity*, 90.

the alternative that Troeltsch advocated, namely, accepting the onus of "discerning norms" in history, committed the historian to bear his or her task as one of strife, as the struggle of envisioning those norms "as a unified whole." Unification, moreover, could not come without its own risks, because without constant vigilance it could become its own repose in a discursive clarity that released the tension of its subject matter in a forgetfulness of its own implication in time, its own failure to recognize its "merely potential" absoluteness. The historian's task therefore had to be seen as a limited engagement, one involving skeptical self-criticism that refused to uncouple itself from the anxiety of beginning and beginning again to take account of its own situation and effort, and to strain toward a wholeness of vision that always retained the character of a question.

How one approached that question, whether as a threat or as a promise (and it might be both) would depend on a variety of factors that rarely admit of neat arrangement and classification. And that left room for hope, a point for which Troeltsch's own life proved illustrative: from the outset of his career, his political hopes, his restlessness with the accepted canons of theological, philosophical, and historical inquiry, and his almost "pastoral" apologetic concern to make Christian faith credible combined to induce in him a profound confidence that the more one engaged in historical investigation the more it would become apparent that history is edifying.[49] Mark D. Chapman, in *Ernst Troeltsch and Liberal Theology*, commented on the hopeful character of Troeltsch's writing:

> Troeltsch's teleological religious a priori, which appeared to many to be closely "bound up with the destiny of an epoch" long since past, seems on closer analysis . . . to be a genuine search for reconciliation

---

49. Edification, like unification, is both risk and promise. I think particularly of Richard Rorty's commentary in *Philosophy and the Mirror of Nature:* "The attempt to edify (ourselves and others) may consist in the hermeneutic activity of making connections between our own culture and some exotic culture or historical period, or between our own discipline and another discipline which seems to pursue incommensurable aims in an incommensurable vocabulary. But it may instead consist in the 'poetic' activity of thinking up such new aims, new words, or new disciplines, followed by, so to speak, the inverse of hermeneutics: the attempt to reinterpret our familiar surroundings in the unfamiliar terms of our new inventions. In either case, the activity is (despite the etymological relation between the two words) edifying without being constructive — at least if 'constructive' means the sort of cooperation in the accomplishment of research programs which takes place in normal discourse. *For edifying discourse is supposed to be abnormal, to take us out of our old selves by the power of strangeness, to aid us in becoming new beings*" (p. 360, emphasis added).

between spirit and nature, and thus it continues to allow for the ethical transformation of the historical world. His combination of realism and optimism, where there can be no easy solutions within history, no immediate perception of absolute truth, but where nevertheless there is always the hope that history might be moving to its goal, perhaps better reflects the continued need not to escape or to evade but to transform history; that is, to discipline it ethically. For Troeltsch, it is the dare to accept the meaningfulness of history that ultimately provides the justification for religion.[50]

While Chapman rightly captured the tentativeness of Troeltsch's hope, two of his suggestions are problematic. In the first place, escape and evasion were not meaningful for Troeltsch *as alternatives* to transforming history. If I read him correctly, Troeltsch thought that the possibility of escaping or evading history was delusional. The hope in or effort toward "escape" (indeed, did Troeltsch ever use this word apropos of history, and if not, is it other than a Christian realist overlay?) itself would always be historical, a *Gestalt* with its own political possibilities and limitations. Thus, from Troeltsch's perspective, one should not ask, "Escape or transformation?" but, "What politico-ethical, that is, *historical,* effect does an 'escapist' configuration of one's posture toward the historical have?" This latter is precisely the kind of question he asked in discussing *askesis* and sectarianism in *The Social Teaching*. Having begun to set out the differences between the church-type and sect-type, Troeltsch wrote:

> The asceticism of the sects . . . is merely the simple principle of detachment from the world, and is expressed in the refusal to use the law, to swear in a court of justice, to own property, to exercise dominion over others, or to take part in war. . . . The ascetic ideal of the sects consists simply in opposition to the world and to its social institutions, but it is not opposition to the sense-life, nor to the average life of humanity.[51]

The examples Troeltsch elicited in this passage are crucial — not detachment as such, perhaps not even detachment at all, since one might render *Weltenthaltung* as "moderation toward the world," but rather detachment as "expressed in . . ." This is certainly not escape or evasion — it is not even

---

50. *Ernst Troeltsch and Liberal Theology: Religion and Cultural Synthesis in Wilhelmine Germany* (Oxford: Oxford University Press, 2001), 136.
51. *The Social Teaching,* 1:331-32.

clear escapist posturing (that would use "escape from history" as a metaphor for separation from certain aspects of social life) — and it is explicitly not a hostility to "the average life of humanity." Therefore, while Chapman argues that "Troeltsch's combination of realism and optimism . . . reflects the continued need not to escape or to evade but to transform history," it is not at all clear that Troeltsch would have recognized himself in the description.

In the second place, Chapman, in characterizing Troeltsch's task as disciplining history ethically, introduced to the discussion a separation between history and ethics that Troeltsch resisted. Chapman argues that Troeltsch thought

> The Christian religion had . . . to be clear about the historical conditions within which it was working. Part of the task of theology was thus to describe the modern world and in turn what differentiated this world from the past. Only after this descriptive task could the construction be attempted: the broader social and political context thus determined the possibilities for theological action.[52]

No: the point for Troeltsch is not merely to construct a history that can be used ethically, but rather to see how our implication in and constitution by history is already an ethical relationship that opens up some political possibilities while closing off others (at least in part because Troeltsch thought being "clear about the historical conditions" with which one worked demanded a recognition of one's own capacities for blindness).

Despite these problems, Chapman rightly evokes the pathos-laden hope with which Troeltsch circled around the problems of historical thinking. His peculiarly desperate confidence that one could be hopeful about the direction of history stemmed from his assumption that the historical synthesized the absolute and the individual, and it produced another tension in his work that was both constructive and constricting. On the constructive side of things, Troeltsch understood that his commitment to the historical method could never allow him to rest on the laurels of his findings. *Der Historismus* demanded constant reworking and revision and was always an unfinished task of clarification. History comes with no guarantees. Moreover, Troeltsch did not think the theologian/historian's task was explanatory. But (and this proved to be the constricting factor in his ap-

---

52. Chapman, *Ernst Troeltsch and Liberal Theology*, 138.

proach) Troeltsch thought history did have a certain illustrative quality.[53] The very assumption of the possibility of synthesis that configured the theologian's task as one of ongoing engagement with history also inflected that engagement teleologically, such that if the results of the historical investigation of religion pointed in the direction of dissolution and disintegration, then those findings could not be considered true in any final sense: conceptual unification remained, after all, the purpose of historical inquiry.

Troeltsch refused to envision ethics primarily as a response to the past. For him, ethics and history were both matters of the present (and therefore of the future), the configuration of a world more than a form of response to a world already given and needing only to be represented. There could be no ethically neutral relation to history; rather, our relation to history is (always already?) ethical.[54] The revision of historiography

---

53. Chapman argues that Troeltsch understood "himself as developing Lessing's dictum that 'the historical serves only as illustration, not as demonstration'" (*Ernst Troeltsch and Liberal Theology*, 118, with reference to Troeltsch, "Das Historische in Kants Religionsphilosophie. Zugleich ein Beitrag zu den Untersuchungen über Kants Philosophie der Geschichte," in *Zu Kants Gedächtnis. Zwölf Festgaben zu seinem 100-jährigen Todestage*, ed. Hans Vaihinger and Bruno Bauch [Berlin: Reuther und Reichard, 1904]). Though this indeed seems to have been Troeltsch's self-understanding, "illustration" might be taken to presuppose a static or representationalist account of the absoluteness of religion that Troeltsch did not hold. Because the absoluteness of religion must be characterized as a future goal, there is no idea of religion of which history provides a set of illustrations. Or, to put it slightly differently, the historical does not illustrate a principle that appears episodically; it sketches a goal "in outline and general direction" (see *The Absoluteness of Christianity*, 100). History, as the context for the realization (albeit a partial, fragmentary, and broken one, but not just the bringing to light) of the religious goal toward which the unity of reality is moving has for Troeltsch a constructive and demonstrative quality. There is no representable concept of a goal that appears in history. Rather, it is only on the basis of historical instantiations of a future goal that one can begin to describe that goal. Chapman is right, however, to draw attention to Troeltsch's ambivalence toward demonstration. Beneath it, to my mind, lies a more fundamental ambivalence to the very idea of a synthetic unity of reality, the affirmation of which Troeltsch characterized as "a creative deed and hazardous venture" ("schöpferische Tat und Wagnis"). See Troeltsch, *Der Historismus und seine Probleme*, 771-72.

54. Glossing Derrida's comments on the archive, I might say that *der Historismus* is "not a question of a concept that we can dispose or not dispose of *already*, a subject *of the past, a historicisable concept of historicism*. It is a question of the future, the question of the future itself, the question of a response, of a promise and of a responsibility for tomorrow. Historicism: if we want to know what we will have wanted to say, we will only be able to know that in times to come. Perhaps. Not tomorrow, but in times to come, right away, or perhaps never. A spectral messianicity is at work in the concept of historicism and ties it . . . to a very singular experience of the promise." Cf. Jacques Derrida, *Archive Fever: A Freudian*

Troeltsch undertook in *The Absoluteness of Christianity* explicitly denied notions of history and experience as thematizable totalities. As such, Troeltsch aimed his historicism at the "Hegelian" understanding of history as the progressive sublation of experience and difference into a complete knowledge, an "artificial absoluteness" that reflected the self-identity of consciousness. Equally, however, Troeltsch also explicitly denied notions of ethics that derived from a radical, "supernaturalistic" rupture with history. The idea of a radical difference from history, a "Sunday causality" that relied on an ahistorical signification in the midst of historical occurrences, was for him a "naïve absoluteness" that also evaded the lessons of modern epistemology stemming from Hume, Kant, and Lessing.[55]

Troeltsch thus set himself in opposition to two currents of inquiry he thought insufficient to the task of engaging Christian thought historically. The two currents can be described as the dogmatic approach and evolutionary theory.[56] Each of them attempted, in Troeltsch's estimation, to secure the absoluteness of Christianity in a way that insulated it against the need to think in the light of time. As he said:

> [B]oth the evolutionary and the orthodox schools of thought desire to attain . . . normative value by placing Christianity, as a matter of prin-

---

Impression, trans. Eric Prenowitz (Chicago: University of Chicago Press, 1996), 60/36. The truth of *der Historismus* lies for Troeltsch in the future, an object of hope and anticipation, which energizes, or at least could energize, politics in the present. That we might (then) know what we will have wanted to say (in the interstices between now and then) commands study and criticism of the past to expose the falsity, the presumption, and also the truth of the present — and, in particular, the sense of the past as we inherit it that produces a set of possibilities and limitations, real and illusory (both can be spectral), for change, for the continuance or the re-founding of the chance for hope.

55. For the reference to "Sunday causality," see *The Absoluteness of Christianity,* 52. Drescher, in *Ernst Troeltsch,* replaced Hume in the list above with Herder, arguing that "For Troeltsch, Lessing, Kant, and Herder pioneered this approach in the philosophy of history: it comes to consummation in Schleiermacher and Hegel" (p. 160).

56. In *The Absoluteness of Christianity* Troeltsch referred to what I am calling the dogmatic approach variously as the stance of "orthodoxy" (die Zurückführung des Christentums [e.g., 125]), a "supernatural apologetic," or simply "supernaturalism." I use "dogmatic" here in an advisedly negative way, not as the activity of teaching and expounding key elements of the Christian faith, but in the pejorative sense of intransigent belief in the teeth of the evidence. While I do not accept such a use of the word "dogmatic" in general, I think the pejorative connotations capture the tone of Troeltsch's prose. But cf. Troeltsch's foreword to *The Social Teaching,* where "dogmatic tradition" seems shorn of any pejorative undertones (1:xix).

ciple, in a unique position. They are not content with a *de facto* supremacy and ultimacy but want to make it into the sole truth to which everything else stands opposed in accordance with the requirements of theory.[57]

To be sure, Troeltsch did not consider each current an equally bad alternative. The dogmatic method "that derives . . . from an absolutizing of Christianity that is determinative from the outset," rested its claim to Christianity's absoluteness in an a priori assertion of special revelation and a uniquely religious causality in a way that evolutionary theory did not.[58] Thus, Troeltsch maintained that

> We are left . . . with the idealistic-evolutionary theory as the only one that calls for serious critical consideration. In itself this theory is an attempt to rule out every means of isolating Christianity from the rest of history on the basis of miracle, and it is an attempt to present in a purely historical way the validity and significance of the Christian religion in statements as unequivocal as the doctrinal formulations of the early church.[59]

Yet the demand for unequivocal validity in the evolutionary approach and the attempt to isolate a principle of religion from history troubled Troeltsch, leading him to argue that this view, too, was beset by insoluble problems. He wrote, "The modern idea of history knows no universal principle on the basis of which the content and sequence of events might be deduced."[60] An idealist-evolutionary theory, therefore, in which Christianity's absoluteness was guaranteed by claiming that it articulated what was immanent and obscurely ascertained in all non-Christian religions, depends on the abstraction of a universally valid and timeless principle of authentic religion that is and could only be, Troeltsch argued, itself the contingent upshot of Christianity viewed from a particular historical perspective. In adopting this stance, evolutionary theory found itself paradoxically committed to preserving the principle of religion that it allegedly

---

57. Troeltsch, *The Absoluteness of Christianity*, 51. Alternatively, "Both the orthodox and the evolutionary theories thus take it for granted that the proof of normative religious truth can be provided only by the doctrine of a theoretically necessary and uniquely confirmed development of the religious powers of mankind" (p. 55).
58. Troeltsch, *The Absoluteness of Christianity*, 107.
59. Troeltsch, *The Absoluteness of Christianity*, 60.
60. Troeltsch, *The Absoluteness of Christianity*, 70.

discovered in a historical way against the detailed historical scrutiny in which it was otherwise invested.

In other words, the idealist-evolutionary theory required the simultaneous maintenance of two mutually exclusive axioms. On the one hand, it required the presupposition that all religions develop in history and are the subjects of ongoing development. On the other hand, it also required imposing a causal logic or law upon the temporal process whereby one could demonstrate that the development of Christianity in history exhausts "its inner principle."[61] But the two axioms, Troeltsch argued, could not go together. Because history is the arena of the unique and individual, it cannot admit of description in terms of any strict law, and therefore any attempt to conceive of a principle of religion that guaranteed Christianity's absolute validity would in the final analysis be a refusal to think in the light of time.

Troeltsch therefore maintained that Christianity's validity could never be guaranteed via a conception of absoluteness "as a humanly realizable and exhaustible idea." Instead, he sounded a cautionary note: "The modern idea of history, as it has taken shape in connection with the object of its inquiries, knows no concept of a universal principle that embodies a law governing the successive generation of individual historical realities."[62] Moreover, he wrote,

> The Christian religion is in every moment of its history a purely historical phenomenon, subject to all the limitations to which any individual historical phenomenon is exposed, just like the other great religions. It is to be investigated, in every moment of its history, by the universal, verified methods of historical research.[63]

The overall point, Troeltsch thought, was that because Christianity is subject to historical investigation, and because historical investigation concentrates on individual events, any conception of absoluteness that proved durable to modern historical thought had to be characterized only in terms "of a goal discernible in outline and general direction."[64] Here the

---

61. Troeltsch, *The Absoluteness of Christianity*, 100.
62. Troeltsch, *The Absoluteness of Christianity*, 64.
63. Troeltsch, *The Absoluteness of Christianity*, 85. Troeltsch at this point seems untroubled by the petitionary nature of the claim. How would one judge whether the "methods of historical research" were indeed "universal" and "verified"?
64. Troeltsch, *The Absoluteness of Christianity*, 100.

eschatological horizon of historicism emerged into view. Ultimately, for Troeltsch, the only way to speak confidently of meaning in history was via eschatology.

In sum: the "absoluteness" legitimately pertaining to Christianity is limited by the recognition that thought always occurs temporally. On this view, one could speak of Christianity's absolute validity in two ways that do not constitute obstacles to thinking in the light of time: (1) empirically and (2) as a matter of faith. On the empirical side of things, only Christianity, Troeltsch said, had been able to work out consistently "the distinction between the higher and lower worlds" that every world religion has struck upon but could not prioritize because of lingering vestiges of "natural religion."[65] Christianity "is simply the highest value discernible in history and the certainty of having found the way that leads to perfect truth."[66] Only Christianity, that is, recognized in its idea of a personal God both a value that transcends everything existent and the possibility of human participation in that value. Every other religion that has emerged in history finds itself stuck with an insurmountable either/or: the religions of law (Judaism and Islam) recognize a realm of transcendent value but could not conceive of the transformation of human nature necessary to participate in that realm, whereas the non-Christian religions of redemption properly grounded humanity in ethical action but, in so doing, evacuated the realm of transcendent value of all distinctiveness in content.

Troeltsch did, however, think his estimation of the "empirical" superiority of Christianity was falsifiable. He thought both that his conclusions were those of sober historical judgment and that only such judgment warranted the conclusion that Christianity is absolute. So, if one could have shown on the basis of a reevaluation of the history of religion that Christianity is not "the highest value discernible in history," Troeltsch would have had to revise his claims. He courted just this challenge throughout his career, both from others and in himself. The historical method limited and refined what it could mean to ascribe absoluteness to Christianity, but it could not guarantee the truth of that ascription in a way that freed it from all possible future revision.[67]

---

65. Troeltsch, *The Absoluteness of Christianity*, 112-14.
66. Troeltsch, *The Absoluteness of Christianity*, 118.
67. See Troeltsch's reflections on *The Absoluteness of Christianity* in *Christian Thought*, where he noted concerning evolutionary theory that "The point at issue was not whether Christianity was as a matter of fact universal, or at least implicit in all religion, but whether it possessed ultimate truth, a truth which might easily depend on a single instance

Nevertheless, there remained a fiduciary dimension to Troeltsch's claim for Christianity's absoluteness, which ensured against any radical revision of his argument for Christianity's absolute validity. In the fourth and fifth chapters of *The Absoluteness of Christianity* Troeltsch ran the risk of undermining his commitment to historicism. He took that risk to be unavoidable, in order to distinguish his position from thoroughgoing historical relativism. That he was conscious of the need to end his book on a stirring note required him to modulate his tone — he characterized himself as moving into a "sermonic" register that had an ironic quality about it.[68] As a matter of faith, Troeltsch claimed, we are justified in considering Christianity's validity to be absolute for us because we cannot conceive of anything that might supplant it. Indeed, he argued, if Christianity were to die out today by means of some cataclysmic destruction of European civilization, we would be justified in believing that whatever religiosity arose in its wake would be Christian. In shifting the emphasis from truth to epistemic justification, Troeltsch essentially argued that only human limitation in history warranted an ascription of absolute validity to Christianity.

The difficulty of Troeltsch's work derived from the need to say two contradictory things at once. On the one hand, Troeltsch needed to maintain that Christianity is thoroughly historical, while on the other he needed to justify the claim that Christianity is the highest religion in which we dare hope. Troeltsch was at his best when he allowed the uneasy fit to persist — in *Christian Thought,* for instance, he encountered it as generative, not needing to be overcome. But in the final revision of *The Absoluteness of Christianity* Troeltsch tried to weave the historical and fiduciary dimensions of Christian faith into a seamless garment. Thus, he wrote,

---

itself" (p. 46). Troeltsch took this claim as a warrant to speculate about truth, or moments of truth, in every religion. He might have taken it rather to warrant further christological reflection, which is the direction, one might suggest, in which Yoder pushed. For Troeltsch, who never felt the force of Barth's *Romans,* Lessing's ditch still loomed large; hence, he admitted, "The recognition of this truth is, however, an intuition which is born of deep personal experience and a pure conscientiousness" (p. 46). Cf. Drescher, *Ernst Troeltsch,* 163: "It is clear from the perspective of theological tradition that Troeltsch relates the concepts of God and history in such a way that an idea of revelation mediated christologically is not determinative."

68. Troeltsch, *The Absoluteness of Christianity,* 120: "It is the tone of the sermon or meditation that we have sounded. However, in view of the question under consideration, it can hardly be otherwise."

When the clouds of research have lifted, this final result will remain forever, and he who sympathetically involves himself with the diverse truths and values of mankind and seeks his way accordingly will discover in this completely free spontaneity, which is at the same time the expression of the purest and most concentrated religious power, an indication of the highest revelation of the divine life that holds sway over us. He will not deny the naïve limitations of even this claim to absoluteness, and he will not recoil when this religious orientation, developing close connections with new ideas, enters into new forms of existence.[69]

No dualism, but also no difficulty, except, perhaps, the difficulty of not yet having seen the clouds of research clear.

Yoder and Troeltsch: Eschatology, Certainty, and History

Troeltsch's difficult balancing act between history and hope provoked an eschatology that was divested of all "primitive" and "dogmatic" elements — divested too, though somewhat less radically, of notions of progress — in a better and more inhabitable future. Eschatology enjoyed but a shadowy life in *The Absoluteness of Christianity*, where Troeltsch consistently limited himself to talk of history's "final goal" or "consummation." In contrast, his dogmatic theology lectures of 1912 and 1913, published in English as *The Christian Faith*, as well as his article on eschatology in *Die Religion in Geschichte und Gegenwart*, discussed specific aspects of Christian teaching on the last things.[70] In both texts, Troeltsch argued that eschatology was analytically related to religious thought. He wrote, for instance, that

> Every religion that seeks to achieve a clear self-understanding and self-expression has a doctrine of last things, an eschatology (to use the technical term), however, mythical its form may be. More than a poetic impulse gives rise to it; it proceeds from the religious idea itself. For religion itself is, if not a doctrine, yet surely a sense of "last things";

---

69. Troeltsch, *The Absoluteness of Christianity*, 161.
70. See Troeltsch, *The Christian Faith*, ed. Gertrud von le Fort, trans. Garrett E. Paul (Minneapolis: Fortress, 1991), 300-304, and "Eschatologie: IV Dogmatisch," in *Religion in Geschichte und Gegenwart*, (Tübingen: J. C. B. Mohr, 1910), 2:622-32; translated into English as "Eschatology" in *Religion in History*, 146-58; hereafter, "Eschatology."

that is, of ultimate realities and values that are absolute and unconditioned, uniform and inherently necessary, in contrast to finite realities and values that are relativized more and more by reflexion.[71]

Troeltsch argued that gaining a sense of the last things is a matter of course for any inquiry into the nature of reality that involves itself with questions of what is ultimate. That sense would be inchoate and metaphorical, a poetic representation of what lies beyond the limits of human knowledge, rather than a matter of strict exposition. Indeed, any attempt to specify, circumscribe, or describe the last things would be hubristic dogmatism, a premature bid to tame history's complexity resting on a "deliberate misrepresentation" of "the relational nexus" and needing chastening by modern historicism.[72] But once the last things were passed through the sieve of modern historical consciousness, once eschatology had been purified of its superstitious elements, its subject matter could competently be limited to two finally unanswerable questions: "(1) the question of the essence of the consummation, or the question of a definitive redemption; and (2) the question of whether all or only a few will participate in this final salvation, or the question of the universality and particularity of grace."[73]

Troeltsch's rationale for the reduction of eschatology to these fundamental questions appeared, at first blush, to have positivist underpinnings. Indeed, many accounts of Troeltsch, both positive and negative, assume he took for granted the intellectual hegemony of the rational methodology of scientific historical inquiry.[74] Consequently, it is easy to view his reduction

---

71. Troeltsch, "Eschatology," 146.

72. Troeltsch, "Eschatology," 147. Modern historicism, Troeltsch says in this text, leads to relativism if practiced consistently.

73. Troeltsch, *The Christian Faith*, 302. I have harmonized Troeltsch's two accounts of eschatology to a certain extent. In "Eschatology," for instance, Troeltsch parsed the problems differently. There, eschatology is schematized under four problems: (1) the question of life after death; (2) "the antinomy between the Kingdom of God and the infinite worth of the human soul"; (3) the problem of universalism; and (4) the problem of the nature or essence of the end (pp. 152-54). Two things about this deserve comment. First, in *The Christian Faith* redemption and the value of the human soul are handled in their own right as discrete topics. There was thus no need to deal with them again under eschatology. Second, Troeltsch's list of four problems in "Eschatology" can be grouped under the two headings in *The Christian Faith* with little difficulty, problems 1, 2, and 4 falling under the essence of consummation, and problem 3 standing on its own.

74. See Van A. Harvey, *The Historian and the Believer: The Morality of Historical Knowledge and Christian Belief* (New York: Macmillan, 1966), 3-6. But cf. Harvey's reflections on his own project thirty years later in his introduction to the 1996 edition of *The His-*

of Christian eschatology as an extension of his historicist opposition to traditional Christian dogmatics. While to some extent this was clearly the case, on closer inspection his eschatological claims were grounded not so much by a conception of science (though Troeltsch took science to provide additional warrant for his position) as by his understanding of practical rationality.

Troeltsch hung practical rationality on a neo-Kantian frame, such that the limitations of his eschatological hope left their mark in the fissure between history and holiness. He coupled a historicist emphasis on the necessary provisionality of all judgment with a conception of holiness as a totalized sphere in which religious hope is exhausted (because realized).[75] Like most of his contemporaries, Troeltsch owed his conception of holiness to Kant's attempt to limit dogmatic theology's ability to take refuge in metaphysical speculation. Indeed, much of the continental theological appropriation of philosophy in the late nineteenth and early twentieth centuries can be conceived as an extended argument over how to formulate Kant's authentic legacy so as to best respond to the rising tide of materialistic monism.[76]

---

torian and the Believer (Urbana and Chicago: University of Illinois Press), where Harvey registers his unease with having been read as making rationalist/Enlightenment/historicist criticisms of Christian belief, and adjusts his view accordingly, especially in the following: "What we call historical inquiry is really the formalization by professional historians of our modern, Promethean desire to know, a desire that is actually rooted in everyday life. Historical reasoning is merely the formalization of one method that has, over time, proved to be our best guarantor of achieving this desire of holding in check the special pleading, obscurantism, and tendentiousness that are omnipresent in human existence" (pp. xx-xxi). See also John Milbank's claim in *Theology and Social Theory* that Troeltsch, like Weber, "quite evidently maintained" "several features of the positivist mentality." Milbank continues: "One can mention, at the outset, the association of 'the social' with given permanent categories; a dualistic conception of humanity as caught between 'real' nature and 'spiritual' values; an identification of 'the religious' with irrational and arbitrary forces which are irreducible and unexplainable; the importance still given to functional causality; an empiricistic attitude to 'facts,' and a historical narrative which compares the post-religious stage to the stage of primitive religion. And like Durkheim, Weber, Simmel, and Troeltsch seek in their political outlook to combine liberal freedom with a positivist attitude to law and sovereignty. Like Durkheim, also, they modify the sociological tradition with an infusion of Kantian and neo-Kantian philosophy" (p. 75).

75. This view of holiness is of a piece with Troeltsch's criticism of evolutionary theory in *The Absoluteness of Christianity*, where the problem lies in an idea of absoluteness that is immanently realized.

76. See Chapman, *Ernst Troeltsch and Liberal Theology*, 75-88.

Seizing Godlikeness

At least one special caution needs to be taken in discussing Troeltsch vis-à-vis Kant. Whereas Kant thought both the dogmatic slumber of imagined convictions and its equally intransigent alternative, skeptical hopelessness, euthanogenic to thought,[77] Troeltsch's historicism, while rarely accused of fostering dogmatic slumber, has often been seen as issuing in the skeptical hopelessness Kant resisted.[78] Against such a view, however,

---

77. See Kant, *Critique of Pure Reason*, trans. and ed. Paul Guyer and Allen W. Wood (Cambridge: Cambridge University Press, 1997), 460. So also, for Kant, holiness was a matter of hope that could not be guaranteed or historically realized. Just as human thought is confronted with a necessary contradiction between the freedom of the will and the laws of nature, so also the human being is confronted by the necessity of recovering the supreme ground of all maxims (the moral law in its purity) and its contradiction in the phenomenal character of virtue. Virtue, Kant argued, is acquired little by little as one is habituated into acting in accordance with duty, regardless of the motive(s) for action. See *Religion within the Boundaries of Mere Reason and Other Writings*, ed. Allen Wood and George di Giovanni (Cambridge: Cambridge University Press, 1998), 67. Such habituation, however, cannot be called holiness because for that all actions must result from duty alone. Holiness cannot therefore be a product of gradual reform in the mode of sense, but must rather be a revolution in the mode of thought. As such, holiness retained an ideal character for Kant. We are justified in assuming the possibility of holiness because the moral law commands it, and the moral law commands only what can be done. Yet, we are not justified in ascribing holiness to ourselves, insofar as under the conditions of space and time each of us encounters the moral law as an imperative. Thus, in *Religion*, Kant paralleled his negotiation of the third antinomy, i.e., that "there is no freedom, but everything in the world happens solely in accordance with laws of nature," (*Critique of Pure Reason* A444/B472, A445/B473), writing: "If by a single and unalterable decision a human being reverses the supreme ground of his maxims by which he was an evil human being (and thereby puts on a 'new man'), he is to this extent, by principle and attitude of mind, a subject receptive to the good; but he is a good human being only in incessant laboring and becoming; i.e. he can hope — in view of the purity of the principle which he has adopted as the supreme maxim of his power of choice, and in view of the stability of this principle — to find himself upon the good (though narrow) path of constant *progress* from bad to better. For him who penetrates to the intelligible ground of the heart (the ground of all the maxims of the power of choice), for him to whom this endless progress is a unity, i.e. for God, this is the same as actually being a good human being (pleasing to him); and to this extent the change can be considered a revolution. For the judgment of human beings, however, who can assess themselves and the strength of their maxims only by the upper hand they gain over the senses in time, the change is to be regarded only as an ever-continuing striving for the better, hence as a gradual reformation of the propensity to evil, of the perverted attitude of mind" (*Religion*, 68).

78. Sarah Coakley commented on Troeltsch's skepticism in the opening pages of *Christ without Absolutes: A Study of the Christology of Ernst Troeltsch* (Oxford: Clarendon, 1988), 1-2. See also, e.g., Emil Brunner, *The Theology of Crisis* (New York: Charles Scribner's Sons, 1929), 7. Cf. Brunner, *The Mediator: A Study of the Central Doctrine of the Christian Faith* (Philadelphia: Westminster, 1947), 69; Barth, *Church Dogmatics* IV.1, 387.

one should insist that Troeltsch did not think historicism led to nihilism, because historical thinking could not foster the certainty required for hopelessness.[79] The process of relativizing that moves from the historical to plausible final ends also moves from the material to the formal, and, in a Kantian framework, it is notoriously difficult to make adequate reference to the purely formal.[80] So, for Troeltsch, precisely *because* humans require an eschatology in order to think historically, and eschatology deals with final ends, one cannot invest whatever last things happen to be posited with certainty. The analogy to Kant remains clear: any time one imports particular content into a requirement for reasoning, one has left the realm of pure formality and has entered the realm of the culturally conditioned and the historically specific. Troeltsch saw that this need to posit final ends required equivocation, because thoroughgoing certainty (or hopelessness, for that matter) was out of place — not warranted by the margin of error — in a situation where one could deal only with conditioned specificities, contingencies, and the things that can be otherwise.

If Troeltsch thought that thoroughgoing certainty and despair were equally ahistorical postures, what kind of certainty did he think properly attached to Christian convictions? The answer is that "The religious man needs . . . the certainty that he is on the right path, that he is following the right star."[81] The certainty that Christian belief can give cultivates open-

---

79. So, for instance, in *The Absoluteness of Christianity*, Troeltsch limited his notion of relativism, noting first that "It appears to many that the inevitable consequence of historical thinking is an unlimited relativism. History, in this view, takes certain temporally related elements and produces a transitory uniqueness, and since this is a repetitive process, it means that history itself turns into an incalculable welter of evanescent forms" (p. 86). Three pages later, he corrected this view, writing: "Relativity simply means that all historical phenomena are unique, individual configurations [*individuelle Bildungen*] acted on by influences from a universal context that comes to bear on them in varying degrees of immediacy. It means, therefore, that every independent structure leads one to a perspective that embraces broader and still broader horizons till finally it opens out onto the whole. It means that a comprehensive perspective of this kind allows one to form universal judgments and evaluations. Relativity does not mean, however, denial of the values that appear in these individual configurations, that are oriented in the same direction, that have the power to encounter and influence one another, and that as a result of such interaction lead men to discern their inner truth and necessity and thus make a choice among them" (p. 89).

80. This is, I take it, one of the perplexities attendant upon the Second Critique. The categorical imperative demands different inflections, not because Kant requires it to do different work in different cases, as is sometimes argued, but because no words are adequate to the austerity of the moral law.

81. Troeltsch, *The Absoluteness of Christianity*, 120-21.

ness to the future, but it does not need to speculate as to the specific shape of that future. In refusing material specification of the eschatological hope, however, Troeltsch denied the erotic character of his ethics, since desire is not oriented by futurity as such, but only by particular imaginings of possible futures. Troeltsch's delimitation of eschatology to openness to the future thus cut his theology off from any potentially countercultural narration of history, making it not so much the servitor of the dominant culture as entirely incidental to that culture, whatever it happened to be.

Troeltsch's historicism, by a circuitous route, can therefore be seen as epistemologically imperialist — not primarily in the sense that he developed a set of sophisticated strategies that allowed him to acknowledge the evidence of "incompleteness" in the writing of Christian history while retaining the idea of a general historical movement culminating in modern European (German) Christianity, but in that he claimed to have uncovered the necessary conditions for and limits of thinking in the light of time. In this he exhibited tendencies Yoder criticized as "Constantinian." Indeed, it is at the intersection between eschatology and history, rather than in a typological account of Christian ethics, that Yoder's thought most clearly responds to Troeltsch. However, Yoder can also be seen as picking up a set of tasks bequeathed to him by Troeltsch. Yoder, like Troeltsch, thought that Christianity had to be political (though they would not always have agreed as to what constitutes the "political"), that the gospel must be "hearable" in whatever context it is found, and that the search for a distinctively Christian epistemology denies the fundamentally historical nature of the faith.

Yet it is nevertheless the case that Yoder took these tasks in directions Troeltsch could not, at least in part because Yoder was not concerned to secure Christianity's cultural hegemony. That is to say, the apologetic aspects of Troeltsch's project were absent in Yoder's theology. Yoder did not think to ask, much less answer, how Christianity could be legitimated in light of modernity. Instead, it might be said that Yoder rendered aspects of Troeltsch's theology more consistent than Troeltsch was able to on his own terms in at least two interrelated ways: Yoder (1) uncoupled Troeltsch's conception of history from its idealist undercurrents (for example, the constitutive tension between the absolute and the individual), and (2) reinscribed Christian content into the eschatological hope that Troeltsch reduced to a purely formal source of motivation.

Let us take each of these points in turn. In "But We Do See Jesus" Yoder responded to the problem of Lessing's ditch ("Accidental truths of history can never become the proof of necessary truths of reason"), out of which Troeltsch took himself to be working. The first thing to notice is that Yoder did not allow the tension between the absolute and the individual to go unquestioned:

> It would be wrong to think that the issue of the credibility of particular claims is best represented only by some quite recent reformulation of historical skepticism, or religious pluralism, or the death-of-God language, or by the gap between contingent facts of history and necessary truths of reason posited by Lessing, the dean of modern ditchdiggers. Each of those formulations is important. Yet none of them is at the bottom of our problem. None of them can find *beyond the ditch* a place to stand which would be less particular, more credible, less the product of one's own social location.[82]

That insight ought, in a sense, to be credited to Troeltsch, for Troeltsch's historicism labors in the ditch. The difference between him and Yoder is that Troeltsch allowed the terms of the question to remain unchallenged. However, Yoder showed that one never encounters a problem of the absolute and the individual in general, but only by dint of the background of comparison enabled by an often excluded third term. So Yoder, in contrast to Troeltsch, particularized (that is, located temporally and spatially) and politicized the terms of the question: the life of any particular community one encounters is always characterized by the movement from "smaller worlds into wider ones," always threatened by the assimilative force or "psychic dominance" of the "next wider world" it encounters.[83] This is not to claim that some people are less modern than others, or that some are legitimately anxious about a period of preparation they need to undergo before encountering perceived cultural elites as peers. It is not, in other words, to assume a progressivist paradigm, as the movement from small (parochial) communities to wide (cosmopolitan) ones might seem to suggest, because Yoder coupled such movement with the claim that the "wider world, in any one person's experience or pilgrimage or in any interface between two groups, is still a small place."[84] Rather, it challenges us to look. It is just to say that if we examine the life of any community, we find that it is always in flux, always encountering that which is different, new, and un-

---

82. Yoder, *Priestly Kingdom*, 46.
83. Yoder, *Priestly Kingdom*, 47.
84. Yoder, *Priestly Kingdom*, 49.

precedented. Consequently, everyone, even the representative of various "wider worlds," lives in, so to speak, the green room of history.

In shaping the issue this way, Yoder released the tension between the absolute and the individual. If, he argued, we attend to how debates actually occur, we find that claims in favor of absoluteness are often ideological, that is, arguments that characteristically mask some degree of provincialism. The question Yoder asked was therefore neither Lessing's nor Troeltsch's, but was altered accordingly. He did not ask how one could claim absoluteness for this or that particular view, but rather "How can particular truths be proclaimed publicly?"[85] For Yoder, publicity, not absoluteness, is the *telos* of the Christian message.[86] If every wider world is one more ghetto, then the "certainty that one is following the right star" is not at stake. What is at stake is a challenge to proclaim the gospel as good and as news. Thus, Yoder described the Christian relationship to the history of movement from smaller to wider worlds as "evangelical":

> I take the term in its root meaning. One is functionally evangelical if one confesses oneself to have been commissioned by the grace of God with a message which others who have not heard it should hear. It is *angelion* ("news") because they will not know it unless they are told it by a message-bearer. It is good news because hearing it will be for them not alienation or compulsion, oppression or brainwashing, but liberation. Because this news is only such when *received* as good, it can never be communicated coercively; nor can the message-bearer ever positively be assured that it will be received.[87]

In conceiving of the Christian's task as publication, Yoder displayed the relationship to the past as a question of and responsibility for the future, but not as one that attempts to guarantee the shape of that future. Rather, he argued, "What we are doing now . . . leads to where we are going."[88] As part and parcel of his picture of salvation as the creation of a community of Jesus' followers, "where we are going" was an admittedly

---

85. Yoder, *Priestly Kingdom*, 49.
86. Yoder, *Priestly Kingdom*, 56-57: "We shall not ask whether Christianity, or Jesus, or anything, is absolute or unique or universal in some way that could be supported, kept dry above the waves of relativity. A claim to absoluteness can be adjudicated meaningfully only in the frame in which it is pronounced, and then only if the way that that frame is self-understood provides some kind of fulcrum and a place to stand to make such a judgment."
87. Yoder, *Priestly Kingdom*, 55.
88. Yoder, *The Politics of Jesus* (Grand Rapids: Eerdmans, 1994), 241.

complex concept for Yoder. It both presupposed a spatial and/or experiential site of departure (what we are doing now) and had a "revolutionary" edge, where the destination is not a return to an original state but to a state transformed unpredictably and given to us as anamnetic renewal, which means that the (present) memory of our wandering, of our turning and turning again *(metanoia)*, of our seeking to actualize, repress, extinguish, and use "what we are doing now" will no longer be recognizable except under the signs of promise — all of which is to say that Yoder recognized the extent to which the continuity that pertains to where we are going, that "leads" there, will also involve revolutionary discontinuity with what we are doing now.

Chris Huebner refers to the revolutionary character of Yoder's thought, and particularly to his rejection of absoluteness or some other conceptual machinery that would underwrite the outcome of history, as his "methodological non-Constantinianism."[89] Here, and as the second site of commonality/difference between Yoder and Troeltsch, I want to supplement Huebner's discussion with a consideration of the non-Constantinian registers of Yoder's substantive eschatological claims.

At the beginning of "Peace without Eschatology?" Yoder noted that "Christian thought is learning to give increasing attention to the importance of the Christian hope for the Christian life."[90] He continued,

> Christian thought in the decades prior to the second World War was strongly influenced by thinkers and preachers who hoped for the brotherhood of man just around the corner and who therefore thought they had no time to waste on eschatology. The very word frightened them; it seemed to suggest weird speculations and wild-eyed fanatics out of touch with the world's real needs.[91]

---

89. Chris K. Huebner, "Unhandling History: Anti-Theory, Ethics and the Practice of Witness" (Ph.D. diss., Duke University, 2001), 192-285.

90. In John Howard Yoder, *The Original Revolution: Essays on Christian Pacifism* (Scottdale, PA: Mennonite Publishing Network, 1971), 55-90. The essay was originally presented as "Peace Without Eschatology" at Heerewegen, Zeist (The Netherlands) in 1954 and was circulated as a *Concern* pamphlet reprint after 1961. When it was incorporated into *The Original Revolution* it was renamed "If Christ Is Truly Lord" to reflect the WCC initiative in its Evanston (IL) conference. The current republication is "Peace without Eschatology?" in *The Royal Priesthood: Essays Ecclesiastical and Ecumenical* (Scottdale, PA: Herald, 1994), 143-67.

91. Yoder, *Royal Priesthood*, 144.

The reference to the brotherhood of man in this passage makes it seem unlikely that Troeltsch was on Yoder's horizon here. The target was much more likely Walter Rauschenbusch and the social gospelers, which seems to be confirmed considering that Yoder went on to speak of "[t]heir simple confidence that they could be sure of the meaning of life" as itself an eschatology, "a doctrine of what is ultimate."[92] Troeltsch, however, was in no way sure he could say what is ultimate; his confidence lay rather in the fact of the necessity of the question of ultimacy, of eschatology, for ethics.

Here too, then, Troeltsch's and Yoder's thought moved in the same direction, at least initially. Yoder indicated as much when he cited approvingly the WCC's recognition that "[t]here is no significance to human effort and, strictly speaking, no history unless life can be seen in terms of ultimate goals."[93] Yet, in another sense, Troeltsch was as much the target of Yoder's criticism as Rauschenbusch and liberal pacifists, for (as I noted in Chapter One with respect to O'Donovan) when Yoder defined "eschatology," he called it "a hope which, defying present frustration, defines a present position in terms of the yet unseen goal which gives it meaning."[94] This (to be sure) complex definition holds together a stance in the present (which may often be obstructed) with a "yet unseen goal" that does no more than let the present make sense. Yoder's unspoken premise is that if the present is to make sense, the goal that gives it its meaning must be specifiable. Troeltsch's "following the right star" "in outline and general direction" and Yoder's eschatology do therefore diverge. For Yoder, eschatology was not simply or merely a question of futurity as it was for Troeltsch. Rather, Yoder claimed that the gospel is "from beginning to end eschatological, a declaration about events and their place in the unfolding of God's purposes."[95]

In other words, what it means to speak of "history" has been transformed in the victory of the Lamb that was slain. Christ's activity is what history is for. Yoder's mantra in this regard is that the meaning of history is displayed in the church's obedience to and suffering with Christ. To be historical in this sense means to have time for God, to receive history in praise as God's gift.[96] History, received (and only thus seen) in the light of Christ's resurrection, cannot be based on an epistemology of dominance

---

92. Yoder, *Royal Priesthood*, 144-45.
93. Yoder, *Royal Priesthood*, 145.
94. Yoder, *Royal Priesthood*, 145.
95. Yoder, *Original Revolution*, 57.
96. Cf. Yoder, *Original Revolution*, 64; von Balthasar, *A Theology of History*, 34.

and security that harbors some sort of reservation about the future, because if the church thinks in terms of mastering time and contingency, or even in terms of ameliorating the threat they pose to its (self-generated) hopes, then it fails to participate in history as the promise of the gospel. For Yoder, our uses and conceptions of history are false and unhistorical to the extent that they generate an ethos of political and epistemological mastery, because they do not imitate the faithful obedience and self-denying patience of Christ.[97]

In sum: I have argued in the preceding pages that despite his sense that the conditions of modernity placed insurmountable constraints on the Christian faith, Troeltsch never gave up on the project of securing Christianity's cultural hegemony. His historicism grew out of the attempt to find a religiosity adequate to the social situation of early twentieth-century Germany, which demanded an emphasis on historical contingency and particularity. Troeltsch tried to hold this emphasis in tension with the need to speak of ultimate values and final ends, but in order to do so he had to evacuate those ends of any specific content. So, in assuming the difficult burden of articulating Christian faith in ways that relevantly addressed modernity (that is, rendered it politically effective), Troeltsch delimited Christian eschatology in accordance with the Kantian requirements of reason. In other words, hand in hand with his elision of the church, viewed as a social agency capable of producing historical change in keeping with the demands of modernity, went suspicion of "pie in the sky by and by" eschatology. But Troeltsch did draw the link between eschatology and ethics, and he did articulate a powerful vision of what it means to think in and with a sober recognition of historical finitude. In both of these respects he needs to be reconsidered as a source for Yoder's theology, as more of a ghost than a marker pointing down a road Yoder refused to take.

---

97. Yoder's eschatological refraction of history places him in close proximity to an under-appreciated teaching of the so-called Spiritualists of the sixteenth century, namely, "the gospel of all creatures." All creatures through suffering and death participate in and recall Christ's renunciation of sovereignty over his own existence. This reminds us that the reception of history as gift is not triumphalistic; it will entail a recognition that its fulfillment is also a matter of the growing barrenness and loneliness of the history of sin and loss.

CHAPTER 3

Constantinianism Before and After Nicaea: Issues in Restitutionist Historiography

[O]ne cannot say that every life, every age, has its own self-contained meaning. The significance of past ages and individual destinies is not irrevocably fixed, and they remain accessible to us; their meaning can always be newly defined and be transformed with the passage of time.

Hans Urs von Balthasar,
A Theology of History

In every era the attempt must be made anew to wrest tradition away from a conformism that is about to overpower it. The Messiah comes not only as the redeemer, he comes as the subduer of Antichrist. Only that historian will have the gift of fanning the spark of hope in the past who is firmly convinced that even the dead will not be safe from the enemy if he wins. And this enemy has not ceased to be victorious.

Walter Benjamin,
"Theses on the Philosophy of History"

The ministry of remembrance, which is the task of the historian, is . . . at heart a christological task. Its vocation is to trace the sameness of Jesus across the generations.

John Howard Yoder,
"Historiography as a Ministry to Renewal"

TO SEE HISTORY DOXOLOGICALLY

Introduction

The three epigraphs above set a constellation of themes within which to clarify some of the issues at stake in Yoder's understanding of history. First, they highlight a certain political danger, call it the danger of fixity, conformism, or establishmentarianism in attempts to envision the past, and they issue a call to mobility, dynamism, or reformation, not only in the representation of the past but also in the activity of representation, which Yoder calls the "ministry of remembrance." Second, they locate the raison d'être of the past's mobility and (more important) our uses of the past christologically. Our image of the past is yoked to and configured by our image of redemption: correspondingly, a lack of hope in the future may correlate with not having attempted an evangelical reading of the past.[1] Here I argue that Yoder's critique of Constantinian ecclesiologies is of a piece with his broader commitment to what he called "evangelical revisionism" or restitutionist historiography.[2] This is to say that a doxological vision of history requires a non-Constantinian picture of salvation. For Yoder, nonviolence is at the heart of non-Constantinianism, and restitutionism is at the heart of an attempt to envision a nonviolent way of "being historical" within the practice of theology, that is, a way of being historical that disavows the use of narratives involving the mastery of risk and the conquest of contingency — the very tropes a Constantinian posture demands. My argument here thus extends that of Chapter Two and further distinguishes Yoder's thought from Troeltschian historicism, which I there discussed in terms of a failure to hit upon an appropriate register of equivocation for thinking in the light of time. Put succinctly, in this chapter I will show how Yoder cycled historiographical practice through a reading of the gospel that allowed him to strike a mode of equivocation appropriate to christological pacifism.

But my task in this chapter includes at least two other foci. In the

---

1. Cf. Walter Benjamin, "Theses on the Philosophy of History," in *Illuminations: Essays and Reflections*, ed. Hannah Arendt (New York: Schocken, 1968), 254; Yoder, "Reply to 'Christianity and Democracy, a Statement of the Institute on Religion and Democracy,' by Richard John Neuhaus," *Center Journal* 1:3 (Summer 1982): 86; Yoder, *The Original Revolution: Essays on Christian Pacifism* (Scottdale: Herald, 1971), 166-67.

2. Yoder, "The Burden and the Discipline of Evangelical Revisionism," in *Nonviolent America: History through the Eyes of Peace*, ed. Louise Hawkley and James C. Juhnke (Newton, KS: Mennonite Press, 1993), 20-37; Yoder, *The Priestly Kingdom: Social Ethics as Gospel* (Notre Dame: University of Notre Dame Press, 1984), 123-34.

first place, it is to give a brief description of Yoder's use of Constantinianism as a trope for picturing a certain set of compromised ecclesiologies (and a certain way of compromising ecclesiology). In the second place, I wish to begin to address a set of historiographical and methodological problems Yoder's use of Constantinianism provokes, especially as it regards his own understanding of evangelical revisionism. That set of problems can be stated generally as a question: What difference ought the revisionist imperative make to Yoder's use of Constantinianism as a description?[3] Stated differently, does Yoder's actual account of Constantinianism live up to the aspirations embedded in his own restitutionist historiographical commitments?

In the introduction to this book I suggested that one way of thinking about the task I set for myself is as a set of theological and philosophical engagements necessary to a complex and faithful presentation of Yoder's work. Whom do you need to read and how in order to understand Yoder? That way of conceiving this work bears with it a set of related questions about the audience(s) for whom I am writing. I suspect that this chapter will be of particular interest to those who approach Yoder from a "Radical Reformation" or "Free Church" perspective. I am particularly interested in addressing those for whom the legacy of Constantine points out the fourth century as "where it all went wrong" with institutional Christianity. I will argue that Yoder, among others, constantly invoked but rarely engaged deeply the history of the fourth century: sketching something of the contemporary "Radical Reformation" or "Free Church" culture both reveals why this is so and suggests the shape of a possible deeper engagement.

---

3. In the last quarter of the twentieth century historians and theologians alike began to rethink their relationship to the fourth century, particularly concerning themselves with the trinitarian and christological controversies. Yet in much of the investigation Constantine's political program and the role he played in the developing ascendancy of Christianity has come under scrutiny. Notably diverse accounts include those collected in Michel R. Barnes and Daniel H. Williams, eds., *Arianism after Arius: Essays on the Development of the Fourth Century Trinitarian Conflicts* (Edinburgh: T&T Clark, 1993), as well as the monographs by T. D. Barnes, *Constantine and Eusebius* (Cambridge, MA: Harvard University Press, 1981); Elizabeth DePalma Digeser, *The Making of a Christian Empire: Lactantius and Rome* (Ithaca, NY: Cornell University Press, 2000); H. A. Drake, *Constantine and the Bishops: The Politics of Intolerance* (Baltimore: Johns Hopkins University Press, 2000); and R. P. C. Hanson, *The Search for the Christian Doctrine of God* (Edinburgh: T&T Clark, 1988). Arguably the renaissance in fourth-century studies was configured by John Henry Newman's *The Arians of the Fourth Century* (Notre Dame: University of Notre Dame Press, 2001), originally published in 1833.

It will undoubtedly seem that the argument here vacillates wildly across a temporal spectrum — from now back to the fourth century and back again — especially in comparison with the other chapters of this book, where I have tended to treat the people with whom I deal as contemporaries in a conversation (largely of my own construction) even where that is patently not the case. The rationale I offer is limited, but I think central to Yoder's practice as a theologian — namely, that history writing as an evangelical mandate requires attention not only to "what happened back then" but also to our stakes in characterizing "what happened" in the particular ways we characterize it. Often, our attentiveness to the past, which is driven by intellectual honesty, blinds us to how our uses of the past are less than honest. So this chapter jumps back and forth through time because it, more than any other chapter, asks about historical vision as a necessary ingredient to ecclesiology.[4] I hope too that, because one chapter would not suffice as a definitive statement on the history that is being foregrounded and contested here (we might even have good reasons to question the notion of a definitive statement), the argument I present will be viewed as an outline for future engagements about the possibility of a contemporary "non-Constantinian" theology.

Before beginning this discussion, I need to offer an account of where I think I am in the argument of this book. The focal contention of the first chapters has been that Yoder's ecclesiological thought is best understood as a way of being in time that envisions the praise of God as at least in part constituted by an often-discordant relationship to our pasts. Rather than conceiving of holiness as a matter of "getting it all straight" right now, I have argued that Yoder conceived of doxology as a series of practices that cultivate patience — a nonviolent and equivocal or difficult *habitus* — as the necessary context within which to confess the church as holy. It is within this context that Yoder's non-Constantinianism is most appropriately interpreted.

As I hinted in the introduction to the book, it seems to me that the more one sees doxology as a matter of history and our uses of our pasts,

---

4. "Jumping back and forth through time" seems to me a dangerous metaphor, because it posits time as a thing, or perhaps as a unit of measure; anyway, as a homogenous singularity. I wonder whether the appropriate way to discipline such a metaphor is via reference to Wittgenstein on games: just as there is no organizing concept "game" that makes all games games, so there is no time that makes all times times. In this sense, "time" is a misunderstanding of the role of the ideal in our language. Cf. Ludwig Wittgenstein, *Philosophical Investigations* (Oxford: Blackwell, 1997), §100.

the more one sees the deep inadequacy of engagement with the fourth century in much modern theology. This is, I think, the case in at least two respects. First, with respect to the "Radical Reformation" audience, who have seen the fourth century as a period of disavowing the gospel and apostasy, I want to suggest that a doxological vision of history prompts the perhaps painful recognition that this past of disavowal and apostasy is effective for us; that, precisely because it is a compromised and conflict-ridden past, it cannot be set aside as "the road not taken." Second, as a claim on the attention of those within "mainstream Christianity," I would also suggest that the more one explores history as an evangelical responsibility, the more it seems inexcusable to defend an "orthodoxy" that is, or has ever been, politically and socially uninvested. Once one argues that the way you tell the story of your past is a matter of praising God, then one has to learn to reckon honestly with the difficulties that the past presents, and this is a comment about biography as well as about Christian traditions: if memory is doxological, it will also be equivocal.

Constantinianism as a Narrative Trope for Yoder

To the first part of the task, then. How did Yoder describe Constantinianism, and how did he use it to analyze a certain kind of ecclesiological pitfall? As I have suggested, Yoder's theological practice involved invoking and deploying narratives of theological development in the pre-modern era. In this, he shared a strategy of thought with many competing theological styles, but I want to suggest that theological history was indispensable for Yoder in a way that it was not for many of his contemporaries — to the degree, then, that Yoder attended to how history shapes politics and theology (and the influence flows both ways), his historical practice needed to be more careful and consciously self-critical than that of his contemporaries. Yet because of his dependence on and self-differentiation from inherited modes of historical thought that assumed a basic distinction between modern and pre-modern theology (Troeltsch is the example I elicited in Chapter Two; H. S. Bender would be another), Yoder's thought relied on summary narratives of the developments preceding modernity, the contents of which I will return to in due course. At this point I would say, however, that such summaries were deployed in their original contexts primarily as historicist strategies whose rhetorical effect is to posit time as a measure of cultural distance between the historian and his or her object of study.⁵ Yoder's account of the development of Constantinianism is one of the clearest examples of this process in his work, and this is borne out by his dependence on older secondary sources, the polemical contexts and concerns of which he does not examine.⁶

Why are these important considerations for understanding Yoder's version of Constantinianism and his governing assumptions about the doing of history? One should not, of course, present dependence on older scholarship as such as a problem, but it is also part and parcel of Yoder's theological practice to recognize the extreme complexity of the development of theological traditions: "Because there is in the [believing community's] storeroom of memories a bewildering variety of 'treasures,' know-

---

5. See, for an examination of historicism as the cultivation of the distance of false superiority, Dipesh Chakrabarty, "The Time of History and the Times of Gods," in *The Politics of Culture in the Shadow of Capital*, ed. Lisa Lowe and David Lloyd (Durham: Duke University Press, 1997), 35-60; cf. Chakrabarty, *Provincializing Europe: Postcolonial Thought and Historical Difference* (Princeton: Princeton University Press, 2000). Hans-Georg Gadamer describes another distancing in *Truth and Method* (New York: Continuum, 1997) as the donation of otherness necessary for understanding, where the very possibility of history requires engagement of the other as other *and* as a constitutive moment of the self: "[T]he experience of the Thou throws light on the concept of historically effected experience. The experience of the Thou also manifests the paradox that something standing over against me asserts its own rights and requires absolute recognition; and in that very process is 'understood'" (p. xxxv). I will look more extensively at the analogies between Gadamer and Yoder at the end of this chapter.

6. So, for example, Yoder relied on the following texts, all of which are summational in character and reliant on nineteenth-century historiography: Roland Bainton, *Christian Attitudes to War and Peace* (Nashville: Abingdon, 1960); C. J. Cadoux, *The Early Church and the World* (Edinburgh: T&T Clark, 1925); Arthur Holmes, *War and Christian Ethics* (Grand Rapids: Baker, 1975); Albert Marrin, *War and the Christian Conscience: From Augustine to Martin Luther King, Jr.* (Chicago: Regnery, 1971). Yoder does not debate these authors' presentation of their stories. One other clear indication of Yoder's reliance on narratological tropes in historiography is his repeated references to "Greek" thought as static, "metaphysical," and unconcerned with history. See, e.g., Yoder, "Historiography as a Ministry to Renewal," *From Age to Age: Historians and the Modern Church: A Festschrift for Donald F. Durnbaugh*, ed. David B. Eller, *Brethren Life and Thought* 43:4 (Summer and Fall 1997): 216-28, at p. 216; *Preface to Theology: Christology and Theological Method* (Grand Rapids: Brazos, 2002), 165 and passim; cf. Yoder, "The Message of the Bible on Its Own Terms," in *To Hear the Word* (Eugene, OR: Wipf and Stock, 2001), 136-37, where Yoder contrasts "Greek" with "Hebraic" thought. Notice that here, however, Yoder says, "It would . . . be misleading to consider 'Hebraic' as 'better.' It suffices that we be warned against screening out dimensions of the biblical witness because of our unavowed, perhaps unconscious commitment to Greek (or for that matter Roman or Germanic or British) thought modes" (p. 137).

ing which of them to bring out and how they fit is itself a charisma."[7] Because a community's memory is prudentially governed as effective for the ongoing process of discernment that constitutes the community's shape, its relation to the past should not be presented as a monolithic story, either of an unambiguously positive inheritance — this is the risk of appeals to the *depositum fidei* — or of an equally straightforward narrative of disavowal and apostasy, which Yoder associates with primitivism. The problem with such narratives is not simply that they disambiguate history, nor is it that they are invested readings of history. The problem is rather that they disambiguate history in order to justify their investment in their unstated set of contemporary theological polemical concerns. On Yoder's view, that combination of disambiguation and justification is dishonest historiography. As he put it, "The most honest historiography is not that which claims to be value free but rather that which is open about its prejudices and includes in its methodology a check against their leading it to distort the record."[8] To the extent that Yoder relied on such narratives without explicit attention to the concerns that shaped them, his narrative concerning Constantinianism risks further authorizing theological narratives that do not locate equivocation and difficulty as partly constitutive of what it means to think historically. Yet this is only part of the problem. Once one sees that Yoder's account of Constantinianism is shaped by monological and polemically invested readings of the early church, then one is in a position to ask further questions regarding how the adoption of such readings might serve as a narratological prolegomenon to Yoder's own "constructive" attempt to develop a nonviolent mode of historical theological practice. In order, however, for the profile of those questions to emerge, I need to inquire as to the basic shape of Yoder's account of the Constantinian temptation.

In "Peace without Eschatology," Yoder put the matter succinctly: Constantinianism "refers to the conception of Christianity that took shape in the century between the Edict of Milan and the *City of God*."[9] The markers are important, for here Constantinianism emerges as a distinct problem in the fourth and early fifth centuries, between two documents, the

---

7. Yoder, *The Priestly Kingdom: Social Ethics as Gospel* (Notre Dame: University of Notre Dame Press, 1984), 30.

8. Yoder, *The Original Revolution: Essays on Christian Pacifism* (Scottdale: Herald, 1971), 167.

9. Yoder, *The Royal Priesthood: Essays Ecclesiological and Ecumenical*, ed. Michael G. Cartwright (Grand Rapids: Eerdmans, 1994), 153-54.

first of which grants "freedom of religion" to Christians — the legal right to practice Christianity publicly — and the second of which deals at least in part with the necessary invisibility of the true church.[10] The choice of texts signals that the problem from Yoder's perspective was not simply one of visibility, or whether or not the church is visible, but rather of how the church conceives of itself as being visible in the world; it therefore concerns the institution during this period of sociopolitical obstacles that inhibit the concrete identification of a determinate body of believers as the church.

The creation of such obstacles was, for Yoder, not solely a fourth-century phenomenon and could not exclusively be connected to Constantine I. Rather, Gerald Schlabach observes that, though Constantine's politics do "mark a watershed in church history," his significance for the church "was conferred upon him" by Christians, who were the inheritors of a whole host of cultural and philosophical assumptions that enabled them to see this as a reasonable thing to do. It is that set of assumptions, Schlabach says, that Constantinianism consists in.[11]

Elsewhere, Yoder confirms Schlabach's view:

> The Roman emperor who began to tolerate, then supported, then administered, then finally joined the church, soon became and has remained until our time the symbol of a sweeping shift in the nature of the empirical church and its relation to the world. Constantine neither initiated that shift nor concluded it, and our present interest is not in the extent to which he knew what he was doing. The shift is what matters. That it took place, was far-reaching, and changed much of the concrete social meaning of Christianity, all historians agree.[12]

---

10. "Freedom of religion" remains a problematically anachronistic way of stating what it was that Constantine extended to Christians in the Edict of Milan. Perhaps "toleration" is better, since there was no talk in 312 of disestablishing pagan rites. On this, see now Lester R. Fields Jr., *Liberty, Dominion, and the Two Swords: On the Origins of Political Theology in the West, 180-395* (Notre Dame: University of Notre Dame Press, 1998), 65-81.

11. Gerald Schlabach, "Deuteronomic or Constantinian: What Is the Most Basic Problem for Christian Social Ethics?" in *The Wisdom of the Cross: Essays in Honor of John Howard Yoder,* ed. Stanley Hauerwas, Chris K. Huebner, Harry J. Huebner, and Mark Thiessen Nation (Grand Rapids: Eerdmans, 1999), 452. Cf. 449-50: "[I]n Yoder's reading of church history and social ethics, Constantinianism is not simply a fourth-century phenomenon but is emblematic for a thoroughgoing and oft-repeated Christian unfaithfulness."

12. Yoder, *Royal Priesthood,* 245. Cf. Yoder, *Christian Attitudes to War, Peace, and Revolution: A Companion to Bainton* (Elkhart, IN: Goshen Biblical Seminary, 1983), 39.

"The shift is what matters." If one refrain throughout Yoder's analysis of Constantinianism remains puzzling, this is it. Constantine is emblematic of "a new era in the history of Christianity,"[13] and "he inaugurated the age of Christianity's being the official religion,"[14] but we are not interested in the man; our business is to attend to the shift. In part, at least, this has to do with Yoder's skepticism — in marked contrast to most other inquiries into the Constantinian era since Jacob Burckhardt's *Die Zeit Constantins des Grossen* — that much can be known about the man. There is, it might be said, a "problem of the historical Constantine," that Yoder tried to steer clear of; whereas other historians venture conclusions about Constantine's psychology or character, Yoder's account was functional. He asked, echoing the other historians, "Was Constantine sincere or was he only using Christianity as a political tool? . . . Why did he postpone his baptism? Why did he convene and control the Council of Nicea? Did he see himself as the savior of the church . . . ? *Are these questions that can fruitfully be posed?*"[15] I suspect that Yoder's implied answer to that last question was, "Probably not." Far too many layers of interpretation and reinterpretation lie between Constantine and us to allow investigation into his life to yield results we could deem veridical. Moreover, apart from those layers of interpretation and reinterpretation, a process that commenced with Eusebius of Caesarea's *Vita Constantini,* there is no history to which we might turn to get Constantine the man straight. Constantinianism, like the Jeremian turn in the life of ancient Israel and the New Testament itself, demands exposition "in a larger than life way . . . as 'legend,' as something having to be recounted, bigger in its meanings than what the historians' questions about documents and causation can contain."[16]

This may be to dismiss the pertinence of the historians' questions too quickly. While I agree with Yoder that it is important to de-center Constantine to a certain extent when considering the Constantinian revolution, it is nevertheless crucial to take care to recognize that individual agency mattered, that "Christianity" or "the Roman Empire" were not simply "impersonal structures." At the very least we should ask questions about the argumentative importance of establishing Constantine's character. Why was that something historians felt compelled to do? Why was it

---

13. Yoder, *Priestly Kingdom,* 135.
14. Yoder, *Priestly Kingdom,* 209n3.
15. Yoder, *Priestly Kingdom,* 245n3. Emphasis added.
16. Yoder, *For the Nations: Essays Public and Evangelical* (Grand Rapids: Eerdmans, 1997), 8.

important for Burckhardt and his heirs? While these are not questions to which Yoder posed an answer, H. A. Drake has posed them recently in *Constantine and the Bishops*. From Drake's text we can see something of the stakes in nineteenth- and twentieth-century historiography for inquiring after Constantine the man.

Drake's main point regarding Burckhardt is that he was not guilty of discounting the role of political processes in Constantine's conversion to Christianity, but that he erred in a subtle way, by relying on the "conceptual anachronism" of "assuming . . . that the disdain for established institutions which he saw all around him prevailed in the fourth century as well."[17] Burckhardt's logic was almost syllogistic in its clarity: a committed Christian would not continue to support pagan institutions after conversion; Constantine did continue to support pagan institutions; therefore, Constantine could not have been a committed Christian. These assumptions are, however, deeply intertwined with Protestant academic polemics against Roman Catholicism's perceived hegemony in Europe through the Reformations and carry on to the conclusion only if one grants the terms in which the premises are posed. Drake challenges the assumption that conversion was understood in the fourth century in the terms Burckhardt recognized; thus, his project miscarried at a fundamental level. By and large scholars since Burckhardt have continued to pose the question of Constantine's conversion in terms with which Burckhardt would have been satisfied, and this has at least partly to do with the continuing utility of older Protestant polemics against Roman Catholicism for "secular" academia: a universalizing religion or comprehensive set of doctrines like Catholicism contains within in it anti-liberal seeds of intolerance. This narrative, however, is question begging, for it presumes rather than establishes the truth of a fall narrative for which Constantine stands as the figurehead to locate and explain contemporary Catholicism as entailing an ecclesiology of which one should be wary.

It should be said that historiographical engagement with Constantine was and remains motivated by reasons other than anti-Catholic bias. It also has to do with the complex negotiations of how to "own" the legacy of the Council of Nicaea, and particularly with acknowledging how the creed that council promulgated continues to bind Christians. The Reformers already connected Constantinian Christianity and the Nicene Creed: if, some of them argued, the former was corrupt, then the latter

---

17. Drake, *Constantine and the Bishops*, 17.

could hardly be an indispensable touchstone for Christian faith and practice. That logic remains powerful today. Yet, while many of the contemporary restatements of this problem are guilty of the genetic fallacy, two things are nonetheless worthy of note for this discussion. The first is that the role of this narrative, *compromised ecclesiology = compromised doctrine*, in shaping contemporary historical interaction with the fourth century, demands the sustained attention of the kind it has begun to receive in D. H. Williams's *Retrieving the Tradition and Renewing Evangelicalism*.[18] The second is that negotiating the continued pertinence of the Nicene Creed for contemporary radical Protestant Christianity was not at the forefront of Yoder's work.[19] Indeed, the claims he made regarding the Nicene Creed characteristically affirmed the theology he advanced as more radically pro-Nicene than that of many theologians in traditions that claim Nicaea's authority in a way he did not. To put the point rather bluntly, one searches Yoder's texts in vain for a decisive contemporary non-Constantinian refutation of pro-Nicene theology.

Again, Yoder's focus is on the shift — not only because historians have been telling us for decades not to blame Constantinianism on Constantine, and not only because we lack the resources to investigate the man in any way that would be less than futile, but also because it is the shift and not the man that accounts for the distance of most contemporary ecclesiologies from the New Testament church.[20] But attending to epoch-making "shifts" is risky business, particularly because shifts foreground fractures, discontinuities, and dislocations that render the historical and epistemic ruptures they represent enigmatic. Why call Constantinianism a shift? Why not a development? An evolution? A maturation? Each description is loaded, and each deploys a different narrative about the past. Constantinianism, when described as a shift, can be taken to represent a deep breach in the span of continuity, a fracture profound enough that it

---

18. Daniel H. Williams, *Retrieving the Tradition and Renewing Evangelicalism: A Primer for Suspicious Protestants* (Grand Rapids: Eerdmans, 1999), esp. 107-31.

19. The eighth and ninth chapters of *Preface to Theology* are the only places I know of in Yoder's work where pro-Nicene theology is subjected to critical inquiry. The lecture format of that material makes it difficult to assess as a measure of Yoder's considered views, but even there the point is not to discredit Nicaea so much as it is to ask for a historically thoughtful approach to its legacy.

20. Yoder, *Priestly Kingdom*, 144: "The fourth-century shift continues to explain much if not most of the distance between biblical Christianity and ourselves, which is a distance not simply of time and organic development, but of disavowal and apostasy."

cannot be "explained" or even adequately referenced in this single word. Part of the difficulty here lies in appropriately assessing the criteria for analysis. After the shift, how will you know how to talk about it? What are the alternatives? Do you cut to the root of its history, hoping to find a secure site, free from doubt, that will fund critical engagement across the breach? Or do you examine an aggregate of specificities as they show themselves to you, hoping to discern there a function or set of functions, marked by discontinuities and cleavages, but plausibly narrated in some continuity? Is that a genuine choice, and what tools do you have at your disposal to help you decide? Constantinianism as a shift, more than any event or series of related events, is like what Michel Foucault called an *episteme*: it is marked by "a *radical* event . . . distributed across the entire visible surface of knowledge, whose signs, shocks, and effects it is possible to follow step by step."[21] But if we follow effects step by step, with attention to minute detail, how long will it make sense to continue to speak of a shift? Perhaps now we begin to see how close Yoder remained to the problems with which Troeltsch wrestled.

I will return to these questions about criteria, about what it could mean to speak of a Constantinian shift, later in the chapter. At this point I want to focus on Yoder's claim that at base the Constantinian shift represents a "reorientation of the meaning of history . . . when it became obvious, because of the victory of Constantine, that the God of Moses is on the side of the people who come out triumphant in a particular course of events."[22] In other words, the question "How does God work in history?" received a new answer at a systemic level.[23] Whereas prior to the age of Constantine God's governance of history remained mysterious, even though Christians knew "as a fact of lived experience that there was a church" through which God worked in the world, after the Constantinian

---

21. Michel Foucault, *The Order of Things: An Archaeology of the Human Sciences* (New York: Random House, 1970), 217. Emphasis added.

22. Yoder, *Christian Attitudes to War, Peace, and Revolution*, 50. One might ask the following question: To whom did it become obvious that the God of Moses is on the side of the victorious? It is arguably never "obvious" to Eusebius, who goes to great lengths to make the point sound reasonable, and it is certainly not obviously the case until after Constantine's death a quarter century later than his victory (and conversion?) at the Milvian Bridge. Lactantius, writing during Constantine's reign, evidences discomfort with such an equation, as does Augustine a century later in *The City of God*. But if not unambiguously to these three, then to whom?

23. Yoder, *Christian Attitudes to War, Peace, and Revolution*, 42.

settlement God's dominion was evident (through the arm of the empire), but one must "take it on faith that there is a church."[24] This reorientation of the meaning of history is deeper than the changes in church polity and Christian ethics that followed upon it, and it is more basic than the "more recent turns, which Western Christians call 'the Reformation' and 'the Enlightenment.'"[25]

The shift can first be detected, according to Yoder, during the latter part of the second century, when Christian theologians like Tertullian, Origen, and Cyprian began to address the way the Christian church should comport itself vis-à-vis the empire. Each of these theologians acknowledged that Christian attitudes toward the empire were changing and becoming less oppositional, and yet put "his pacifism within a more global rejection of the Caesar system as a diabolical system as it . . . [was then] encountered."[26] The implication in Yoder's view is that, though the theologians continued to argue strongly against Christian involvement with the sword, the imperial cult, and oath taking, nevertheless at the popular level at least two things were in flux. In the first place, the extent to which Christianity in large measure viewed itself as a set of moral rules to be followed was less significant than it had been earlier in the second century. Correlatively, and in the second place, the repercussions on Christians who stepped outside the bounds of Christian doctrine loosened as the century neared its end.[27] These two factors, taken together, were both symptomatic of and contributed to the church's increasingly acculturated self-perception. Moreover, such acculturation prompted the apologetic concerns that dominated Tertullian's ecclesiological thought and, though to a lesser extent, were noteworthy in Origen's and Cyprian's writing as well.

When Yoder links apologetics and nascent Constantinian views of the church, it is interesting that he never ties Christian apologetic concerns in the late second and early third centuries to major changes in the imperial stance toward Christianity. Yet the writings of the apologists arose in a context in which the edges between the church and empire were becoming more habitable from both perspectives. This, of course, was not simply a

---

24. Yoder, *Christian Attitudes to War, Peace, and Revolution*, 44.
25. See Yoder, *Christian Attitudes to War, Peace, and Revolution*, 41, and *For the Nations*, 8, where Constantinianism is placed in parallel to the "other ancient turning point" represented by Jeremiah.
26. Yoder, *Christian Attitudes to War, Peace and Revolution*, 30.
27. Yoder, *Christian Attitudes to War, Peace, and Revolution*, 34.

matter of dialogical rapprochement, though Christian and pagan discourses did fertilize each other, but it was also a matter of inescapably sharing a politics. Consider, for instance, the effects on Christians initiated by such legal institutions as the dramatic revision of the Roman constitution, which commenced with Caracalla's edict of 212. Elizabeth DePalma Digeser, in *The Making of a Christian Empire*, argues that the Antonine Constitution unified the empire in new way:

> From a loose collection of *civitates*, each under the central authority of the emperor but also maintaining its own laws and citizenship, the empire became one great *civitas* under Roman law. In the early empire, religious pluralism survived in the interstices between peregrine and Roman law. But after the passage of the Antonine Constitution, Decius, Valerian, and Diocletian were quite willing to use force against groups whose refusal to worship the gods called into question their loyalty to the laws.[28]

While the use of force to suppress religious dissent was one important (pre-Constantinian) effect of the Antonine Constitution, a number of other factors deserve consideration. Prior to the passage of the Antonine Constitution, many if not most Christians were not Roman citizens.[29] But the Constitution granted rights of citizenship to all imperial subjects, Christians included. Indeed, the Antonine Constitution represented an unprecedented reevaluation of the meaning of empire. At one level — by and large the stated one — it was a reformative legislation, designed to return Rome to its republican roots. At another level, it simply broadened the tax base for the imperium, as commentators from as early as the third century noted.[30] At yet another level, however, it radically reconfigured how the borders of the empire were to be conceived, and this through a process of internalizing and homogenizing the effects of power. Let me explain: prior to the passage of the Constitution the empire could be conceived primarily in spatial terms — it was wherever the local government acknowledged allegiance to the emperor. But the Antonine Constitution, while not doing away with the spatialized concept of empire, also subjectivized it by making citizenship constitutive of what it meant to be

---

28. Digeser, *The Making of a Christian Empire*, 119.
29. Ramsey MacMullen, *Christianizing the Roman Empire (A.D. 100-400)* (New Haven: Yale University Press, 1984), 32-33.
30. Cf. Digeser, *The Making of a Christian Empire*, 50.

inside the empire. The edges of the empire were thus made coterminous with its citizenry, and this produced something like what Foucault (in a very different connection) called a "discipline-mechanism," where each person, by the mere fact of having been made a citizen, internalized and policed his or her relation to the empire.[31] In this context, many Christians found themselves face to face for the first time with the requirements of the empire in a way that demanded self-aware, legal, and public display.

Consequently, legal measures like the Antonine Constitution created some of the conditions for the increased social mobility and conspicuousness of Christians that Yoder cites as a motivating factor in third-century apologetic theology. This is not to suggest that the Constitution's effects were an unmixed blessing for Christians, for it initiated, in a way that had never been the case before, imperial policy regarding the cultic affiliation of all citizens of the Roman Empire. As Digeser's account intimates, after 212 failure to participate in the imperial cult, which Christians had always refused to do, became a treasonable offense.[32] The point to be learned in this connection is simply that the Christian apologists of the early third century responded not only to a process of acculturation initiated by, as Yoder put it, "second, third, and fourth generation Christians, who . . . [had] never really, deeply suffered for being Christian."[33] Their apologies for Christianity were also prompted by the imposition of the imperial cult on all subjects of the empire, newly defined as citizens — and this latter should be seen as the basic polemical context for their theologies.

The problem this example presents to thinking through Yoder's account of the Christian slide into Constantinianism, namely, that the "history" he adduces to support his case is surprisingly monological, is evident elsewhere in his work. To extend the example above: it is easy to get the impression, reading *Christian Attitudes to War, Peace and Revolution,* that second- and third-century Christianity can be configured as a contest between the martyrs, who represent Christian conviction and exclusivism, and the apologists, who represent hellenization and acculturation. On this narrative trope, the Constantinian settlement appears as but the logical outworking of the apologetic tradition — Tertullian sets the stage for

---

31. Michel Foucault, *Discipline and Punish: The Birth of the Prison* (New York: Vintage, 1979), 202-4.
32. Digeser, *The Making of a Christian Empire,* 50.
33. Yoder, *Christian Attitudes to War, Peace, and Revolution,* 30-31.

Theodosius.[34] But inasmuch as legal measures like the Antonine Constitution forced Christians into a context where they had to both legitimate their practice and begin to make a case for religious toleration in terms recognizable to the imperium, the registers in which a contemporary account of the birth of Constantinianism must be pitched are modulated, and in ways that Yoder's telling of the story does not take into account.

Given these considerations, Yoder's argument for increasing acculturation in the pre-Constantinian church and a slow but perceptible drift into a comfortable relationship with the empire begins to look like an attempt to retell the past in order to furnish it with a suitable denouement. Here then, Yoder's work on Constantinianism reflects something of an older, primitivist account of Christianity, which, though he took pains to distance himself from it — slow drifts do not make for golden ages — nevertheless shows itself in his uncritical adoption of the narrative trope of apologists/inclusivists versus martyrs/moral rigorists.

As Yoder continues the story of the Constantinian shift other instances emerge that prompt questions about the argumentative orientation of his historiography. He writes, "In the fourth century an age of toleration and accommodation begins. There was still, in the early part of the century, some persecution of Christians, but it soon ended."[35] Elsewhere he notes that the "last wave of persecution was not successful. The alternative for the Empire was then: 'if you can't lick 'em, join 'em.' It is that alliance that Constantine represents."[36] In these passages Yoder gives two impressions: (1) that the persecution under Diocletian and Galerius was in fact not terribly consequential for the formation of Christian consciousness in the fourth century, and (2) that the empire conceived of itself as waging an ongoing and losing battle with Christianity. Both impressions deserve much more careful attention than Yoder gives them. At the very least it needs to be said that the persecution of Christians under Diocletian

---

34. While Tertullian's *Apologia* is dated from around 197, the dates of *De corona militis* and *Contra Marcion* are at least a decade later — possibly, though not certainly, under the edict of 212. But, the Severan persecution out of which the *Apologia* grew is another instance of a largely external pressure that prompted Christian theologians into apologetic inquiry, which Yoder does not mention.

35. Yoder, *Preface to Theology*, 195.

36. Yoder, *Christian Attitudes to War, Peace, and Revolution*, 39. Stylistically, this quotation sticks out like a sore thumb (to use another cliché). I am aware it could be argued that Yoder's lecture transcriptions are unfair sources to which to turn for his considered views on the matter.

and Galerius was remembered as the "Great Persecution," distinct from its predecessors in both scope and systematic focus. Moreover, at this point Yoder's arguments about the fourth century still focus on the accommodation of the church "to the culture of the surrounding world."[37] He fails to mention that by the end of the third century the "surrounding world" had itself cultivated assumptions regarding the importance of the singular divine mind in human affairs that were increasingly similar to those already held by Christians.

What has been at stake in the preceding paragraphs is the lingering presence of contestable narrative tropes in Christian historiography that shaped Yoder's account of the Constantinian revolution. Yoder's discussion of the age of Constantine is governed by a fall motif, which shows itself in his assumptions regarding second- and third-century apologetics, as well as in his inattentiveness to imperial legislation that created an inescapable proximity between Christians and the imperium. In the next section of this chapter I will show why Yoder's own assumptions about history as an evangelical mandate ought to have led him to challenge the effectiveness of these tropes in his ecclesiology. In the next few paragraphs, however, I will discuss a second argumentative orientation that provided a subtext for many of Yoder's sources' accounts of the development of Christianity in the age of Constantine, namely, the ease with which the politics of the fourth century prompted analogies with the politics of early- to mid-twentieth-century Europe.

Eusebius of Caesarea and Augustine of Hippo are only slightly less central figures in Yoder's account of the age of Constantine than is Constantine himself. Indeed, Eusebius and Augustine are the dominant theological touchstones in Yoder's narration of the fourth and fifth centuries. Eusebius, who authored the *Ecclesiastical History,* the *Life of Constantine,* and the *Oration in Praise of Constantine,* deservedly plays a major role in the history, historiography, and hagiography that surrounds Constantine's reign, and was himself been the subject of intense inquiry in the nineteenth and twentieth centuries. That inquiry goes back at least to Jacob Burckhardt, who in 1852 denounced Eusebius as "the first thoroughly dishonest historian of antiquity."[38] As we have seen, Burckhardt's argument left something to be desired in terms of foregrounding his own

---

37. Yoder, *Preface to Theology,* 195.
38. Jakob Burckhardt, *The Age of Constantine the Great,* trans. Moses Hadas (New York: Pantheon, 1949), 283.

prejudices, but the outlook that dominated the twentieth century was heavily influenced by his polemics.

Recent scholars, including Michael J. Hollerich, have put a more refined point on Eusebius's political propagandism. In *Eusebius of Caesarea's Commentary on Isaiah: Christian Exegesis in the Age of Constantine*, Hollerich notes that "much of the work on Eusebius has been done with one eye on the crisis which convulsed Europe in the 1930s and 1940s; the involvement of Christianity in the fate of the Third Reich has left its mark on scholarship."[39] The implication of Hollerich's claim is that in the second third of the twentieth century European historians and theologians projected their own political anxieties onto the fourth century. In this context, Constantine became a potent symbol not simply of the established church's moral decadence, which had been the case in the writings of religious dissenters since at least the twelfth century, but also of the specific dangers concomitant on Christianity's cultural accommodation, of the fusion of church and world.[40]

In slight variation from Hollerich, T. D. Barnes locates the projection of modern politics onto the fourth century in the Germany of Bismarck and Kaiser Wilhelm II.[41] Then, significantly, Yoder's relationship to Troeltsch's historical method might require extended inquiry particularly as regards thinking about Constantinianism, insofar as Troeltsch thought of his vision of a new cultural synthesis as recapitulating the Constantinian revolution. The extent to which Yoder's own analysis of the Constantinian settlement was marked by a concern to distance himself from Troeltsch remains unclear: he did not write about Troeltsch's theology as the fusion of church and world. It is, however, indubitably the case that Yoder was influenced by theologians and historians for whom the accommodation of the *Deutsche Christen* to Nazism was a major issue (Barth and

---

39. Michael J. Hollerich, *Eusebius of Caesarea's Commentary on Isaiah: Christian Exegesis in the Age of Constantine* (Oxford: Clarendon, 1999), 193.

40. Interestingly, Rowan Williams, in *Arius: Heresy and Tradition*, rev. ed. (Grand Rapids: Eerdmans, 2001), hazards an analogy between Barth's position vis-à-vis the Deutsche Christen and Athanasius's championing of pro-Nicene theology, while acknowledging that such juxtapositions can be badly misleading (pp. 237ff.). This indicates, and there are a few other indications throughout the text, that while Williams altered many of the parameters for considering the "Arian crisis," he too remained attracted to older and questionable narratives and polemics that configured historiography of the fourth century.

41. T. D. Barnes, "Constantine, Athanasius and the Christian Church," in *Constantine: History, Historiography, and Legend*, ed. Samuel N. C. Lieu and Dominic Montserrat (New York: Routledge, 1998), 7-20, esp. 8-9.

Berkhof both leap immediately to mind), and he appears to have learned much from this strand of criticism, which associates pro-Constantinian theology with christological subordinationism. Hendrik Berkhof, in both *Kirche und Kaiser* and *Die Theologie des Eusebius von Caesarea*, detected subordinationism in Eusebius's theology, which he then correlated to his panegyrics for the emperor.[42] If Christ was not God in the way that the Father was God, Berkhof's logic runs, then the emperor and Christ could exercise more or less parallel rules, Christ in heaven over the cosmos and Constantine on earth over the *imperium*.

Berkhof's account resonated powerfully throughout the mid-twentieth century. Perhaps Erik Peterson, in *Der Monotheismus als politisches Problem*, gave the clearest expression to the equation between Constantine and Christ: "The one monarch on earth — and that for Eusebius is only Constantine — corresponds to the one divine monarch in heaven."[43] Berkhof and Peterson were followed in large part by George Hunston Williams and Per Beskow.[44] Williams argued forcefully that

> The facility with which Eusebius could assimilate the Constantinian with the Messianic peace is connected . . . with the fact that for Eusebius the Logos was a subordinate *deuteros theos*, a mediator primarily in the cosmological rather than in the religious sense. Hence salvation was understood as coming through the might of a godly ruler.[45]

Williams is especially interesting in counterpoint to Yoder. As I indicated above, Yoder detected an ambiguous relationship between pro-

---

42. Hendrik Berkhof, *Kirche und Kaiser: Eine Untersuchung der Entstehung der byzantischen und der theokratischen Staatsauffassung im vierten Jahrhundert*, trans. Gottfried W. Locher (Zürich: Evangelischer Verlag, 1947), 100-102, and *Die Theologie des Eusebius von Caesarea* (Amsterdam: Uitgeversmaatschappij Holland, 1939), 53-59, 83-85.

43. Erik Peterson, *Der Monotheismus als politisches Problem: Ein Beitrag zur Geschichte der politischen Theologie im Imperium Romanum* (Leipzig: Jakob Hegner, 1935), 71ff. (see especially p. 81: "Der *eine* Monarch auf Erden — und das ist für Euseb nur Konstantin — korrespondiert dem *einen* göttlichen Monarchen im Himmel").

44. Per Beskow, *Rex Gloriae: The Kingship of Christ in the Early Church*, trans. Eric J. Sharpe (Uppsala: Almqvist and Wiksells, 1962), esp. 161-75. This despite Beskow's quite trenchant but negative assessment of Williams at pp. 316-24 and of Berkhof at pp. 325-28.

45. G. H. Williams, "Christology and Church-State Relations in the Fourth Century," *Church History* 20:3 (September 1951): 3-33; Williams, "Christology and Church-State Relations in the Fourth Century," in *Church History* 20:4 (December 1951): 3-26. The quotation comes from 20:3, p. 18.

Nicene orthodoxy and Constantinianism. While he did not maintain that pro-Nicene theology was wrong, he did attempt to decenter Nicaea in the contemporary imagination, and this in three related ways.

First, he argued that it is useful to regard Nicaea as the solution to a specific set of problems prompted by the attempt to maintain fidelity to the gospel in the idiom of the late third through early fifth centuries, but that it is improper to see the statements of Nicaea as conveying saving truth. In this light, pro-Nicene theology appears as the struggle for what Yoder elsewhere called the application of an "interworld transformational grammar to help us discern what will need to happen if the collision of the message of Jesus with our . . . world is to lead to a reconception of the shape of the world, instead of to rendering Jesus optional or innocuous."[46]

Second, Yoder also argued that doctrines are basically rules for how one uses words, such that to view them as revelation is to misapprehend their role in the faith.[47] Two things are important to see in connection to these first two decentering moves. One is that the Nicene Creed, on this understanding, does not summarize the content of the faith so much as it aids in producing and regulating readings of scripture that attempt to be faithful to the tradition as it has been passed on and received. And the other is that finding new grammars in which to maintain fidelity to scripture is a process that goes on in and is partly constitutive of any vital Christian community — yet this is not to suggest that the community will not also find new ways to apprehend the uses of old grammars, as is arguably demonstrated within the formation of the canon itself.

Yoder's third move to decenter Nicaea consisted in an attempt to problematize any easy relationship to the Nicene Creed for a contemporary "Radical Reformation" audience by highlighting the messiness of the politics that surrounded its negotiation. He wrote, for instance, that "it must mean something to us that the Arians and the Nestorians . . . were less nationalistic, less politically bound to the Roman Empire, more capable of criticizing the emperor, more vital in missionary growth, more ethical, and more biblicist than the so-called orthodox churches of the Empire."[48] Though Yoder gave no sources for these claims, they align with a series of counter-histories written by radical Protestants since the mid-sixteenth century, including *The Chronicle of the Hutterian Brethren* and

---

46. Yoder, *Priestly Kingdom*, 56.
47. Yoder, *Preface to Theology*, 199.
48. Yoder, *Preface to Theology*, 223.

The Martyrs' Mirror, both of which include Arius among the persecuted faithful.[49] G. H. Williams's view, however, is diametrically opposed to Yoder's: "All who have worked through the fourth century have sensed some affinity between Arianism and Caesaropapism on the one hand and on the other between Nicene orthodoxy and the recovery of a measure of ecclesiastical independence."[50] Indeed, Williams takes up Peterson's mantle in terms of arguing that only "a fully understood Trinitarianism proved itself capable of resisting the exploitation of Christian monotheism as a means of sanctioning political unity and securing social cohesion."[51] Williams, as I have indicated, identified "Arianizing" or subordinationist christologies in the fourth century as contributing to the uncritical linkage of church and state. He wrote:

> Over against the Catholic insistence on the consubstantiality of the Son ... are the various forms of subordination of the Son and the Holy Spirit worked out among the different Arianizing parties of the fourth century. Roughly speaking these two Christologies gave rise to, or are at least associated with, two main views of the Empire and the relationship of the Church thereto. According to one view the emperor is bishop of bishops. According to the other, the emperor is within the church.[52]

---

49. *Das große Geschichtbuch der Hutterischen Brüder*, trans. the Hutterian Brethren (Rifton, NY: Plough, 1987); Thieleman J. van Braght, *The Bloody Theater or Martyrs' Mirror of the Defenseless Christians Who Baptized Only Upon Confession of Faith, and Who Suffered and Died for the Testimony of Jesus, Their Saviour, From the Time of Christ to the Year A.D. 1660*, trans. J. F. Sohm (Scottdale: Herald, 1938). Cf. D. H. Williams, *Retrieving the Tradition*, 113-14.

50. G. H. Williams, "Christology and Church-State Relations," 20:3, p. 10. For Yoder's most concise assessment of the ambiguity surrounding pro-Nicene theology and the Constantinian settlement, see *Preface to Theology*, 204: "If we look back at the politics between 325 and 431, at some of the theologians' methods and motives, at the personal quality of Constantine, or if we ask in what sense he was a Christian when he dictated this dogma [the *homoousion*], then we have to be dubious about giving this movement any authority."

51. G. H. Williams, "Christology and Church-State Relations," 20:3, p. 6.

52. G. H. Williams, "Christology and Church-State Relations," 20:3, p. 9. Here, Williams essentially builds upon Newman's thesis in *The Arians of the Fourth Century* that after the Council of Nicaea an Arianizing party led by Eusebius of Nicomedia and Eusebius of Caesarea ingratiated itself to Constantine, leading him to attempt to reinstate Arius and later to exile Athanasius. Further treatment of Yoder in relation to Newman's *Arians*, as well as the *Essay on Development* would be illuminating, particularly in terms of Yoder's adoption of the Antioch vs. Alexandria trope and his correlative assumptions (1) that the process

The pro-Nicene view, with its insistence that the Son is consubstantial with the Father, was in Williams's estimation the view that preserved the New Testament's logic concerning the deity of Jesus. It was therefore easier for "Arians" than for "Catholics" to accommodate themselves "to the assimilation of pagan conceptions of kingship" and to "lavishly compensate the ruler for relinquishing purely pagan attributes and honors."[53] Put more simply, Williams argues that "Arianizing" theologies contributed to the Constantinian captivity of the church in a way that pro-Nicene theologies did not.

Williams and Yoder thus offered starkly opposed views of the consequences of Nicaea. One of the problems with both views is that they shared a set of assumptions that recent scholarship is calling into question, particularly as regards the propriety of speaking in terms of an Arian party in the later fourth century, as well as showing just how flexible the word "God" was during the discussions leading to and following Nicaea. Nicaea should not be considered an argument between some Christians who claimed Christ was God and others who claimed he wasn't. Rather, the situation seems to have been much more about striking on the appropriate set of rules for using the word "God" in any context.[54]

Another problem common to Yoder and Williams is that the history

---

of translating the gospel into the terms of middle Platonism had gone badly astray and (2) that Christian theology was more marred where it had naturalized its break with "Judaism." On the polemical context of Newman's Arians, see now Rowan Williams's very helpful introduction to Newman, *The Arians of the Fourth Century,* ix-xlvii.

53. G. H. Williams, "Christology and Church-State Relations," 20:3, p. 5.

54. Cf. Lewis Ayres, "Rethinking Nicaea," TMs (photocopy). Another problem elicited by noting the flexibility with which the word "God" was used in the fourth-century debates is the absence in most contemporary discussions of any sustained reflection on what might be called the "angelology" of Christian theologians in the age of Constantine. This lacuna is apparent in, for instance, Glenn F. Chestnut's *The First Christian Histories: Eusebius, Socrates, Sozomen, Theodoret and Evagrius,* Théologie Historique 46 (Paris: Éditions Beauchesne, 1977). Chestnut cites Eusebius of Caesarea's reference to iconography of Constantine slaying/putting down the dragon of the Apocalypse (*Vita Constantini* 3.3) as fitting smoothly with Eusebius's tendency to identify Constantine as an icon of the Word (as the Word is an icon of the Father). Yet, in the Apocalypse (ch. 12) it is Michael and his angels, not Christ, who defeat the dragon and his armies. If Michael is the proper prototype for this image of Constantine, then it is clearly not christological or "subordinationist," but "angelological." I raise this as an interesting way to reflect on Eusebius's Christology and eschatology only because later in the Apocalypse the angel who accompanies the seer identifies himself as "a fellow servant" with the seer — language Eusebius also used to characterize Constantine's relationship to the authorities of the church.

on which they drew is messy enough to support either of their conclusions. And in such a situation it is reasonable not only to ask what other motivating factors were at play that turned each historian in such sharply divergent directions, but also to draw attention to the differences in these authors' theological uses of historiography. For Williams it remained important to get the right handle on history, in order to show what political and theological implications could be justifiably drawn from the record. Hence, only if it could be shown that pro-Nicene theologies assert a basic distinction between the word and creation was it licit for him to assume that pro-Nicene theologies also safeguarded a measure of ecclesial independence from the empire.

For Yoder, by contrast, even if pro-Nicene theology safeguarded the Christology of the New Testament in the "hellenized" idiom of the late empire, its politics have not necessarily been vindicated. Rather, he drew attention to the following difficulty: politics cannot be abstracted from doctrine, and there is rarely any easy one-to-one correspondence between doctrine and politics. We do not have to agree with Yoder's specific claims about "Arian" and "Nestorian" theo-politics in order to take the point. Yoder's account, as we have seen, contrasts with the assessment of the political implications of pro-Nicene theology that runs from Peterson to Williams and on to contemporary historiography, particularly in the work of T. D. Barnes. It also contrasts with the attempts by recent historians of Christian doctrine to offer a more complex account of the range of theological "positions" both leading up to the Council of Nicaea and in the years between the council and its ratification, so to speak, in Constantinople, Ephesus, and Chalcedon.[55] To clarify: for Yoder, theology is not merely theology; it is politics, institutional arrangements, and practices as well. It is therefore not credible on Yoder's grounds either to defend pro-Nicene theology *in spite of* the politics associated with it or to repudiate it *on the basis of* its politics. And this perspective has everything to do with Yoder's evangelical outlook on historicism. For instance, he wrote,

> The creeds are part of the only history we have. It is a fallible history and a confused history. A lot of dirty politics were involved in defining the creeds, in explaining their meaning, and still more in applying

---

55. See particularly Lewis Ayres, "Re-thinking Nicaea, Chapter 1: The Emergence of the Christian Doctrine of God, AD 300-360," TMs (photocopy); Michel R. Barnes, "The Fourth Century as Trinitarian Canon," in *Christian Origins: Theology, Rhetoric, and Community*, ed. Lewis Ayres and Gareth Jones (New York: Routledge, 1998), 47-67.

their authority, but this is the history with which God has chosen to lead a confused people toward at least a degree of understanding of certain dangers and things not to say if we are to remain faithful.[56]

We do not have another history than that which is described as turning out both pro-Nicene and Constantinian to which we can appeal in our theological judgments. Theology is never vindicated in spite of its history, and history is the only arena in which we have to play the theological game. This is however, not to insist that the way things are is the way they have to be. It is, rather, to stake a claim in favor of the ongoing task of historiographical revision. And it is also to say that revisionist historiography will itself be but another part of "the only history we have."

Before exploring these last two claims more fully, let me summarize what the preceding discussion has shown with respect to Yoder's use of Constantinianism as a way of describing compromised ecclesiologies. Constantinianism is not a problem. It is a totalizing discourse. This is to say a number of things, among which is that the resources one has by which to see oneself out of Constantinianism will themselves likely be implicated in Constantinianism. It is also to acknowledge an ambiguous distinction between the narratives one tells about Constantinianism (regarding, for instance, genesis, legacy, and so on — Constantinianism as an object of knowledge) and the architectonic discourse that conditions the possibility of the narratives themselves (Constantinianism as episteme). There is in Yoder's work a certain "transcendental function" for Constantinianism. Apropos of Constantinianism and the priority of the shift to the man, Yoder makes a clear argument for historical complexity — that a linear genetic account is out of the question. Constantinianism has historical, social, and economic conditions that arise within and as complex relations: between people, between institutions, between patterns of power and knowledge that constitute people, institutions, and the relations between them; that it was not formed independently of these particular relations as they were configured in this or that place at this or that time; in short, to echo Foucault, that Constantinianism "constitutes a history of human knowledge that could both be given to empirical investigation and prescribe its forms."[57]

That it prescribes the forms of knowledge that would constitute and

---

56. Yoder, *Preface to Theology*, 223.
57. Cf. Foucault, *Order of Things*, 319.

govern empirico-historical investigation is what I mean when I say that Constantinianism has a transcendental use. Constantinianism conditions the possibility for its own investigation. To be blunt: centuries of history written by winners create the criteria by which we know what counts as history. That is why Constantinianism resists historical dissection; that is why there could be no definitive display of its mechanisms and logic; that is why it must be recounted "as legend" and in "a larger-than-life" way; that is why it is more basic than what the historians' tools can uncover. That is also why it is so difficult to make much sense of Yoder's claim that "the relationship between the obedience of God's people and the triumph of God's cause is not a relationship of cause and effect but one of cross and resurrection."[58]

But the distinction between the empirical and the transcendental uses of Constantinianism is not basic for Yoder. More fundamental is the distinction between historicist and eschatological discourse, where historicism stands in for the priority of empirical investigation to the truth of the discourse produced in and as that investigation (that is, where the individuality of an object determines the discourse that describes its formation), and eschatology stands for the anticipation of a hope — that is, a posture of hopefulness — whose nature and history are defined in and as the present. Yet, just as with the empirical and transcendental uses of Constantinianism, it would be wrong to think of the distinction between historicist and eschatological discourse as diremptive. Foucault claimed that "a discourse attempting to be both empirical and critical cannot but be both positivist [historicist?] and eschatological,"[59] and Walter Benjamin noted that "only a redeemed mankind receives the fullness of its past — which is to say, only for a redeemed mankind has its past become citable in all its moments."[60] Yoder's way of putting the point is even more imaginative: the true meaning of history is in the church. And this history is, at least in part, one of disavowal and apostasy.

To put the point in yet more provocative terms, Constantinianism is us. When Yoder describes Constantinianism as a general identification of churches (whether Protestant or Catholic) "with the power structures of their respective societies instead of seeing their duty as that of calling these powers to modesty and resisting their recurrent rebellion," we see that

---

58. Yoder, *The Politics of Jesus*, 232.
59. Foucault, *Order of Things*, 320.
60. Benjamin, "Theses on the Philosophy of History," 254.

Constantinianism is sufficiently malleable to withstand (even perhaps to invite) revision and to implicate churches today in its anatomy.[61] This use of Constantinianism is close to what I have called "transcendental," in that it schematizes the possibilities for how one sees the world. But, as I have stressed, it also has methodological implications for the historian, in that it cultivates assumptions about history as a discipline that are shaped by the drive to secure a single master narrative of events "as they really happened." While Yoder explicitly rejected this methodological use of Constantinianism, he nevertheless continued to foster historical narratives that were methodologically Constantinian in origin and use in the aspects of his work that I have examined in the preceding pages.

That Yoder saw the danger of Constantinian epistemological and political postures for the doing of history has extensive implications for how he thought about the church. He rejected the politics of reductive historicisms, because the empiricities of history will not serve as methodological scratch. He also refused, in Rowan Williams's words, "a normative time in which the scholar stands" that could be "opposed to the distant or 'other' time in which the objects of study exist."[62] Once such normative time has been rejected, the presumptions of distance separating the scholar from her or his object of study, as well as the (positivist?) notions of superiority and objectivity that are concomitant upon distance, are undermined. Those methodologically Constantinian notions are replaced, Yoder argued, by patience.[63]

Constantinianism and Restitutionist Historiography

It is in this connection that I turn now from describing Yoder's views on Constantinianism to inquiring after his claims about the way Christians need to practice the doing of history. On the one hand, Yoder's theses regarding Constantinianism are historical: a shift in the relation of church and world occurred, such that Christians today do not reason as early Christians did. On the other hand, Yoder repeatedly skirted, and in some instances flubbed, the historical coordinates of the shift. His inattention to

---

61. Yoder, *Original Revolution*, 150.
62. Williams, *Arius: Heresy and Tradition*, 23.
63. Yoder, "'Patience' as Method in Moral Reasoning: Is an Ethic of Discipleship 'Absolute'?" in Hauerwas et al., eds., *The Wisdom of the Cross*, 24-42.

the effects of Roman law on Christian self-perception and theology, as well as his unnuanced account of the political implications of pro-Nicene theology are only two instances in which this is to be the case. Another instance might be cited in brief. Yoder's claim is that Constantinianism created a "two-tiered ethic," wherein the "evangelical counsels" are reserved only for the "religious and the highly motivated," and the less demanding "precepts" suffice for the baptized laity. Before Constantine, the Christian was "a minority figure, with numerous resources not generally available to all people: personal commitment, regeneration, the guidance of the Holy Spirit, the consolation and encouragement of the brotherhood, training in a discipleship life-style."[64] Christian ethics was for Christians. After Constantine, when "Christian" means everyone, Christian ethics must either be watered down or, if retained, become supererogatory.

Certainly thought about the nature of Christian discipleship changed during the age of Constantine.[65] But it is less clear than Yoder took it to be that the early church had a more rigorous account of Christian ethics than did the church in the post-Constantinian era. And here we are again implicated in a fall narrative that served to legitimate, among other impulses, radical Protestant primitivism. The situation in the fourth century, however, seems to have been much more complex, as Hal Drake has shown. While the Council of Nicaea prompted ever increasing theological sophistication and historical reflection through the subsequent century and a half, the rising rate of conversion also "prompted new thinking about what it meant to be a Christian and a longing to reconnect with an unspoiled and innocent primitive church." Drake continues:

> On both levels, the effect was to prompt new thinking about what was essential to Christianity, and the side effect was to raise and tighten the standard by which Christian performance was measured. . . . [A] by-product of this effort to establish ties with an idealized past was a reconstruction of that past as one of fortitude and resistance which resulted in a tightening of criteria, a raising of the threshold of Christian identity.[66]

64. Yoder, *Priestly Kingdom*, 139.
65. Cf. the essays collected in Alan Kreider, ed., *The Origins of Christendom in the West* (Edinburgh: T&T Clark, 2001).
66. Drake, *Constantine and the Bishops*, 432-33. That Yoder might well have objected to Drake's distinction between "definitions of Christian belief" and "thinking about what it

To at least some extent, if Drake is right, the Constantinian church helped to create the narrative that later voices of religious dissent extended in order to fund a context in which their reformative impulses could be justified. As with the previous instances, the point is not to provide grounds for discounting Yoder's use of Constantinianism to describe an ecclesiological pitfall.

Nor is the point to claim that the Constantinian settlement did not represent the "fall of Christianity," though I have reservations, which I think are held on Yoderian grounds, about the usefulness of the very notion of *a fall* of Christianity. In this respect I disagree with Gerald Schlabach, who claims, "One thing . . . explanations for church-state accommodation have in common is their attempt to trace backwards toward . . . a point at which early Christians begin to fall into temptation. . . . Of course it might be hard to conclude such digging without eventually questioning the apostolic wisdom of calling Jesus 'Lord' and thus vindicating the language of dominance."[67] To the extent that Schlabach takes these reflections to characterize Yoder and to implicate him in the search for a basic problem in Christian ethics, I think he has missed much of the significance of Yoder's particular claims about the nature and shape of restitutionism. Yoder argued, in distinction from the view Schlabach articulates, that "[i]t is not claimed that history always goes wrong or always needs to be reversed. A particular fall necessitates a particular restitution."[68] So there was, for Yoder, no basic or (worse) unavoidable ecclesiological pitfall, and this is what distinguished his restitutionist view of history from other views, which Schlabach rightly characterizes. But neither did Yoder assume that the church's vision of history was by its nature faithful. Rather, "Any existing church is not only fallible but in fact peccable. That is why there needs to be a constant potential for reformation and in the more dramatic situations a readiness for the reformation even to be 'radical.'"[69]

That there is no basic ecclesiological problem and that every ecclesiology encounters its own particular problems elicit the recurrent theme in Yoder's work toward which I have been working: "remembrance

---

meant to be Christian" does not, I think, invalidate the point that the idealized pre-Constantinian church was at least partly a reconstruction.

67. Schlabach, "Deuteronomic or Constantinian," 452.
68. Yoder, *Priestly Kingdom*, 129.
69. Yoder, *Priestly Kingdom*, 5.

... is ... a christological task,"⁷⁰ "historiography is theologically necessary," or, as he puts it slightly later in the same passage, theologians committed to a restitutionist view of history accept "the challenge to be critical of history and thereby to take it more seriously than do those for whom some other criterion than the New Testament determines the faithfulness of the church."⁷¹

In what, precisely, does Yoder's restitutionist view of history consist? In three related exercises of christologically inflected patience, at least. For one, it dissolves the relation between history as object and history as discipline. For another, it foregrounds the necessity of open reception of voices that are disharmonious with one's own. And finally, as an outgrowth of the other two points, it advocates the adoption of a "middle distance" to debates as they are encountered.

To take each facet of patience in turn: in "Anabaptism and History," he maintained that among "a limited number of possible ways to take history seriously," including spiritualizing, rejecting, or Constantinianizing it, one can claim "to critique the course of history using as criterion a point within history, namely the Incarnation, or the canon."⁷² Here Yoder erases the distinction between history and criticism, because when one claims to have a view of history decisively shaped by a point of that history, one's posture toward history is itself encountered as historical, that is, as part of the story of the past one tells. Thus, on Yoder's restitutionist view of history, the church's integrity consists in its evaluation of its past as contributing to the sense in which the present furnishes it "with the choice between fall and renewal," with the possibility of judging our reception of our past faithful or not on the basis of "the very particular story of the New Testament."⁷³

Put more simply, the restitutionist argues that the church can and must engage in continuous criticism of its own story, where that criticism is conceived as an evangelical task. It "can" because the norm by which it engages its history is itself historical — "to be found fully within the researchable, debatable particularity which according to the New Testament witness is the meaning of Incarnation."⁷⁴ It "must" because "the wholesome growth of a tradition is like a vine: a story of constant inter-

---

70. Yoder, "Historiography as a Ministry to Renewal," 216.
71. Yoder, *Priestly Kingdom*, 127.
72. Yoder, *Priestly Kingdom*, 127.
73. Yoder, *Priestly Kingdom*, 128.
74. Yoder, *Priestly Kingdom*, 128.

ruption of organic growth in favor of pruning and a new chance for the roots."[75]

In "The Wild Patience of John Howard Yoder," Romand Coles reflected on the possibilities opened up by (and risks attendant upon) Yoder's metaphor of tradition growing like a vine. Coles argues that Yoder's perspective toward the past resists deploying aprioristic conceptions of the future that legitimate a particular past at the expense of permeable engagements with other visions of the future (and, hence, the past): "There is no worthy directionality that would not repeatedly have to pass through vulnerable encounters with other directions and indirections."[76] In the next two chapters I will probe this attitude of the church toward itself as it is displayed in the practices that govern the church's negotiations of insideness and outsideness. Here, the point is to see how this dispossessive perspective configures the historiographical task.

So, in the second place, Yoder sees as part of the task of restitutionist historians the search for "disciplined, accountable ways to sustain the argument [in favor of nonviolence] against mainline historiography, with a concern for defending the 'good news' quality of the peace church/free church stance that this particular perspective is just generally grumpy, or 'sectarian,' or self-righteous."[77] Restitutionist historiography is here not motivated because some historians dislike the dominant historiographical trends, or because they are members of a ghettoized in-group whose voice goes consistently un(der)acknowledged by the power brokers of contemporary society, or because they claim aprioristically to possess a more faithful account of the world than their non-restitutionist peers. All of these things might be true, but they are not necessary (and may be unhelpful) characteristics of restitutionism.

Restitutionism, or "evangelical revisionism," is motivated by "love of the intellectual adversary, including intellectual respect for the holders of positions one must in conscience reject."[78] Such respect for the position of the adversary involves refusing to reject the adversary's claims because he or she is the adversary. The alternative to this basically ad hominem posture is to look again at the sources that the adversary takes as warrant for his or her claims and thereby to attempt to envision alternative plausible readings

---

75. Yoder, *Priestly Kingdom*, 69.
76. Romand Coles, "The Wild Patience of John Howard Yoder: 'Outsiders' and the 'Otherness of the Church,'" *Modern Theology* 18:3 (July 2002): 309.
77. Yoder, "The Burden and Discipline of Evangelical Revisionism," 21.
78. Yoder, "The Burden and Discipline of Evangelical Revisionism," 22.

of those sources, which the adversary could in principle (that is, if he or she is honest about the nature of his or her commitment to the sources) accept. Yoder described the search for alternative readings of sources that may be seen as plausible by those with whom one disagrees as reading history "against the grain," a phrase he borrowed from Walter Benjamin.[79] I do not know whether Benjamin was Yoder's only or initial source for using the metaphor of a piece of wood to describe his brand of theological realism. Yet, in "Armaments and Eschatology" Yoder claimed that those who work in cross and resurrection have their hands with the grain of the universe, a comment that prompted Stanley Hauerwas's Gifford Lectures, entitled *With the Grain of the Universe*. Hauerwas's argument is that the story of God revealed in Jesus of Nazareth tells Christians how the world really is and that that story is accessible and justified only in terms of attending to the lives of people who have been shaped by that story. While I suspect that Yoder shared Hauerwas's convictions, he did not characterize the restitutionist's task as one of adopting or finding the right perspective on history.[80] Rather, Yoder said that "[t]he reason history needs to be reread is . . . that at certain points there is specifiable good news about the human condition, the goodness or the newness of which those who hitherto have been controlling the storytelling had not appropriated."[81]

The focus on "certain points" suggests that restitutionist historiography need not be preoccupied with systematicity or comprehensiveness à la John Milbank's metanarrative realism, or, for that matter, Troeltsch's

---

79. While the analogies between Benjamin and Yoder are striking, the disanalogies are also significant. When Benjamin wrote that the historical materialist "regards it as his task to brush history against the grain," the tone was not as straightforwardly self-critical and repentant as Yoder's. Benjamin saw "against-the-grainness" as implying dissociation "as far as possible" from historiography that "benefits the rulers." But he did not foreground the necessity of listening to voices with which one disagrees as a necessary corrective to the stance of the historical materialist that distinguishes it from mainline historiography. See Walter Benjamin, "Theses on the Philosophy of History," 256; cf. Yoder, "The Burden and Discipline of Evangelical Revisionism," in Hawkley and Juhnke, eds., *Nonviolent America*, 22.

80. It is not clear that Hauerwas is committed to finding the "right perspective" on history either, at least not if that means "getting the story straight." But there does seem to be a sense in which Hauerwas does not subject witnesses to the same scrutiny (testing the spirits) as Yoder did. Thus, Hauerwas trusts Dorothy Day to have had the right handle on history (even though that handle might be one that foregrounds dispossession — and is this the same as not having a handle?). I suspect that this has to do with Hauerwas's more "Catholic" belief in the "communion of saints."

81. Yoder, "Burden and Discipline," 22.

historicism, both of which vacillate between the modes of grand narrative and ever more exact attention to minute detail. For Troeltsch, at least, that tension could not be overcome, since it was constitutive of responsible historical scholarship. Neither for Troeltsch could either horn of the tension be resolved in its own: grand narratives can never be grand enough and attention to detail can never be appropriately exacting. In each direction the historian is limited by his or her own historicity.

Yoder accepted Troeltsch's diagnosis of the historiographer's dilemma, at least at one level. He called it the "'modest' patience of sobriety in finitude." "Although," he continued, "we have good grounds (if we have adequately studied a matter) to believe that in its main lines the things we are sure of are worthy of that assurance, we must always keep open spaces where sometimes our ignorance and at other times our sinfulness have kept us from seeing all the truth."[82] By cultivating such openings, Yoder inserted a posture of equivocation into Troeltsch's binary between grand narratives and attention to historical uniqueness. Rather, because "[o]ur recognition that we may be wrong must always be visible,"[83] the restitutionist is limited to envision the task of critical historiography as "entertaining seriously founded hunches about what may have made things go wrong in the past." He continued: "It is quite fitting that such illuminating alternative biases should best be stated neither on the highest level of generality nor as simple moral judgments, but as middle-level aphorisms about the nature of things."[84] Each of the alternatives to the mid-level perspective reifies history in a complementary way. The short view (preoccupation with *das individuelle* in history, situationalism in ethics, "strong perspectivism" in epistemology) characteristically lands one in the vicinity of Lessing's ditch. The long view (grand narrative, universal moral theory, foundationalism) characteristically reinforces the assumption that the way

---

82. Yoder, "'Patience' as Method in Moral Reasoning," in Hauerwas et al., eds., *Wisdom of the Cross*, 31.

83. Yoder, "'Patience' as Method in Moral Reasoning," 31.

84. Yoder, "Burden and Discipline," 23. Notice that this claim develops or recasts Yoder's use of middle axioms in *The Christian Witness to the State* (Newton, KS: Faith and Life Press, 1964), 32-33, 35-44, 72-73. Middle axioms were for Yoder a way to focus on how debates actually went when they happened, rather than on the logical presuppositions of each party to the debate: "The conception of middle axioms . . . permits meaningful communication of a significant Christian social critique without involving extended speculation about the metaphysical value of the principles appealed to" (*Christian Witness*, 33). Yoder also thought that focusing on conversation as it happened was a way to avoid demonizing or valorizing the people in dialogue by casting them as ideal types.

things are is the way they have to be. A mid-level perspective, however, arises "out of watching the debate as it happens."[85]

Finally, Yoder's recommendation of the middle distance gives some purchase on his preference for working in an occasional way. The restitutionist's work is not self-generated. It is generated by an awareness that the telling of history makes "a difference for how the world is to go and what is to happen to our neighbors."[86] History is an evangelical enterprise, and for the restitutionist it is done well when it lays bare its own moral commitments as a way of opening it to challenge and change by other voices.

Adopting a middle view aids the task of clarifying the ethical stakes of historical inquiry because it facilitates rendering "the decisiveness of the choices people make." What people do makes a difference for how things turn out. Though this may seem self-evident, Yoder claimed that "often the historian puts a premium on being able to lay over events the grid of an explanatory cause/effect connectedness such that things really had to go the way they finally did."[87]

Conclusion

A comparison between Yoder and another prominent thinker might be fruitful at this point for further spelling out Yoder's conception of history and historiography. Yoder's stated commitment to evangelical revisionism bears significant affinities with the philosophical hermeneutics of Hans-Georg Gadamer, and the former's account of Constantinianism is a point at which to clarify the commonalities. Yoder, as I have said, was clear that Constantine is not the locus of his critique of Constantinianism. And, as I have argued in this chapter, it should be equally clear that he was not overly concerned with the specific contours of this or that set of events in the third, fourth, or fifth centuries. Rather, his concern was with an ethos, namely, our way of experiencing the history of the shift for which Constantine stands. To use Gadamer's phrase, Yoder's concern was with how Constantinianism has become "historically effective."

By historically effective, Gadamer meant simply that events have his-

---

85. Yoder, "Burden and Discipline," 23.
86. Yoder, "Burden and Discipline," 23.
87. Yoder, "Burden and Discipline," 24.

tories that determine how we become conscious of them. Those historical consequences include a given event's immediate — many would say "causal" — effects, but also, and perhaps more important, the history of interaction with the event, which configures our prejudices for encountering it. As Gadamer put it:

> Real historical thinking must take account of its own historicity.... A hermeneutics adequate to the subject matter would have to demonstrate the reality and efficacy of history within understanding itself.... *Understanding is, essentially, a historically effected event.* ... If we are trying to understand a historical phenomenon from the historical distance that is characteristic of our hermeneutical situation, we are always already affected by history. It determines in advance both what seems to us worth inquiring about and what will appear as an object of investigation, and we more or less forget half of what is really there — in fact, we miss the whole truth of the phenomenon — when we take its immediate appearance as the whole truth.[88]

Historical thought that accounts at least in part for its own historicity seems basic to the restitutionist's task. "At least in part," because Gadamer and Yoder agree that there is no stance purified of contingency to which we can retreat in order to "start from scratch." In a similar connection, Yoder, Gadamer, and possibly Michel Foucault shared a set of sensibilities about how to respond to the methodological captivity that plagues contemporary approaches to history. One response, which each rejected, would be further methodologization. Another, more appropriate response would begin to help us reflect about the fragmentary and reified contemporary experience of history — a thinking about thinking wherein we discover that the character of our historicity is most obvious where there is the greatest rupture with thinking historically. The legacy of Constantinianism is one such site; the scientific ideal of objectivity and the linkages between knowledge and power are others. In terms of the torn character of our historical thought, Alasdair MacIntyre recently made a point in respect to Gadamer that I think pertains to Yoder as well. MacIntyre wrote:

> One of Gadamer's key theses that I take to be unquestionably true [is,] to have become aware of the historically conditioned character of our philosophical enquiries and interpretations is not to have escaped

---

88. Gadamer, *Truth and Method*, 299-300.

from it. There is no standpoint outside history to which we can move, no way in which we can adopt some presuppositionless stance, exempt from the historical situatedness of all thinking . . . [But] a certain kind of awareness, while not providing a standpoint outside history, can transform our relationship to that history.[89]

My question throughout this chapter has been whether Yoder's thought on Constantinianism sufficiently accounts for its own historicity as to transform our relationship to that history. The answer, I think, will have to be equivocal. One wonders whether Yoder's assessment of Constantinianism could admit of a "mid-course correction," as he puts it elsewhere, "a rediscovery of something from the past whose pertinence was not seen before, because only a new question or challenge enables us to see it speaking to us."[90] In principle Yoder affirms the possibility of such "looping back" by denying systematic pessimism in regards to Constantinianism as "not only . . . equivalent to denying the rhetoric of Christian belief in Providence, but also the actual lessons of modern social experience, in which there has been at least some progress in the direction of greater humanity and justice."[91]

Yet it should be clear by now that the question I have attempted to raise is not about principle, but about Yoder's actual textual and historiographical practice. It should also be plain that I approach Yoder's work on Constantinianism as more than a textbook account of church history. If it were indeed giving such an account it would be subject to devastating criticism, as the complicating factors I discussed in part two of this chapter indicate. Yet Constantinianism's importance in tracing the outlines of Yoder's ecclesiology lies not so much in its particular contribution to historiography: as an account of doctrinal or political development in the fourth century it cannot be wholeheartedly endorsed. Its value lies rather in the way that the answers Yoder reached open historians up to new possibilities for envisioning how historiography can be done as Christian ministry, in that Yoder gave specifically theological merit to the process of listening to alternative voices as a way of making Christian inheritance of the past difficult. And this is the case even when his own overly schematic

---

89. Alasdair MacIntyre, "On Not Having the Last Word: Thoughts on Our Debts to Gadamer," in *Gadamer's Century: Essays in Honor of Hans-Georg Gadamer*, ed. Jeff Malpas, Ulrich Arnswald, and Jens Kertscher (Cambridge, MA: MIT Press, 2002), 158.
90. Yoder, *Priestly Kingdom*, 69.
91. Yoder, *Priestly Kingdom*, 146-47.

treatment of the material kept him from listening to those voices as patiently as he might.

Yoder therefore did not articulate a clearly non-Constantinian theology. But he did formulate a task: that to begin to discharge the burden of proof that rests on non-Constantinian ecclesiologies will necessarily involve one in a patient and thorough willingness to reassess the stories we have inherited about Constantine's legacy. It will require a renewed focus on the political and doctrinal history of the Patristic era — a focus that cannot be content with a "take it or leave it" attitude, but that is willing to labor through and tarry with the process of negotiating "the only history we have," the same history "with which God has chosen to lead a confused people toward at least a degree of understanding of certain dangers and things not to say if we are to remain faithful."[92]

---

92. Yoder, *Preface to Theology*, 223.

CHAPTER 4

Memory in the Politics of Forgiveness

It is part of the psychic and social condition of the victim that he cannot receive compensation for what was done to him. History is still working through that condition, and so above all is the principle of brute force behind it.

W. G. Sebald,
On the Natural History of Destruction

Cain murdered Abel, and blood cried out from the earth; the house fell on Job's children, and a voice was induced or provoked into speaking from a whirlwind; and Rachel mourned for her children; and King David for Absalom. The force behind the movement of time is a mourning that will not be comforted. That is why the first event is known to have been an expulsion, and the last is hoped to be a reconciliation and return. So memory pulls us forward, so prophecy is only brilliant memory — there will be a garden where all of us as one child will sleep in our mother Eve, hooped in her ribs and staved by her spine.

Marilynne Robinson,
Housekeeping

Introduction

Each of the preceding chapters has converged on the following point: for Christians charitable relations with both non-Christians and other Christians depend upon robustly eschatological conceptions of the faith. Eschatology is not simply the speculative anticipation of future events, whether imminent or not; it entails an account of the place and function of memory within the church. In this chapter I argue that the church embodies the memory of God's work in Jesus by institutionalizing processes and practices of forgiveness and reconciliation and thereby activating charity, both in the sense of a capacity to receive the other as gift and in the sense of a pouring out of oneself for the other. Eschatology and ecclesiology intertwine as the "conditions of possibility" for practices of charity by creating, sustaining, and shaping the memory of redemption. I examine these claims by bringing Miroslav Volf into conversation with Yoder. Yoder's eschatology is displayed within an ecclesiology that centrally locates processes of negotiating communal memory as necessary constituents of peaceable practice. Volf's eschatology, alternatively, is enabled by "a certain kind of forgetting," the primary agent of which is God, that eradicates the persistence of injurious memory in the future consummation of Christ's kingdom.[1] I argue that Volf's hope in a "nontheoretical act of nonremembering" repeats a modernist account of subjective agency that (1) makes forgetting crucial to peaceable practices, (2) applies not only to humans, but paradigmatically to God, and (3) requires radical discontinuities with central elements of the Christian story.[2] For Yoder, on the other hand, reconciliation is doxological in character, and praise is an activity that takes, as well as makes, time. Consequently, Yoder's eschatology is neither static nor grounded in forgetfulness of past injuries, but proceeds as the patient labor of redeeming "the things we can never undo."[3]

---

1. Miroslav Volf, *Exclusion and Embrace: A Theological Exploration of Identity, Otherness, and Reconciliation* (Nashville: Abingdon, 1996), 131. In what follows, I examine memory and forgetting as they appear in *Exclusion and Embrace*. Volf has, since *Exclusion and Embrace*'s publication, continued to write about memory and redemption, particularly in *The End of Memory: Remembering Rightly in a Violent World* (Grand Rapids: Eerdmans, 2006). The argument of that book reinforces that made in *Exclusion and Embrace* without substantially revising it. For a compelling account and critique of *The End of Memory*, see Jonathan Tran, *The Vietnam War and Theologies of Memory: Time and Eternity in the Far Country* (Oxford: Wiley-Blackwell, forthcoming), esp. ch. 5, "Saving Our Lives with a Story: Memory and Narrative." Tran's analysis of memory leads him to argue rightly that redemption does involve "a type of forgetting, for every remembering is a forgetting. However, this forgetting is not due to redemption's limits, as if 'the memory of horror' exists apart from God's redemption" (p. 102). What Tran recognizes philosophically about the selectivity of memory, Yoder celebrates in John's vision of the slaughtered lamb.

2. Volf, *Exclusion and Embrace*, 135.

3. Cf. Paul Wadell, CP, "Redeeming the Things We Can Never Undo: The Role of For-

History and the War of the Lamb

Near the end of *The Politics of Jesus,* Yoder asked about the "meaningfulness of history."[4] The question arose in a discussion of contemporary Christians' obsession "with the meaning and direction of history."[5] Contemporary Christian social ethics, Yoder contended, seeks the "right 'handle' by which one can 'get a hold on' the course of history" to subject it to social engineering.[6] The "handles" approach to history had three characteristics, according to Yoder. First, it isolated one focal point in history that served as a fulcrum for determining the purpose and direction of history. Second, because that handle had to be pursued in order to make history come out right, it justified the sacrifice of lives (one's own and others'). And third, effectiveness in getting and maintaining control over the handle became the sole criterion in judging the seemliness of human action.

Given these three assumptions, Yoder argued, moral reasoning in recent centuries has been dominated by commitments to pre-Enlightenment stability and post-Enlightenment progressivism. These two stances, prima facie at odds with each other, share the perspective that the apostolic witness is irrelevant in determining the meaning of history.

Yoder juxtaposed the "handles" approach to history with the answer given to the question by the "series of visions and their hymns" that comprise John's Revelation. John's answer was "not the standard answer," because the "image of the sealed scroll in the hand of the 'one that was seated upon the throne'" tells us that the question of the meaning of history "cannot be answered by the normal resources of human insight."[7] Instead, to the angel's question, "Who is worthy to open the scroll and break its seals?" (Rev. 5:2), all the creatures and elders around the heavenly throne, together with myriads of angels cry out, "The lamb that was slain is worthy to receive power" (Rev. 5:12). John said this, according to Yoder, not as an "inscrutable paradox but as a meaningful affirmation, that the cross and not the sword, suffering and not brute power determines the meaning of history."[8]

---

giveness in Anne Tyler's *Saint Maybe,*" *New Theology Review: An American Catholic Journal for Ministry* 8:2 (May 1995): 34-48.

4. Yoder, *The Politics of Jesus: Vicit Agnus Noster,* 2nd ed. (Grand Rapids: Eerdmans, 1995), 232.
5. Yoder, *Politics of Jesus,* 228.
6. Yoder, *Politics of Jesus,* 228.
7. Yoder, *Politics of Jesus,* 232-33.
8. Yoder, *Politics of Jesus,* 232.

TO SEE HISTORY DOXOLOGICALLY

Yoder fleshed out John's "meaningful affirmation" in the following way: history's course is subject to the power of the resurrection rather than to any calculation of causes and effects or to the proportionally greater strength of the so-called "good guys." God's triumph is not *caused* by the kind of might that justifies the use of violence; rather it is testified to by the *obedience* of God's people *as demonstrated in the exercise of patience*. Moreover, Yoder claimed that the practice of patience embodies the "biblical philosophy of history," which itself is nothing more than the "logical unfolding" of Christ's own work, namely, choosing suffering servanthood, love to the point of death, and faithfulness to God's enemy love over violent lordship, righteousness backed by force, and prudential calculations of effectiveness. In other words, by the very shape of its life the New Testament church related the meaning of history to the incarnation and ministry of Jesus, through whom the will of God is "affirmatively, concretely knowable."⁹

As I argued in Chapters One and Two, Yoder offered an eschatological account of history: what we are doing now not only leads to where we are going, but also makes sense of the present in light of its participation in the future Christ promises.¹⁰ What, however, about the past? I have claimed that Yoder's eschatology was inseparable from his account of the place and function of memory in the church. In what does that claim consist?

At least in part, memory is a constituent element of Yoder's eschatology in the simple sense of contributing to historical awareness. If cross and resurrection, rather than cause and effect, are the "first principles" for making judgments about the meaning of history, then we will use memory to survey past events and make sense of them in light of cross and resurrection.¹¹ More important for Yoder, however, memory is ingredient to

---

9. Yoder, *Politics of Jesus*, 233.
10. Yoder, *Politics of Jesus*, 241.
11. Yoder did not employ the concept of "first principles" in exactly this sense. I take that concept from its use in Alasdair MacIntyre's "Aquinas Lecture," in *First Principles, Final Ends and Contemporary Philosophical Issues* (Milwaukee: Marquette University Press, 1990). In that text, MacIntyre discussed first principles as constituent of practices. He wrote:

> Aquinas . . . uses *"principium"* [Greek *"archē"*] of an axiom furnishing a syllogism with a premise . . . and speaks of a principle as composed of subject and predicate . . . But Aquinas also uses *"principium"* in speaking of that to which such principles refer, referring to the elements into which composite bodies can be resolved and by reference to which they can be explained as the *"principia"* of those bodies. In fact, *"principium,"* as used by Aquinas, names simultaneously the principle (in our sense)

eschatology because without it doxology is rendered impossible. In "To Serve Our God and to Rule the World" Yoder called doxology central to the Christian task. "To see history doxologically," Yoder said, is to "describe the cosmos in terms dictated by the knowledge that a once slaughtered Lamb is now living."[12] As I noted in the introductory pages to this book, doxology for Yoder was a way of seeing that is, for example, displayed by participation in liturgy and the moral life. By learning to see history doxologically the church comes to understand that its memory is "embedded within a larger life process," a process of praise, a process that "rules the world."[13]

To say that the church's praise is part of a process that rules the world is not quixotic. Instead, it makes a realist claim out of the confession that "the lamb that was slain is worthy to receive power and wealth and wisdom and might and honor and glory and blessing" (Rev. 5:12). The doxologies in John's Revelation are therefore not primarily statements about a future hope, though they are that as well. Neither is the force of praise in the first place metaphorical. No, the crucified Jew Jesus is identified as the slain lamb — and it is not the lamb's qualities of innocence, purity, and blamelessness that render praise meaningful, though again these qualities are more than incidental. Rather, it is the life, ministry, and death of the man Jesus of Nazareth that gives force to *this* Lamb's claim to blessing, honor, glory, and power. The eschatological vision of the book of Revelation transforms Jesus' own situation within the political context of first-century Israel by remembering and confessing it as relevant for Christian faith and practice now. Thus, praise of Jesus as the slaughtered lamb is not only relevant as a way of seeing what happened on a hill outside Jerusalem two thousand years ago; it is also relevant as a claim about the church's continuation and revolution of Israel's history. The movement with Christ at its center is distinctive because it shared such crucial characteristics with

---

and that of which the principle speaks, but not in a way that gives to *"principium"* two distinct and discrete meanings, although it can be used with either or both of two distinct references. (p. 4)

That, however, Yoder did not so use first principles nevertheless does not mean that the concept is unrelated to his use of the New Testament terms "powers" *(dunameis)* and "principalities" *(archai)*, which, in his work, name both rebellious agencies in creation and human structures for making sense out of experience.

12. Yoder, *The Royal Priesthood: Essays Ecclesiological and Ecumenical,* ed. Michael G. Cartwright (Grand Rapids: Eerdmans, 1994), 128.

13. Yoder, *Royal Priesthood,* 129.

Israel's own story that it could plausibly be construed as continuing that story.[14]

Formative Judaism and Jesus' own ministry shared ambivalence toward majesty and kingship "as instruments of divine rule."[15] Within Israel's story this ambivalence was demonstrated time and again, through the wars of the Lord in the Deuteronomistic history to Jotham's fable in Judges 8, the Israelites' rejection of the Lord in favor of a human king in 1 Samuel 8, and the Babylonian diaspora in which Jeremiah advocated *galuth* as a positive calling rather than merely a negative judgment. Jesus' own rejection of what Yoder called "the Zealot option" stands squarely within this stream of Jewish experience, such that Christians differ from Jews not in their low expectations for what kings can do, nor in their form of life as a minority people persecuted under the powers, but rather (a) in their incorporation of Gentiles into the promises reserved for Israel according to the flesh, and (b) in their knowledge, belief, or faith that the powers to which they found themselves subjected have been placed under the lordship of the Lamb.

Because the life, ministry, death, and resurrection of "the slaughtered lamb" is the major anamnetic focus of a doxological vision of history, Yoder argued, Christians derive their behavior from the gospel of Jesus Christ and not from an *ex ante* concern for effectiveness: "That action is right which fits the shape of the kingdom to come."[16] But interpreting history as praise risks generating tremendous complacency in the face of injustice, violence, suffering, and death. Christian ethics in America from Walter Rauschenbusch to Stanley Hauerwas could be depicted as the history of Christians confronting just such complacency. How does Yoder's doxological vision fit or fail to fit that story? Moreover, does construing doxology as the definitive form of Christian participation in history give up on the place of other voices in scripture? Does it drown out with "praise before the throne" intonations of penitence, intercession, and lament? Does seeing history doxologically reproduce Marx's claim that religion is the opiate of the people by encouraging contentment under the conditions of oppression? In a word, does praise silence persistent cries for justice? In recent theology, few have asked these questions with more force than Miroslav Volf.

---

14. Cf. Robert Jenson, *Systematic Theology*, 2 vols. (New York: Oxford University Press, 1996-99).
15. Yoder, *Royal Priesthood*, 133.
16. Yoder, *Politics of Jesus*, 137.

Memory in the Politics of Forgiveness

The Rhetoric of *Exclusion and Embrace*

Volf's *Exclusion and Embrace* offers a complex picture of salvation, as even the most cursory reading will suggest. Throughout his inquiry, Volf introduces many of his reflections and themes with questions to the reader: "Could I be serious in suggesting 'forgetting' as the final act of *redemption*?" "Do not the victims have excellent reasons for *never forgetting* the injustices suffered and hurts endured?" "What 'right' does God have to forget all the brutalities done to so many human victims? Would not a loss of *this* memory amount to an embrace between the perpetrator and God . . . ?"[17] Characteristically, Volf's answer to this kind of question is, "Not exactly — a good answer will be more complex than simply 'yes' or 'no.'" In what follows I will not pretend to deal with every aspect of Volf's work, nor will I attempt to summarize *Exclusion and Embrace*. Rather, I will probe the role memory plays in Volf's picture of salvation. Before that, however, a few comments regarding the rhetoric of *Exclusion and Embrace* (the book) and exclusion and embrace (as focal concepts) need to be made, because if Yoder was right that the gospel is gospel only if it can be received as such, then Volf's picture of salvation and reconciliation might not be as charitable as it first appears. So, what do questions of the form I have just sampled do rhetorically? At least two things deserve noting.

Take, in the first place, a question like, "Do not . . . victims have excellent reasons for *never forgetting* the injustices suffered and hurts endured?" Volf often uses this form of question at a point in the text where he has piqued his reader's sense of moral outrage. *Of course* those who have suffered the most brutal atrocities have excellent reasons for never forgetting. *Of course* God's forgetfulness of victims in some sense sanctions the perpetrator of violence. The very form of the question promotes a nearly visceral response from the reader. And well it should; put so starkly, these questions evoke strongly polarized reactions, only one of which seems genuinely moral.

Ingredient in Volf's method is the conviction that starkly binary moral alternatives are rarely helpful. At the beginning of his third chapter, entitled "Embrace," Volf asks whether "the inner logic of exclusionary polarities [is] irresistible?" He answers:

---

17. Volf, *Exclusion and Embrace*, 131-37. Hereafter, page references to this book will be given parenthetically in the text.

> There may indeed be situations in which "there is no choice," though we should not forget that to destroy the other rather than to be destroyed oneself is itself a choice. In most cases, however, the choice is not constrained by an inescapable "either us or them." If there is will, courage, and imagination the stark polarity can be overcome. Those caught in the vortex of mutual exclusion can resist its pull, rediscover their common belonging, even fall into each other's arms. (p. 99)

This is a vision of moral heroism. The implicit assumption behind both Volf's question and his answer is that stark dualisms like "forget or remember," "us or them," are the natural responses to tough questions. Behind that assumption lies a second assumption: only a well-trained moral imagination will be able to envision an alternative to binary and dualist logics. But both of these assumptions are questionable. In the first place, seeing the world in terms of hard choices or "exclusionary polarities" itself requires moral training and can as easily be characterized as a way to avoid the pluriformity of human perceptions as it can be described as part and parcel of an acknowledgment that people have competing and even contradictory interests and accounts of the world. In Yoder's terms, the kind of rhetoric could be described as a way to get a handle on history. In the second place, the assumption that it takes moral training to resist cutting the world into opposing pieces needs to be challenged because it fosters notions of ethical expertise, that is, the idea that only the very willful, courageous, or imaginative will be able to negotiate such a stark moral landscape with a truly human appreciation of complexity. But this is still an engineering approach to ethics: the world is not cut into neat halves, so in order to manage it you need a conceptual apparatus that can take stock of just how complex things really are.

Volf's similarity to Yoder should not be overlooked. Both resist answering questions in ways that allow dualisms to go unchallenged. However, where Volf resists polarities by demonstrating how binary thought often masks the complexity of the issue at hand, Yoder characteristically suggested that the very impulse to answer the question positively or negatively ignores the possibility that the question itself is ill-formed. He did this as a way of reminding the reader that questions have political histories. If a theological question is asked in a way that elicits a "yes" or "no" answer (and often "both" or "neither" answers as well), this typically means that the voices that say "that's the wrong question to be asking in the first place" have already been silenced. One example of this kind of reasoning in Yoder's work was his critique of the book *Christ and Culture* in "How H. Richard Niebuhr Reasoned."[18] Niebuhr assumed that "Christ" and "culture" named distinct categories, such that the perennial question before the church is always about how to relate Christ, on the one hand, to culture, on the other. Yoder noted that the very way Niebuhr set up the categories ruled out a priori the possibilities that (a) Christ was himself "cultural" and that (b) the church in fact embodies its own culture, no doubt distinct in some ways from other cultures, but not *categorically* different from them.

Even within a generally similar approach, then, Volf and Yoder are not entirely in accord on why or how one should resist simple oppositions. Indeed, the prima facie similarities highlight a deeper set of rhetorical differences between the two. Whereas Volf renders the *answers* given to standard questions more complex, Yoder persistently changed the very *questions* asked. The effects of this difference can be seen by considering a second function of Volf's rhetoric in *Exclusion and Embrace*, namely, the way it harnesses fear of the other.

In a part of the book entitled "The Politics of the Pure Heart," Volf excerpts a powerful story from Željko Vukovic's book, *The Killing of Sarajevo*. Volf writes:

> One of the most distressing stories from the war in former Yugoslavia comes from a Muslim woman. Here is how she tells it:
>
> I am a Muslim, and I am thirty five years old. To my second son who was just born, I gave the name "Jihad." So he would not forget the testament of his mother — revenge. The first time I put my baby at my breast I told him, "May this milk choke you if you forget." So be it. The Serbs taught me to hate. For the last two months there was nothing in me. No pain, no bitterness. Only hatred. I taught these children to love. I did. I am a teacher of literature. I was born in Ilijas and I almost died there. My student, Zoran, the only son of my neighbor, urinated into my mouth. As the bearded hooligans standing around laughed, he told me: "You are good for nothing else, you stinking Muslim woman...." I do not know whether I first heard the cry or felt the blow. My former colleague, a teacher of physics, was yelling like mad, "Ustasha, ustasha...." And kept hitting me. Wherever he could. I have become insensitive to pain. But my soul? It hurts. I taught them to love and all

---

18. Cf. Glen Stassen, Diane Yeager, and John Howard Yoder, *Authentic Transformation: A New Vision of Christ and Culture* (Nashville: Abingdon Press, 1996).

> the while they were making preparations to destroy everything that is not of the Orthodox faith. Jihad — war. This is the only way.... (p. 111)

Commenting on the story a number of pages later, Volf continues:

> One could object that victims should no more repent for what the perpetrators have done to the moral makeup of their souls than they should repent for what the perpetrators have done to the integrity of their bodies. Have not "the Serbs . . . taught" the Muslim woman to hate, as she put it? In an important sense, they did; the kind of violence and disgrace she has suffered creates hate. And yet even under the onslaught of extreme brutality, an inner realm of freedom to shape one's own self must be defended as a sanctuary of a person's humanity. (p. 117)

The Muslim woman's story, combined with Volf's commentary, not only exemplifies the first characteristic of Volf's rhetoric, namely, asking a question in polarizing terms and then suggesting that the standard answers to the question are insufficiently complex. But by offering a nuanced answer to the question, "Have not the Serbs taught the Muslim woman to hate?" rather than contesting the very assumptions constitutive of the question itself, Volf also activates the fear, disgust, and outrage generated by the question. Not only does he allow the fear to remain, but, more important, he harnesses its energy. The Muslim woman's story is harrowing; a receptive response to her will involve tremendous pain and outrage. I contest none of this. What concerns me is the way Volf uses the woman's story. The stark polarity of "either us or them," "Jihad — war. This is the only way," generates a fear of polarity that is answered only in a further dualism, *either* Volf's nuanced answers to standard questions *or* degeneration into irresoluble antagonism. Volf gets rhetorical mileage out of the very dualisms he purportedly contests, but he does not cease thinking in dualist terms. Rather, he rejects purportedly inadequate dualisms by holding out for a more comprehensive alternative. But, crucially: *Tertium non datur.*

From Exclusion to Paradise and the Affliction of Memory

An important argument in *Exclusion and Embrace* involves forgetting as the final "act" in the drama of reconciliation. The argument is based in a number of fundamental premises about the nature of justice and about what it means to be a person. Volf views reconciliation, for which his dominant metaphor is embrace, as life in a community that resists the exclusionary logic of "either us or them" by making a sustainable peace between the self and its others in a world "threatened by enmity" (p. 100).[19] To learn to live this way, Volf argues, requires repentance, forgiveness, making space in oneself for the other, and the healing of memory as constitutive and "essential elements in the movement from exclusion to embrace" (p. 100). Moreover, these essential elements require that we engage in "the struggle for truth and justice" in the context of self-giving love "modeled on the life of the triune God" (p. 101).

Volf claims that if Christians are to engage in the struggle for truth and justice in a way consistent with their trinitarian and christological convictions, then one of the first principles to test is freedom as it has been construed in the dominant political theories of post-Enlightenment Western culture. Liberal and socialist political theory, Volf argues, has helped to ensconce liberation and oppression as the dominant categories for theological reflection on social realities. The picture Volf paints is familiar: within the liberal tradition, freedom is primarily construed negatively. "All people are equal and all are free to pursue their interests and develop their personalities in their own way, provided they respect the same freedom in others" (p. 101). Liberation is thus being freed from the undue incursions of others into our pursuit of freedom, while oppression entails subservience or heteronomy to those same incursions. A socialist conception of freedom, alternatively, considers negative freedom to be empty. Freedom is instead conceived of as capacities to live with dignity. Liberation is whatever cultivates those capacities, and oppression is whatever inhibits them.

Neither the liberal/negative nor the socialist/positive conception of freedom is satisfactory for Volf, because neither challenges the polarization between liberation and oppression. Human conflicts are often too messy to admit of an easy classification of oppressors or liberators: liberators often "succeed" just to the extent that they become oppressors. In both its liberal and socialist guises, modern freedom is secured only by perpetuating the cycle of liberation and oppression, which nurtures neither reconciliation nor peace. As an ultimate social goal and good, therefore, freedom must be rejected by Christians.

---

19. This is not to say that "embrace" is merely a metaphor for Volf. As he says, reflecting on a similarity in Hegel's *Phenomenology of Spirit*, in his "analysis of the self and the other . . . metaphor and concept are intertwined" (p. 140).

Rejecting freedom as an *ultimate* social goal does not, however, mean that Christians must give up on the *project* of inhibiting oppression and working for liberation. Instead, Christians must contextualize that project, Volf says, within a vision of love as the ultimate social goal. Freedom is at most a step in a process of moving toward the kingdom of love, a process that transforms the project of liberation by liberating it "from the tendency to ideologize relations of social actors and perpetuate their antagonisms" (p. 105). But even as a step in working toward a politics wherein love is the ultimate social goal, freedom as a concept needs to be scrutinized.

For instance, it would be mistaken, Volf thinks, if accepting freedom as a proximate goal in working toward "the kingdom of love" prompted Christians to follow the postmodern critique of "universal emancipation" (p. 105). Such critiques, of which Volf takes J.-F. Lyotard to be a leading exponent, demonstrate how modernity has constructed a single universal history that channels the various competing currents of history into one river that flows toward freedom. Lyotard argued that the cultures out of which universal narratives of emancipation arose were themselves "intrinsically plural, heterogeneous, [and] incommensurable," such that we "need to guard the heterogeneity of language games" as opposed to imposing upon them a hegemonic grand narrative. Volf notes that Lyotard wrote, "Let us wage a war on totality, let us be witnesses to the unpresentable; let us activate the differences and save the honor of the name" (p. 107).[20] But what, Volf wonders, could be a grander or more totalizing narrative than one which suggests that people always and everywhere must resist totality in the name of preserving the incommensurability of language games? Moreover, Volf suggests that not only is a summons to resist the grand narrative of universal emancipation itself a grand narrative, but it is one with deleterious political consequences. By maintaining the conditions under which differences may proliferate in an unregulated manner, a society also maintains the conditions for the proliferation of violence and oppression. Where incommensurability is cultivated, violence is inevitable; or, as Volf puts it, "Unable to settle their differences by reasoning, the gods will invariably fight" (p. 108). The agonistics Lyotard envisions could be playful, but

---

20. Quoted from J.-F. Lyotard, *The Postmodern Condition: A Report on Knowledge*, trans. Geoffrey Bennington and Brian Massumi (Minneapolis: University of Minnesota Press, 1984), 81-82.

[w]hen the play gets serious, when one party breaks what the other party thinks are the rules of fair play and players are being carried off the field, would not continuing to play "in peace" amount to perpetuating injustice? (p. 108)

The use of a game analogy to describe the perpetuation of injustice is potentially misleading to the extent that competing players/teams in a game do not exemplify incommensurable discourses. This is so at least in part because the rules of games often make provisions for the presence and arbitrational authority of referees, for the use of penalty shots or their equivalent, and for fouls that sideline players for a determinate amount of time after breaking the rules.[21] In games such provisions make continuing to play "in peace" after the rules have been broken a logical course of action. This is to say that, because games exist within a larger set of agreements between teams or contestants/players, there is often a background of conversation about the goods internal to and attendant upon playing the game in question that do not leave players resourceless as they determine a just outcome in the face of an infraction of the rules. A game is an institution that creates an analogy between players, and rules are the laws that regulate both the gap between (the *ana* in the analogy) players and the ability for them to play together (the *logy* in analogy).[22] Continuing to play *in any other way* than "in peace" would be, at least in the instance of games of the kind I am describing, to fail to practice the game qua game, to fail to discern the institutions of analogy.

There are, however, situations plausibly described as "games" in which

21. Volf's use of the game analogy to illustrate incommensurability is also misleading in that it is part and parcel of the notion of playing a game that those involved *take themselves to be playing the same game*. Lyotard's account of incommensurable language games is not one in which all speakers of various language games take themselves to be playing the same game as everyone else. The relevant analogy to illustrate a "game" situation in which "continuing to play 'in peace'" would necessarily amount in perpetuating injustice would have to involve players or teams engaged in different games. A soccer team playing soccer "against" a baseball team playing baseball is an example. Notice, though, that what it means to play a game "against" someone playing another game is unclear. So, the example will still fail as an analogy to the "postmodern condition" unless the soccer team thinks the baseball team is (or should be) playing soccer and the baseball team thinks the soccer team is (or should be) playing baseball. Additionally, none of these comments about games should be taken to imply a negative judgment on forms of play that are not rule dependent. See, e.g., Janet Lever, "Sex Differences in the Games Children Play," *Social Problems* 23 (1976): 478-87.

22. Cf. Gillian Rose, *Mourning Becomes the Law: Philosophy and Representation* (Cambridge: Cambridge University Press, 1996), 10.

players will not have a set of deliberative resources on which to draw when the rules have been broken. Some instances of this kind of game might be a backyard football game, a game of kick the can, or a professional wrestling match. The incommensurabilities involved in this kind of game will typically be ones having to do with an unclear account of the good involved in playing the game in question, which, I would suggest, is often an indication that the play has not been taken seriously enough in the first place to warrant deliberation about how the game is encompassed within or reflects a vision of a more determinative conception of the good achieved by engaging in play. Yet Volf describes incommensurabilities as what happens when play "gets serious," which on the account of game-playing I am representing, is deeply to misconstrue the nature of "seriousness."

While that is a relatively minor set of objections, Volf's account of the irresoluble war that follows Lyotard's vision of proliferating difference is a prime instance of the way the rhetoric of *Exclusion and Embrace* cultivates fear. At most Lyotard offered a plea that we might play in peace amid our differences. But Volf, far from noting either the invitational quality of Lyotard's vision of postmodern politics or the fact that Lyotard's *Postmodern Condition* was written as an effort to resist the "computerization" (homogenization of all difference in the name of technocracy) of society, Volf pushes Lyotard into a *reductio ad absurdum:* incommensurable language games entail irresoluble war. Consider how Volf glosses his account of Lyotard with a characterization of Jürgen Habermas's objection to imprincipled incommensurabilities. Volf writes:

> Consider what happens when one tries to replace the modern schema of "oppression/liberation" with a postmodern model of incommensurable "language games." As Jürgen Habermas has argued, intersecting and sequential language games have the unfortunate characteristic that judgments of validity are not possible *between* them. (p. 108)

Habermas accurately assessed what Lyotard said about strict incommensurabilities (in *Just Gaming*), but as a general assessment of postmodernity's political visions Habermas's argument ignores the fact that incommensurabilities among language games do not rule out the possibility of *any* intelligible commerce or shared value judgments among them. An argument that accommodates incommensurabilites among language games simply affirms that agreements are, in many instances, partial. It does not affirm that those agreements are less constitutive of the social fabric than disagreements, nor does it affirm that all shared judgments between language games that are finally incommensurable are invalid. In many instances shared judgments between language games are possible and provide the constitutive conditions under which, as Lyotard himself hoped, people might learn to "play in peace."

Volf acknowledges as much: "[I]ncommensurability is not universal but always local, temporal, and partial, just as the commensurability is" (p. 109). Instead of using this insight to display the resources within a postmodern account of politics to resist totality without committing oneself to Lyotard's struggle to maintain the purity and incommensurability of different language games, Volf translates Lyotard's conviction of the irreducibility of language games into a judgment in favor of principled incommensurability as itself constitutive of postmodern politics *in toto*. Postmodernism, like the modernism of liberal and socialist dreams of emancipation, thus offers only deficient possibilities for envisioning a future of peace, because

> [w]hat stands in the way of reconciliation is not some inherent incommensurability, but a more profoundly disturbing fact that along with new understandings and peace agreements new conflicts and disagreements are permanently generated. (p. 109)

This last claim, however, remains unwarranted. According to it, we have to fear the possibility of *permanent* disagreements and conflict being generated by partial commensurabilities more than we have to fear total incommensurability. What grounds, given the local, temporal, and partial character of the commensurabilities we encounter, could possibly be given for this claim? Conflicts are perhaps always generated, but they are by no means inexorable or permanent, something Lyotard, Michel Foucault, and Gilles Deleuze have helped us all to see.[23] Neither does conflict always lead to war; indeed, sometimes exactly the opposite is the case. Conflict can be part and parcel of the patient labors constitutive of any peace worth the name.

---

23. Albeit negatively, with Lyotard, since in his account we must *strive* to keep language games pure and *protect* their heterogeneities. Clearly this means that conflicts and disagreements, even fairly basic ones, *can* be overcome for Lyotard. His project is to force us to linger with our disagreements, to see in the fact of certain kinds of conflict a set of goods to be preserved from the hegemonic discourses of capitalist economic expansion and computerization.

To return to Volf's argument: the problems involved in the modern schema of liberation/oppression and the postmodern critique of universal emancipation demand that we resist political programs that attempt to "accomplish the final reconciliation." Indeed, for Volf, when the project of final reconciliation is not left to God, it can be a project only of the antichrist. The problem that confronts Christians, then, is not that of finding a way to secure future peace, but rather of searching for the "resources we need to live in peace in the absence of the final reconciliation" (p. 109).

From Volf's point of view, the Christian task is more minimal than securing a peace that cannot be undone. Nevertheless, Christians should not give up hope in a final reconciliation. For what, Volf asks, would Christianity mean if the wedding feast of the Lamb were truly a grand illusion? And what could that supper entail if not "a reconciliation that can neither be surpassed nor undone"? If Christianity gave up on this hope, it would also be giving up on itself. Therefore, Volf advocates "the struggle for *a nonfinal reconciliation based on a vision of reconciliation that cannot be undone*" (p. 110). Seeking such a nonfinal reconciliation involves at least two things: (1) it involves backgrounding Christian hope to serve as the animus for, but not the proximate goal of, Christian ethical/political engagement now, and (2) it involves a readjustment of the self "in light of the other's alterity," without assuming that the configurations of power are symmetrical between them. Indeed, in Volf's analysis Christians should assume the opposite, a vision of "nonfinal reconciliation" that readjusts "dynamic identities *under the condition of inequality and manifest evil*" (p. 110; emphasis added).

Volf argues that Christians need to accept these conditions because of Jesus' proclamation of the kingdom of God. The masses to whom Jesus addressed his message were in conditions of radical inequality and oppression. His message resonated precisely because it was so rife with the "political, economic, and cultural frustrations and aspirations" that animated Israel in first-century Palestine (p. 112).

That Jesus addressed himself principally to the poor and disenfranchised should not surprise us, Volf insists, because any political leader who desires social power needs to command a movement. But Jesus did not aspire to political leadership; rather, he inspired his hearers and "built into the very core of his 'platform' the message of God's unconditional love and the people's need for repentance" (pp. 112-13). Thus, says Volf, "the truly revolutionary character of Jesus' proclamation lies precisely in the *connection between the hope he gives to the oppressed and the radical change he requires of them*" (p. 114). In what does that radical change consist?

Essentially, repentance consists in the uncoupling of our desires from the social mechanisms that generate envy and enmity. Jesus preached his message against devotion to wealth and hatred of enemies, not merely as psychological states but as sets of material practices to be dismantled. For the oppressed, however, who have only limited access to the material things that engender obsession with wealth and enemy hatred, Jesus' injunctions criticize the passions, not as disembodied emotive states but as visceral responses to the effects of an economy that blocked people off from the pursuit of abundant life. The oppressed, Volf argues, heard Jesus' message of God's love and repentance for sin as "release from the understandable but nonetheless inhuman hatred in which their hearts are held captive" (p. 114).

This is to say that repentance must have material consequences for Volf. That is, repentance is only effective if it breaks the seductive power of envy and enmity, whose "social impact . . . is to reinforce the dominant values and practices that cause and perpetuate oppression in the first place" (p. 116). For victims of violence repentance entails minimizing their own oppressive behaviors of exercising reactive violence. Victims, according to Volf, need to repent of what perpetrators do to their souls, for "even under the onslaught of extreme brutality, an inner realm of freedom to shape one's self must be defended as a sanctuary of a person's humanity" (p. 117).

How such an "inner realm of freedom" that is the "sanctuary of a person's humanity" differs from the liberal notion of freedom Volf criticizes as insufficient for Christian practice is unclear. Volf claimed with the socialist tradition that the liberal conception of freedom was substantively empty. He also claimed that the liberal conception of freedom was negative, that is, freedom from undue intrusions into one's own pursuit of the good life. But the notion of "freedom from" presumes that the question "Who is free?" makes sense. In the liberal philosophical tradition following Kant, the "who question" is answered as precisely "an inner realm of freedom" and as "the sanctuary of a person's humanity." Within that tradition, the inner realm of freedom or "higher faculty of desire" allows the subject to step back from its substantive commitments and engage the question "What ought I to do?" in the light of reason alone. So, while beginning his account of reconciliation with a critique of freedom as construed in modernist inquiries, Volf ends up reproducing exactly the conception of freedom that is foundational for the enterprise he meant to critique. This is important because the "sanctuary of a person's humanity" makes forgetting both possible and necessary as a constitutive moment in the movement from exclusion to embrace. How so?

For Volf both repentance and forgiveness, if they are genuine, are truly free activities because they allow people to transcend the normal dynamics of the social fabric. Repentance and forgiveness are practices that uncouple us from our desires for self-justification and revenge, desires that foment envy and enmity. Repentance and forgiveness so uncouple us from misdirected desires precisely because they short circuit the normal channels and expectations of justice. Given repentance and forgiveness, justice cannot be represented as simple retribution, since retribution is what the claims of forgiveness and pleas of repentance ask us to forgo. Neither, however, can justice be construed as strictly restorative. There is no way to undo the past, which is, Volf argues, what a consistent account of restorative justice demands. Instead, repentance and forgiveness illumine the shortcomings of retributive and restorative justice alike, while nevertheless making the claims of justice all the more pressing.

Volf's conception of justice is bound up with his conception of freedom, just to the extent that justice requires heteronomy. While in repentance, one "becomes free from alienation and the determination of his actions by others; he comes to himself, and steps into the light of a truth which makes him free," and in forgiving one "breaks the power of the remembered past and transcends the claims of the affirmed justice and so makes the spiral of vengeance grind to a halt"; on the issue of justice Volf writes, "every act of forgiveness enthrones justice," because it "draws attention to [justice's] violation precisely by offering to forgo its claims" (pp. 120-23). So, while repentance and forgiveness contribute to autonomous self-determination, in the process they foreground the demands of justice even while not satisfying them. And this is no anomaly in Volf's account, because in considering what justice requires we are always in a heteronomous relationship with the past. We forgive and are forgiven, but justice must nevertheless be done, lest autonomous activity have no purchase in the realm of social reality.

Forgiveness is thus but a momentary uncoupling from the spiral of vengeance that determines the demands of justice. As momentary and fragmented, forgiveness nevertheless echoes the activity of Christ on the cross, where Christ prayed for the pardon of his torturers and so created space in the divine life for the other to come in. Thereby he fulfilled the conditions for a determinative peace to take hold and transform the relation between victims and perpetrators.

The forgiveness Christ prayed for and extended on the cross expressed "the *will* to embrace the enemy," according to Volf. "Christ is the victim who *refuses* to be defined by the perpetrator, *forgives* and *makes* space in himself for the enemy" (p. 126; emphasis added). But this construal of Christ's activity on the cross is monological (*he* wills, *he* forgives, *he* makes space) and, as such, is paradigmatic of the sovereign subject of modern critical inquiry, secure in his identity, with nothing to risk or lose by magnanimously engaging the enemy. As, however, a model of vulnerable engagement appropriate to a savior who was "emptied of himself," Jesus the victim can be in no position to refuse to be defined by his oppressors — his relationship to them on the cross was not one of sovereign transcendence, but rather of abject humiliation; it was not one of autonomous detachment from his subjective commitments, but from beginning to end heteronomous and other-determined. Yet God raised him up and used Christ's abjection both therapeutically and pedagogically, not to teach Christians a strategy for making space in oneself for the other, but as a demonstration of the extent to which living in a way consonant with the coming kingdom requires giving up on all social controls, being ready to disavow the handles approach to history, even when doing so seems certain to spell only disaster.

It is certainly important to affirm, as Volf does, an ethos that invites engagement with the stranger and the enemy. But it is equally important to disavow the cultivation of dialogical receptivity as itself one more in a cache of power moves deployed to ensure that I retain control over whatever engagements in which I happen to find myself enmeshed. Thematizing forgiveness as an act of ultimate sovereignty, however, is just such a power move. Moreover, it presents Volf with a nearly insoluble problem.

If, on the one hand, the demands of justice refuse to go away, and if, on the other hand, strict justice is a practical impossibility, such that forgiveness is the only way to get uncoupled from the spiral of vengeance, then the proposed solution is not an answer to the problem at hand. Forgiveness in Volf's account does not redeem unrequited justice — the memories of wrongs done and of unrecoverable pasts of wholeness persist even when forgiveness has been extended and received. A sovereign act of autonomy does not overcome the chains of determination that bind us to our histories. Therefore Volf writes:

> After we have repented and forgiven our enemies, after we have made space in ourselves for them and let the door open, our will to embrace them must allow the one final, and perhaps the most difficult act to take place, if the process of reconciliation is to be complete. It is the act

of forgetting the evil suffered, a certain kind of forgetting, I hasten to add. It is a forgetting that assumes that the matters of "truth" and "justice" have been taken care of . . . that perpetrators have been named, judged, and (hopefully) transformed, that victims are sage and their wounds healed . . . a forgetting that can therefore ultimately take place only together with the creation of "all things new." (p. 131)

For Volf this divine forgetting is the object of Christian hope. It secures final reconciliation. But it is also important to note what this act of forgetting is not. Forgetting the memory of past wrongs is no substitute for justice or forgiveness. Nor does forgetting change the "truth" of the past. But forgetting is a way of redeeming the past, or so Volf claims: "Since memories shape present identities, neither I nor the other can be redeemed without the redemption of our remembered past" (p. 133). Or, and this is subtly different: "As long as we remember the injustice and suffering we will not be whole, and the troubling and unanswerable 'open question' that craves resolution in an impossible harmony will keep resurfacing" (p. 134). In the first quote Volf affirms that redemption of us requires the redemption of our memories. In the second, however, the redemption we require is non-remembering.

In sum: for Volf divine amnesia is the final component in a mechanics of reconciliation that encodes in its center a lapse between the demands of justice and the social transformation attendant upon forgiveness, understood as an autonomous act. Forgiveness cannot change the past, and since the past is precisely where the history of pain that requires justice lies, complete reconciliation requires "a stage of nonremembering" (p. 135).

Volf's argument moves from heteronomous relationships to history, configured in terms of the insatiable demands of justice, to an act of subjective sovereignty (repentance, forgiveness, making space in oneself for the other) that uncouples people from their heteronomous relationships. This act of self-sovereignty is, moreover, secured only by the further act of a higher sovereignty, the "grace of nonremembering" (p. 138). For if it is difficult to imagine how victims might become so free in themselves to forgive those who have wronged them and forgo the demands of justice, it is impossible to imagine, Volf says, an autonomous activity capable of securing a reconciled and non-tragic future between victim and perpetrator if the memory of wrongdoing persists. Thus, the affliction of memory can only be healed by the grace of nonremembering, a grace not grounded in subjective sovereignty, but found in the arms of God, at the center of whose "all-embracing memory there is a paradoxical monument to forgetting, the cross of Christ" (p. 140). God alone is able to erase the memory of the "unredeemed past that un-redeems every present," and so lets former enemies, now "separated only by the boundaries of their identities," "embrace each other within the embrace of the triune God" (p. 138).

If, however, the past has not been redeemed, and if the present memory of the past is not being redeemed and cannot be redeemed without being forgotten, such that God must drown "my sins' black memory" in "a heavenly Lethean flood," as John Donne once put it, then salvation ceases to be temporal, the analogy between creation and salvation has been stretched to the point of breaking.[24] Or, in a somewhat different register, to argue for reconciliation only on the basis of a radical discontinuity with the past is another way for Christians to put "handles on history." How so?

The central question, "Who is to be redeemed?," depends on the analogy between creation and salvation. This question interrogates the limits of redemption both christologically and ecclesiologically. Christologically, because it assumes Gregory Nazianzen's dictum: "Whatever would not have been assumed would not have been healed." Ecclesiologically, because the question requires an account of the church as the body of Christ. Put most boldly, any account of redemption that does not involve our negative memories of past violence and our histories of loss is inadequate, in that who is saved is less than the entire person. If Volf is right about forgetting, it turns out that Augustine was wrong: the God who created us without us will, after all, save us without us, too.

To say this presupposes an account of the person as an embodied story. What makes a person a person is precisely that her or his life can be construed as at least part of a drama, which, as Aristotle said, characteristically consist in beginnings, middles, and ends. Given Volf's account of personhood and personality as notions fundamentally valenced by the Trinity — nonstatic relations that have their "being" in the conversations among the very same relations — Volf has no prima facie reason to object to an account of personhood as being part of an embodied story. But Volf's picture of salvation and reconciliation has human persons redeemed precisely from their stories: the memory of justice undone is a memory that cannot continue if people are to regain their integrity and be

---

24. John Donne, Holy Sonnet 9, in *The Norton Anthology of English Literature*, 6th ed., vol. 1., ed. M. H. Abrams (New York: Norton, 1993), 1116. I have modernized Donne's spelling in this quote.

reconciled to each other. The "creation of all things new" is a radical discontinuity with the old precisely in that it is the beginning of a different story from the story of injustice, oppression, and exclusion that we currently inhabit.

Volf could perhaps argue that in construing his account of redemption as radical discontinuity with the past I am overdrawing the distinction between the here and the hereafter. To be reconciled with each other we need not forget our stories *in toto;* we need only forget the fragments of our stories bound up in the injuries of past violence. Arguably, this is not radical discontinuity, but only partial discontinuity, the constitution of a new language game, to return to Lyotard's idiom, with at most partial incommensurabilities to the language games of which we are currently parts. But I wonder whether the claim — and it is a claim that must hold if Volf's response to the objection of radical discontinuity is to be sustained — that there are memories not bound up in the violences of the past can be plausibly validated. I confess I have no idea how one might test this question in general, but for Christians perhaps a general inquiry is unnecessary. At least we can say that one memory, that of Christ's crucifixion, is a memory both inescapably bound up in violence and, as such, is also central to our stories as Christians. Without the memory of the cross, no Christianity. Without the memory of Jesus' crucifixion and our violent collusion in it, the "creation of all things new" entails a radical discontinuity with a story that claims no less than that this violence at least, the violence that nailed Jesus to the cross, is essential to the story of our salvation.

It is not that Christ's crucifixion was unavoidable. The violence that culminated in Jesus' death was contingent, not categorically different from any other act of violence. But apart from the crucifixion, the story of Christianity would cease to be the same story. Moreover, an account of hope in a final reconciliation that requires the forgetting of this set of injurious memories cannot be Christian hope, at least in part because it secures our future against contingency at the cost of erasing the past that gave that future a possible coherence in the first place.

The very reasons that led us to question Yoder's doxological vision of history — the persistence of the past's injuries, the place of rage before God, the concern that praise might drown out cries for justice — the very questions Volf addressed, remain in his argument deeply problematic. Justice goes unrequited, and reconciliation is possible only at the expense of the central elements of the story that makes Christians who they are. What if, at this point, we turn back to Yoder? Can he offer an account of history as praise that does not, on the one hand, require radical discontinuity with key elements of the Christian story, and, on the other, address the persistence of cries for justice? In the final portion of this chapter, I argue that he can, and indeed does, offer just such an account, by making communal processes of negotiating memory part and parcel of the praise the people of God render before the throne.

Yoder's Politics of Memory

"What would not have been assumed would not have been healed." In some senses it is odd to claim Nazianzen for Yoder, since the statement can be read to presume the kind of incarnational Christology that makes Jesus' obedience to "the one who sent him" merely incidental to Christian theology. What matters about the incarnation, theologians have claimed by citing sources just like Gregory, is that it represents the infinite capacity of Christ to absorb the failures of humanity and transform them "without impairing his own majesty," as Leo the Great put it.[25] To the kind of incarnationalist theology that demands "a full concept of the prior exalted status which [Christ] forsook," for which Jesus' human career and its results were simply an unveiling mechanism, Yoder strongly and persistently objected.[26] But in another important sense it is only natural for Yoder's Christology to resonate with Nazianzen's, for both invite a strong interpretation of Jesus' solidarity with those he came to save. Indeed, solidarity is too weak a word, since precisely what Christian tradition affirms is that Christ was one of those whom he saved, not different from them in any respect, except that he was without sin. In this claim, that of the strongest affirmation of Christ's full humanity, both Yoder and Nazianzen locate Jesus' claim to divinity. That he did not consider "equality with God something to be grasped," but saved us as one of us, is "the profoundest proof of his condescension, and thereby of his glory."[27]

---

25. Sermon 28, in *PL* 54, 221-26. The relevant lines are 97-98: "Deus enim Dei Filius, de sempiterno et ingenito Patre unigenitus, et incommutabiliter atque intermporaliter habens non aliud esse quam Pater est, formam servi sine suae detrimento majestatis accepit, ut in sua nos proveheret, non se in nostra dejiceret."

26. Cf. Yoder, *Preface to Theology*, 86; see also *The Politics of Jesus*, 7-8.

27. This is to quote Yoder somewhat out of context. See *Priestly Kingdom*, 62. I think it is, however, not to quote Yoder unfaithfully. Nazianzen, for his part, says Christ "honors obedience by his action, and proves it experimentally by his passion. For to possess the dis-

The theological sense of Nazianzen's statement can be elucidated by reference to Yoder's Christology. The story of Christ's life would be incomplete without the memory of unjust suffering. Or rather, it is not Jesus' story apart from the suffering of his body. Divested of the memory of unjust suffering, it will not be the same Jesus to whom Christians bear witness. And then what would it mean for Christians to praise him, or to say that praise truly is embedded within a process that "rules the world"? Yoder's Christology pushes these ecclesiological points, namely, that the church's memory loops back to *this* Jesus, "handed over ... according to the definite plan and foreknowledge of God ... crucified and killed by the hands of those outside the law" (Acts 2:23). In so doing, it continues his memory, but not just as a memory of the past, but as a mode of being now, for this same Jesus remains relevant as present and future to a people whose life is shaped by praise of him. When Yoder wrote, for instance, that the primary social meaning of the eucharist is economic sharing, he was affirming the church's continuation of the story of Jesus' earthly presence.[28] The church's eucharist announces the body of Christ — the social process of eating together publishes Christ's body, it makes it present for and available to the world. When the church eats and drinks together in Christ's name it "proclaims the Lord's death until he come." The anamnetic focus of the meal is clear. But precisely in continuing the visible and material dynamics of Jesus' earthly career, this anamnetic activity is encompassed within a wider process than that of a "mere" memorial to a savior now gone and seated far away in heaven. For in repeating and imitating the dynamics of Jesus' earthly ministry, the church continues the story of that ministry, and, as the continuing story of Jesus, continues so also to embody his person here on earth. Memory thus becomes the mode by which Christ's body is made present and available in and for the world.

For Yoder, this was no less true of the practice of forgiveness than it was of the celebration of the Lord's Supper. He argued, "A process of human interchange combining the mode of reconciling dialogue, the substance of moral discernment, and the authority of divine empowerment deserves to be considered one of the sacramental works of the community."[29]

---

position is not enough, just as it would not be enough for us, unless we also proved it by our acts; for action is the proof of disposition." See Gregory of Nazianzus, "Fourth Theological Oration," paragraph 6, English translation in *Nicene and Post-Nicene Fathers*, 2nd ser., vol. 7, ed. Philip Schaff and Henry Wace (Grand Rapids: Eerdmans, 1996), 311.

28. Yoder, *Royal Priesthood*, 365-66.
29. Yoder, *Royal Priesthood*, 362.

Why? Because a process of reconciliation and moral discernment, just like processes of economic sharing — of eating and drinking together as a way of "looping back" to Jesus — continues the story of Jesus here and now by making that story available in and to the world.

What is crucial to see is that the story of Jesus the church is called to incarnate is not the same story without the memory of unjust suffering. Concomitant upon this claim is the further claim that the church's practice of forgiveness and moral discernment cannot be ordered toward a vision of reconciliation, holiness, or redemption that sanitizes the past by erasing it. Since the church remembers Jesus and claims to continue his story, the church's work for reconciliation between victims and perpetrators proclaims the very same work as the work of God in Jesus Christ, the story of which cannot be forgotten if the story is itself to be continued.

"Protestants," Yoder wrote, "have for centuries been arguing that 'only God can forgive,' and that the believer receives reassurance of forgiveness not from another person but in the secret of his or her own heart."[30] While Volf is perhaps not quite as blunt as this, his argument for "nonfinal reconciliation" secured by hope in a final reconciliation enacted by God and grounded in the "grace of nonremembering" in fact repeats the thrust of this Protestant position. The scandal of justice undone and the irrecoverability of the past requires a radical disjunction between the church's work for reconciliation now and the eschatological reconciliation God will effect with "the grace of nonremembering" and "the creation of all things new." But this, according to Yoder, is to misidentify the nature of the scandal in question:

> The heat and vigor of this old Protestant-Catholic debate points us to the difficulty we have in conceiving, and in believing, that God really can authorize ordinary humans to commit him, that is, to forbid and to forgive on his behalf with the assurance that the action stands "in heaven." How can it be, and what can it mean, that such powers are placed in the hands of ordinary people the likes of Peter? The jealous concern of religious leaders, and of all religion, for the transcendence of God, for his untouchablility and his distance from us, might have been able to adjust, or to make an exception, for arrogant claims like this made on behalf of some most exceptional person, a high priest or a grand rabbi, a prophet or king. But the real scandal of the way God

---

30. Yoder, *Royal Priesthood*, 330.

chose to work among humans — what we call the Incarnation — is that it was an ordinary working man from Nazareth who commissioned a crew of ordinary people — former fishermen and taxgatherers — *to forgive sins*.[31]

How indeed can a crew of ordinary people be given God's power to forgive sins? How can the process be integral to a doxological vision of history? I have three suggestions to make.

First, forgiveness and reconciliation are a process that *takes* and *makes* time. Forgiveness does not secure us against the contingencies of our past or against the contingencies of our futures. Nor should we insist that reconciliation can occur only if and when our pasts have been sanitized. If forgiveness is a way of continuing the story of Jesus, then it takes the shape, not of a moment in the drama of embrace — with whatever expansive conception of moment we might wish to adopt — but of an ongoing conversation. As conversation, and by this I mean simply, even if not merely, the desire of victims to talk with perpetrators, forgiveness is not an activity whose primary purpose is to achieve a goal external to the conversation itself. The overriding interest is not with the appropriate punishment for offenders, with reparations for victims, or even with creating a neutral space from which each party may be free to choose to go his or her own way. Rather, forgiveness names the possibility of and desire to continue conversing with the one who has offended, without assuming that one can predict in advance the shape that conversation will take. Moreover, relinquishing control on the shape of forgiveness as conversation requires patience. The needs of the victim and the demands of justice are not self-evident, nor are they assumed to be discrete possibilities that must be "taken care of" before reconciliation can occur. Rather, justice is a good that inheres in the shape of the conversation itself.

Yet, second, to insist that forgiveness take the shape of an ongoing conversation whose particular nature is not specifiable in advance of or apart from the engagement itself is not to counsel radical situationalism. For Christians this is the case at least because forgiveness is a way of continuing the story of Jesus. This means that that story, recorded in the Gospels and interpreted within the church, always requires a set of ongoing deliberations about how the current conversation does or does not plausibly continue the story of Jesus. These ongoing deliberations, too, are open-

---

31. Yoder, *Royal Priesthood*, 330-31.

ended; the concern is with making Jesus' story available in the world, and not with a set of *ex ante* rules and procedural justifications.

Finally, forgiving conversations that are partly constitutive of a doxological vision of history require hope — not hopefulness as such, or hope in final reconciliation, subjective wholeness, or the grace of nonremembering. Some reconciliations will not prove durable, or will not be effected in certain settings when certain persons are involved because of dynamics like willful stubbornness, trauma, or deep elements of mistrust — all of which are inescapably bound up in memories of the past. Some notions of subjective wholeness are terrifying; others are merely chimeric, but each is beholden to the fantasy that "I" am fundamentally other than the stories, deployed through time and so composed of the stuff of memory, of which I find myself a part. Some forgetting is no doubt merciful; but where mercy, truthfulness, constancy, and patience embrace in the arms of God, nonremembering can only be a terrible parody of grace. Seeing forgiveness as part of a doxological vision of history affords none of these hopes. Rather, forgiveness as conversation requires hope that, in the midst of, through, and by tarrying with the ruins of memory, by being committed to the patient labor of giving voice to violent pasts precisely as part of the patient labor of crafting a new future, we may again make the story of Jesus available in the world.

CHAPTER 5

"Love One Another":
Voluntariety Transformed by Dialogical Vulnerability

> *Though we still recognize the feeling of love, we have forgotten how to practice love when we don't feel it.*
>
> Wendell Berry,
> *Sex, Economy, Freedom, and Community*

Yoder's account of the essentially communal embodiment of holiness in the rule of Paul (an open meeting of the church, in which any participant is free to speak and be heard) and the fullness of Christ (diversity of gifts) could be paraphrased as commentary on Paul's exhortation in Romans 13:8, "Owe no one anything, only love one another." Though I know of no place where Yoder explicitly makes this connection, I think it nonetheless apposite. Here Paul subtly draws attention to our propensity to assume that the graciousness of love is dissociable from our normal contexts of negotiating with others, with owing people something. Prima facie, this makes some sense. Love characteristically happens to us. We discover that we love, and in this context it seems strange to think that love is a duty, something we owe, a product of negotiation. Indeed, when love is something we do, it is rarely love. Have you ever *tried* to be in love? Most of us probably have: my teens might be so summarized. But what happens in trying to be in love is almost always that we attempt to secure our subjectivities, and so to become the sole agents of our own ends. Trying to be in love has the profoundly unwanted effect of making the other an extension of myself, and therefore of rendering me incoherent as an agent, since what I do in projecting my fantasies of *self*-fulfillment onto this or that person is deeply at odds with what I profess that I want to do, that is, to love *another*. Perhaps something of our sense of the futility of and the deformations involved in trying to love is highlighted in the refrigerator magnet adage, "If you love someone, set them free." That exhortation is central to our cultural assumptions about love. It is the commonsense expression of our philosophical anthropology, inherited at least partly from a central tenet of the European Enlightenment: rationality means autonomy. In his book *The Fire and the Rose Are One*, Sebastian Moore comments with characteristic clarity on a slightly more sophisticated version of the refrigerator magnet:

> The "Gestalt Prayer" was composed by Fritz Perls as a poetic summing-up of Gestalt Therapy. I've seen it on at least one banner:
>> I do my thing, and you do your thing.
>> I am not in this world to live up to your expectations
>> And you are not in this world to live up to mine.
>> You are you and I am I,
>> And if by chance we find each other, it's beautiful.
>> If not, it can't be helped.
>
> This prayer illustrates the contemporary confusion over guilt. It is a beautiful half-truth, for it assumes that the only "expectations" people can have of each other are those improper expectations which keep us in infantile guilt. Correspondingly, it assumes that the only guilt people feel is the infantile guilt of not living up to other's expectations. Predictably, love shows up in this picture as a happy accident having no place in the structure of being a person. By way of contrast, St Paul describes mutual adult expectations succinctly: "Owe no man anything, but to love one another."[1]

One way of stating a common and powerful objection to the contemporary resurgence of "narrative ethics" — that it is elitist and authoritarian — is that it demands that we cultivate what Moore calls "improper expectations" of others, that having our lives bound by and as stories requires us to owe others things we cannot owe and still "do our thing." One inadequate but commonly adduced response to this is that of a voluntarist, essentially contractual communitarianism. Yoder has, I think unfairly, been indicated as a representative of this response, which crudely takes the following form: once you have voluntarily entered into communal engagements with others, the community is entitled to make otherwise improper

---

1. Sebastian Moore, *The Fire and the Rose Are One* (New York: Seabury, 1980), 59.

"Love One Another"

demands of you; but you can always leave if the going gets rough.[2] This Hobbesian account of community assumes that the only legitimate form of adult human dependence is chosen dependence. In other words, and to twist somewhat Max Weber's famous distinction, the only form of community contemporary people can countenance is associative.

In this chapter, I try with Yoder to unthink the church as a voluntary association conceived along the lines of a species of social contract. The task is not straightforward because Yoder does, after all, conceive of the church as voluntary. The burden therefore has to do with seeing what Yoder's voluntarism does and does not entail, with, that is, undoing a possible equivocation on the word "voluntary." To that end, my discussion falls into two major divisions. In the first part of the chapter, I employ Alasdair MacIntyre's conception of tradition-constituted inquiry as it cycles around notions of dependence and obligation to help to forge a context in which we can begin to discuss the life of the church, not as freeing people from obligation as such or from all forms of dependence on others except those we choose to acknowledge, but as shaping desires so that we can focus on appropriate and inappropriate forms of interdependence. Crucial to that investigation is the realization that relationships of interdependence develop over time and are thus products of negotiation, work, and ongoing discovery in a way that calls into question the voluntarist notion of the church as an aggregate of self-possessed individuals who band together for the purpose of pursuing some set of goals that they have agreed in advance of their formal association would be good to pursue.

---

2. Travis Kroeker notes that this is O'Donovan's sense of what Yoder's commitment to the church as voluntary requires: "According to O'Donovan, Yoder's emphasis on voluntariety and the 'free church' is purchased at the expense of *belief;* that is, it is rooted in an intellectually flabby liberalism that has lost confidence in truth claims and views all social doctrines as inherently coercive" (p. 55). Far from cultivating such a "take it or leave it" attitude to the church, Yoder, Kroeker argues, understands the social doctrine of the church as non-coercive "because it is not in the business of enacting and enforcing judicial authority — it proceeds on a different paradigm of divine rule and justice" (p. 56). Kroeker is close to right, although I think he ought to concede that a "different paradigm of divine rule and justice" will likely put the church in the role of "enacting" "judicial authority," if not of "enforcing" it, once judicial authority has been reconceived along the lines of the different paradigm. My attempt in this chapter to think through the rule of Paul and the fullness of Christ as prescriptions for church order might be understood as such a reconception. See his "Why O'Donovan's Christendom Is Not Constantinian and Yoder's Voluntariety Is Not Hobbesian: A Debate in Theological Ethics Redefined," *Annual of the Society of Christian Ethics* 20 (2000): 41-64.

Yoder's account, I argue, of the fullness of Christ and the rule of Paul is in fundamental continuity with MacIntyre's assumption that specifically human flourishing relies on acknowledgment of what he calls "the virtues of acknowledged dependence."

In the second part of the chapter, I delve more deeply into the fullness of Christ and the rule of Paul as practices that foreground dialogical vulnerability in the life of the church. I do this not by means of an extended exposition of Yoder's thought, for which there is no substitute beside his own texts, but rather by investigation of a conversation that his account of church practice enables. That conversation is with John Milbank's conception of Christianity as installing an economy of the gift, which is instructive, I argue, for thinking carefully about what Yoder does and does not mean when he describes the church as voluntary.[3] Though the argument of this chapter is, I think, intelligible in its own right, it also takes up issues of the need to control and delimit the shape of the church as a historical mover that were prominent in the preceding chapters. Moreover, it fills out my discussion in the previous chapters of the church as a distinctive and imitable way of being in time that sees history doxologically. I begin, then, by noting the initial oddity of proposing a strategic alliance between MacIntyre and Yoder.

Appropriate Dependency and the Shape of Desire

Alasdair MacIntyre, in partial response to his critics, has developed a book-length reply to the view that his ethics is elitist and authoritarian. I find that book, *Dependent Rational Animals*, useful for thinking about Yoder.[4] Before embarking, however, on an extended analysis of MacIntyre's book, a set of comments seems in order concerning this alliance between MacIntyre and Yoder, which many readers may find unlikely. Michael Cartwright's introduction to *The Royal Priesthood*, which makes the connection between MacIntyre and Yoder, seems a good place from which to take our initial bearings.

---

3. Other "conversations" could be had. One important example is of how Yoder's thought about the political practices that constitute the church resonates with aspects of traditional Christian reflection on what it means for humanity to be created "in the image of God."

4. Alasdair MacIntyre, *Dependent Rational Animals: Why Human Beings Need the Virtues* (Chicago: Open Court, 1999).

Cartwright notes that the last two decades of the twentieth century saw a renewed interest "in the role of 'living traditions' in shaping moral discourse in all spheres of society."[5] MacIntyre's conception of tradition constituted inquiry — all discourse is inescapably historical and therefore is both a function of and produces institutions and forms of life that we inhabit, and are themselves the subject of a history that begins at some point in time and extends indefinitely into the future — stands, Cartwright says, as a challenge to both modernist claims to universal "objectivity" and postmodernist "relativism." And with this we can see a clear set of affinities with aspects of Yoder's thought, both with the claim that the search for moral scratch is fruitless, and with the claim that the historical particularity of all knowledge does not deny the possibility of discovering truth.[6]

Yet Cartwright also includes in his account a number of possible cautions on, or at least disanalogies between, Yoder's and MacIntyre's projects. In the first place, Cartwright says,

> Yoder offers no explicit moral theory in the way that MacIntyre does. Second, Yoder's conception of practical reason — oriented as it is within what he has called "The Hermeneutics of Peoplehood" — is much more narrowly focused in terms of what might be called a discipleship ethics, whereas MacIntyre's agenda is broader and more all-encompassing. Third, whereas MacIntyre wants to reconstruct the "local communities" in the midst of "the new dark ages," as we have already seen, Yoder's contention is that the church should be seen as "a sociological entity in its own right." Fourth, MacIntyre is so broadly

---

5. Yoder, *Royal Priesthood*, 36.
6. See, e.g., MacIntyre, *Whose Justice? Which Rationality?* (Notre Dame: University of Notre Dame Press, 1988), 350: "There is no standing ground, no place for enquiry, no way to engage in the practices of advancing, evaluating, accepting, and rejecting reasoned argument apart from that which is provided by some particular tradition or other." And cf. Yoder, *The Priestly Kingdom: Social Ethics as Gospel* (Notre Dame: University of Notre Dame Press, 1984), 7: "There is no 'scratch' to which one can go back to begin, anymore than there is any 'onion per se' to be reached by peeling off one after another the layers of flesh. What must replace the prolegomenal search for 'scratch' is the confession of rootedness in historical community." The affinity has been commented on with respect to MacIntyre's and Yoder's refusals to use ethical theory to master contingency by Chris K. Huebner, "Unhandling History: Anti-Theory, Ethics and the Practice of Witness" (Ph.D. diss., Duke University, 2001), esp. ch. 6, "Practicing Witness, Unhandling History: Christian Ethics Beyond Theory and Anti-Theory."

concerned with foundations in theory that he does not discuss such issues as the love of enemies, war, money, whereas Yoder would argue that such issues as these in relation to the messianic kingship of Jesus are the substance of ethics. Finally, where MacIntyre's interest in the church appears not to exclude the possibility of Christendom-type alliances, Yoder's free church is juxtaposed against any version of Christendom, if "Christendom" means the alliance of church and state for the purpose of governance. In these respects, Yoder's attempt to retrieve the idiom of apostolic apocalyptic as a resource with which to interpret both social and cosmic structure appears to offer a very different way of approaching moral inquiry in contrast to the three approaches MacIntyre identifies, although Yoder's project, like MacIntyre's, is one of recovery or retrieval.[7]

I share Cartwright's concern not to assimilate Yoder to MacIntyre, or vice versa, although the latter is probably not a serious temptation. Yet I do not find Cartwright's admittedly sketchy enumeration of differences between the two thinkers terribly compelling, and this for two reasons.

First, Cartwright's account of the differences between Yoder and MacIntyre is fueled by the assumption that each is essentially "a project of retrieval." MacIntyre's account of tradition constituted inquiry is "cast within a reconstruction of the Aristotelian tradition of ethics and, more specifically, within the Thomistic version of that tradition of moral inquiry," while Yoder's project, as Cartwright says in the passage above, seeks "to retrieve the idiom of apostolic apocalyptic as a resource with which to interpret both social and cosmic structure."[8] It is fair to say that both MacIntyre and Yoder draw our attention to grammars of moral inquiry that remain largely neglected in contemporary philosophy and theology, but "retrieval" seems to me a misleading notion in both their cases, because it can easily conjure up images of recourse to a less-complicated and unadulterated past, which, if we were to take refuge in it, would furnish us with a degree of moral clarity we cannot otherwise come by. So read, both MacIntyre and Yoder become doomsayers, lamenting the loss of a golden age and recommending its recovery.[9] This, however, is a stance each strenuously

---

7. Yoder, *Royal Priesthood*, 37.
8. Yoder, *Royal Priesthood*, 36, 37.
9. The point here is not to charge Cartwright with the ascription of this position to either MacIntyre or Yoder. It is rather to point out that Cartwright's reading of their projects does not disable "golden-age" misreadings.

denies. There are, I think, good reasons to say that the fundamental orientation in each thinker's work is toward the future. The history of the church and the notion that a tradition of inquiry is something of which we are largely inheritors are both deployed in MacIntyre and Yoder as ways of getting our bearings, taking stock of where we are so as to be able to describe where we might go. Retrieval, that is, is not a project in its own right. It is simply one aspect of any coherent reflection on what it means to live in change and exchange, time and language, to find ourselves part of an ongoing story.[10]

Consider, for instance, the charism Yoder describes in many different connections as essential to the church's ministry, namely, the community's "agents of memory."[11] He compares the role to that of a scribe, itself likened in Scripture to a good steward, who knows when to bring out of the storehouse good things, both new and old. The scribe is not an archivist, collecting and collating communal memory simply for its preservation, though indeed preservation is an important constitutive element of his or her task. Rather, agents of communal memory keep their ear to the ground and read the signs of the times, so that they can highlight resources in the past that help us see how to imagine alternative possible futures into which we might live now. The scribe's task cannot be described as "essentially a project of retrieval" — it is more a case of reminding us that, wherever we happen to find ourselves, we didn't get there on our own.

Similarly, MacIntyre thinks that a tradition of inquiry, conscious of itself as a living tradition in varying degrees of continuity and discontinuity with its past, is incapable of making an appeal to the past as such.[12] There is no retrieving the past, only remembering it, and memory is conspicuous for its interest in the present. When memory is not used as a resource for current guidance, we call it nostalgia, which, incidentally, is it-

---

10. Cf. Rowan Williams, *Lost Icons: Reflections on Cultural Bereavement* (Edinburgh: T&T Clark, 2000), 151-52: "My 'health' is in the thinking or sensing of how I am not at one with myself, existing as I do in time (change) and language (exchange). Were it otherwise, the self would not be something that could be thought at all."

11. Yoder, *Priestly Kingdom*, 30-32.

12. Alasdair MacIntyre, *After Virtue*, 2nd ed. (Notre Dame: University of Notre Dame Press, 1984), 215: "What I have called a history is an enacted dramatic narrative in which the characters are also the authors. The characters of course never start literally *ab initio*; they plunge *in medias res*, the beginnings of their story already made for them by what and who has gone before.... Of course just as they do not being where they please, they cannot go on exactly as they please either; each character is constrained by the actions of others and by the social settings presupposed in his and their actions."

self characteristically not without particular uses. Here it is helpful to recall a distinction made by Paul Ricoeur in his short but highly instructive essay "Fragility and Responsibility."[13] Appeals to the past are put to different uses, and these uses stem from differing ways to claim responsibility for our actions. Claiming responsibility, Ricoeur argues, calls for recognition of the fragility of human activity that orients us toward the future. The attempt to claim responsibility for our actions is, thus, incomplete if it consists only "in the ability to designate oneself as the author of one's own acts."[14] It is incomplete because, in drawing us toward retrospection, such an account of responsibility fails in two related respects. In the first place, it fails to direct our sense of responsibility "towards the future of a being in need of help to survive and grow," and, in the second place, it fails in that it directs us away from the recognition that it is "always another who declares us responsible, or, as Levinas says, calls us to responsibility."[15] Projects of retrieval in their retrospective orientation thus characteristically secure their executors against important intersubjective aspects of responsibility that are not called forth in the aftermath of action — the responsibility claimed in "I did that" — but have to do instead with how we are rendered accountable by others for the fragile futures we shall have to learn to inhabit — the responsibility claimed in asking of oneself the question, "How shall I now live so as not to alienate others?"[16] All this is simply to suggest one set of reasons why I find Cartwright's focus on retrieval in his comparison of Yoder and MacIntyre less than helpful.

The second set of reasons is more directly concerned with my present purpose. If, as Yoder claims, "the cross is natural" — and I shall reflect

---

13. Paul Ricoeur, *Paul Ricoeur: The Hermeneutics of Action*, ed. Richard Kearney (London: Sage, 1996), 15-22.

14. Ricoeur, "Fragility and Responsibility," 16.

15. Ricoeur, "Fragility and Responsibility," 16-17.

16. In another context, Ricoeur makes a related set of claims in answering the question, "How is it possible to speak of an ethics of memory?" He writes: "It is possible because memory has two kinds of relation to the past, the first of which . . . is a relation of *knowledge*, while the second is a relation of *action*. This is so because remembering is a way of doing things, not only with words, but with our minds; in remembering or recollecting we are exercising our memory, which is a kind of action. It is because memory is an exercise that we can talk about the use of memory, which in turn permits us to speak of the abuses of memory. The ethical problems will arise once we begin to reflect on this connection between use and abuse of memory." "Memory and Forgetting," in *Questioning Ethics: Contemporary Debates in Philosophy*, ed. Richard Kearney and Mark Dooley (London: Routledge, 1999), 5-11. The quote is from p. 5.

on this phrase more fully elsewhere — then the contrasts Cartwright draws between Yoder and MacIntyre are overdrawn. We should expect to see continuity between Yoder's and MacIntyre's accounts of living in history, continuities that cannot be undone by focusing on Yoder's particular Christian commitments. This is not quite to say that Yoder's ecclesiology is best construed as an example of MacIntyre's tradition-constituted inquiry; it is rather to say that if the church's life is publicly accessible, lay, and at least partially imitable, then Christians should not be surprised when they find general recommendations for the life of local historical communities that mirror the church in important respects. Nor should they be surprised when they find, though the inference that they will be so surprised might not be drawn strictly from Cartwright, that the church, practicing its "discipleship ethics," has much to learn about being the church from those who are not a part of it, even from those with allegedly "broader and more all-encompassing" agendas.

So, given these ambiguities that Cartwright notes in using MacIntyre to read Yoder, is there anything we learn from MacIntyre that will help us think about Yoder and the church? I suggest that there is at least one important lesson; that is, MacIntyre's account of dependency and desire disabuses Christians reading Yoder of voluntarist trends in their ecclesiologies. In *Dependent Rational Animals* MacIntyre investigates two interrelated questions that he thinks have "received insufficient attention within moral philosophy." The questions — "'Why is it important for us to attend to and to understand what human beings have in common with members of other intelligent animal species?' and 'What makes attention to human vulnerability and disability important for moral philosophers?'" — might be seen as MacIntyre's admission that he was too quick in his earlier work to dismiss as irrelevant Aristotle's metaphysical biology, or his view that ethics is partly dependent upon biology.[17] In other words, MacIntyre has come to see that biology has profound implications for ethics and therefore ought to shape how we think about legitimate and illegitimate forms of dependence and independence, precisely the point at which his account of tradition constituted inquiry comes under strenuous attack.

MacIntyre argues the significance of biology for ethics in two interrelated ways. First, he claims that an account of ethics that prescinds from considerations of the characteristics humans share with other animals will tend to misconstrue the forms of life humans inhabit. As he puts it:

17. MacIntyre, *Dependent Rational Animals*, ix-x.

> No account of the goods, rules and virtues that are definitive of our moral life can be adequate that does not explain — or at least point us towards an explanation — how that form of life is possible for beings who are biologically constituted as we are, by providing us with an account of our development towards and into that form of life.[18]

If, in other words, human beings are constituted so as to be tutored into the achievement of a specifically human end or set of ends, then any account of how human nature is so tutored will need to be cognizant of the capacities that direct us toward the achievement of some ends and away from others. For example, Gregory of Nyssa, the fourth-century Cappadocian father, argues in his treatise *De Hominis Opificio* that human beings are rational creatures ordered toward the love of God. Although Nyssa thinks that humans may consider our rational nature in abstraction from our animal nature, nevertheless the way our bodies are shaped is not incidental to our rationality, for our minds operate according to our senses. Consider, he asks in effect, what would happen if humans had no hands but were four-legged like the cattle. We then would need to grasp our food with our mouths, tearing grass out of the ground by its roots, and thereby developing strong lips and tongues, insufficiently subtle for the production of clear speech. And if, Gregory reasons, we were unable to speak clearly, we would lack the rationality proper to us, for which speech and language are constitutive requirements. Not to put too fine a point on it, for Nyssa human rationality is inseparable from speech, and speech-using is inseparable from hand-having.[19]

Second, MacIntyre argues that failing to understand "our initial animal condition . . . and the light thrown upon it by a comparison between humans and members of other intelligent animal species will obscure crucial features of that development."[20] If, to extend Nyssa's illustration, we fail to ask what human hand-having has to do with human life in a way that distinguishes it from bovine life, then we will likely be blind to some of the necessities for human flourishing, like the capacity for clear speech. Another such blindness, MacIntyre says, "of immense importance on its own account, is the nature and extent of human vulnerability and disability."[21]

---

18. MacIntyre, *Dependent Rational Animals*, x.

19. Gregory of Nyssa, *De hominis opificio* 10.1, in *PG* 44:151. Cf. Thomas Aquinas, *Summa Theologiae* I. 91. 3 ad. 3.

20. MacIntyre, *Dependent Rational Animals*, x.

21. MacIntyre, *Dependent Rational Animals*, xi.

My contention is that by attending to MacIntyre's account of the place of vulnerability and disability in any conception of human flourishing — if it is to be robust — we may come to see how the rule of Paul and the fullness of Christ shape Yoder's understanding of the church as a voluntary community in ways that heretofore have been undervalued.

That we are vulnerable, that we all face the prospect, if not the actuality, of living in various forms of disability, may seem so obvious as hardly to need stating. Yet moral and political philosophers, if they treat vulnerability and disability at all, have characteristically accounted for them as exceptions to the norm of practical rationality and, moreover, as exceptions to be avoided where possible. It is by now common enough to hear criticisms advanced against the whole of Western moral philosophy since Plato as adopting "the view from nowhere." Yet that nowhereness is strikingly particular: it consists in the assumption that to be effective moral agents capable of realizing our individual good or goods we must secure the capacity to be free of the forms of dependence on others, social institutions, and even our own bodies, that might inhibit us in the realization of the good. Aristotle, who, it must be said, paid uncommon attention to the place of dependence on others in the moral life, nevertheless located the magnanimous man — gender is not incidental for him — as the paradigm of virtue, for "what is great in every virtue pertains to magnanimity."[22] Now, the magnanimous man

> takes moderate delight in great and desirable honors, receiving good things as his own or less than his due. In his opinion, honor is not an appropriate tribute to perfect virtue, but still he accepts it from men who have nothing greater to bestow on him.... Moreover, he will observe moderation about wealth, power, good fortune, and adversity, no matter what may happen. He will not be exalted by prosperity nor cast down by misfortune, nor does he even regard honor as if it were a very great thing. Power and wealth should be desirable for the sake of honor; and those who possess them seek to be honored by reason of them. But a man to whom honor is a trifle will place little value on the other things. For this reason the magnanimous seem to be disdainful.... The magnanimous person likes to remember those he benefits but not those by whom he is or was treated generously. That man is less noble who gratefully receives benefits than he who bestows them.

22. Aristotle, *Nicomachean Ethics*, trans. Martin Ostwald (Upper Saddle River, NJ: Prentice Hall, 1999), 1123b 29-30.

> Hence it is in the bestowal that the magnanimous man wants to be eminent. . . . The magnanimous person likes to show himself in need of nothing or hardly anything, but to minister to the needs of others promptly.[23]

So construed, magnanimity consists in the structured and habitual denial of dependence, not only on external material goods, but also on other people's estimations of one's worth. Notice, however, that magnanimity is not in Aristotle's terms a species of arrogance, for arrogance pertains only to those who do not legitimately possess a virtue they claim. Rather, magnanimity is as close to happiness, *eudaimoneia*, as one can attain prior to death, for it involves the ability not to be inappropriately affected by things that can change. The magnanimous person is one whose life is constrained by chance in only the barest minimum of ways and who therefore stands the greatest chance of exhibiting true virtue over the unity of an entire life. It follows that the magnanimous man will avoid vulnerability as such, to the point of disliking the memory of those things he received from others that put him in a position to cultivate the virtues in the first place. Disability, no matter how trifling or temporary, will almost certainly involve the loss of magnanimity and therefore of happiness.[24]

Despite Aristotle's focus on magnanimity he not only, as I have said, pays uncommon attention to the place of dependence in the moral life — in books 8 and 9 of the *Ethics*, dependence takes the shape of friendship — but he also furnishes us with a set of tools appropriate for further excavating the place and importance of appropriate dependencies in human life. Therefore he lies at the root of MacIntyre's reflections on dependence and vulnerability. Nevertheless, MacIntyre writes that

> Aristotle . . . anticipated [Adam] Smith — and a great many others — in importing into moral philosophy the standpoint of those who have taken themselves to be self-sufficiently superior and of those who take their standards from those who take themselves to be self-sufficiently superior. And he also and correspondingly anticipated them in being

---

23. Aristotle, *Nicomachean Ethics*, 1124a 5-9, 13-20; 1124b 12-14, 17-18.
24. For further discussions of the importance of the magnanimous man for Aristotle's ethics, as well as a discussion of the differences between Aristotle's conception of human flourishing and that embodied in Christianity, see Stanley Hauerwas and Charles Pinches, *Christians Among the Virtues: Theological Conversations with Ancient and Modern Ethics* (Notre Dame: University of Notre Dame Press, 1997), esp. chs. 1, 2, 3, and 5.

"Love One Another"

unable to give due recognition to affliction and dependence. Nonetheless when we try to remedy this injury to moral philosophy, it will turn out . . . that we have to draw to a quite remarkable extent upon Aristotle's concepts, theses and arguments.[25]

It is not that Aristotle and the modern moral philosophers he anticipated were wrong to place a premium on our capacity for acting as independent rational agents. To MacIntyre's mind, the problem arises when modern moral philosophy so single-mindedly focuses on independence that it is blinded to the forms of sociality, and therefore of dependence, in which independent practical deliberation takes place, and without which it is unintelligible. Thus, MacIntyre argues that "the virtues of independent rational agency need for their adequate exercise to be accompanied by what [he calls] the virtues of acknowledged dependence."[26] Failing such an acknowledgment, we shall be liable to misunderstand distinctively human rational agency.[27]

MacIntyre's description of the virtues of acknowledged dependence asks what is necessary for human beings to develop out of infantile forms of dependence, which consists in "the immediate satisfaction of felt bodily wants."[28] Emerging from infantile dependence involves both the transformation and the management of our desires. But such transformation is insufficiently characterized if it is conceived primarily as a change in the object of desire. That what we want will change over time will generally be the case, yet we will not have successfully developed from infantile desire if we simply substitute new things we want for old ones. Infantile desire, it turns out, is not only about which things we want (food, sleep, clean clothing, attention); it is also about how we want them. As Aristotle might have

---

25. MacIntyre, *Dependent Rational Animals*, 7.
26. MacIntyre, *Dependent Rational Animals*, 8.
27. For the purposes of this discussion I bracket MacIntyre's arguments concerning how human beings share and do not share forms of life with other intelligent animal species. The arguments are not insignificant for moral philosophy, but their importance for Yoder's account of the church as a voluntary society seems to me limited to the recognition that the capacities to hold beliefs and to form judgments require life in and through forms of sociality that contribute to our conception of what it means for a certain species to flourish. The rationalities of intelligent animal species (humans included) have this much at least in common: that they are functions of time (change) and communication (exchange). Cf. the important third chapter, "Ethics as Language," of Herbert McCabe, *What Is Ethics All About?* (Washington: Corpus, 1968), 68-103.
28. MacIntyre, *Dependent Rational Animals*, 68.

said, it is difficult to know how to want the right things, at the right time, with the right people and in the right way. And in our culture, as I have said, most of us have a tough time with difficulty. Rowan Williams, in his book *Lost Icons,* reflects on the contemporary persistence of something like infantile desire. He writes:

> Our (North Atlantic) culture fosters, even in some senses rewards, a privileging of the reactive over the active in our relations with the world. We become used to the pressure of stimuli that are calculatedly and habitually addressed to the more transient kinds of emotion, hunger for rapid gratification; which also means that the frustrated emotional hunger, the desire that meets a shock, an unprecedented check, is overwhelmed with panic, the sort of panic that shuts out other habitual considerations as to how I manage my environment.[29]

Williams here has put his finger on the widespread and subcutaneous demands in late capitalism for immediacy and self-transparency that inhibit our ability to reflect on our wants. Yet MacIntyre says that if we as human beings are to develop from infantile desire and hence dependence on others into the dependencies appropriate for independent practical reasoners, we must learn to evaluate the reasons for our actions. And in the course of developing the capacity to evaluate our reasons for acting, "to make or presuppose a judgment that it is best for me here and now to act so as to satisfy this particular desire," we often find ourselves in situations where practical deliberation is murky at best.[30] This, MacIntyre contends, is the case for at least two reasons.

In the first place, as we learn to identify not only differing desires but also different kinds of desire, we often find it extraordinarily difficult to rank or even name those desires so as to be in a position to deliberate about them.[31] The demand for self-transparency meets altogether proper but nonetheless significant obstacles when I am asked to reflect on what I want and why. Perhaps this kind of unclarity suggests something of why

---

29. Williams, *Lost Icons,* 140. Cf. McCabe, *What Is Ethics All About?:* "A certain distortion of the nature of man is built into the capitalist culture which makes it difficult for us to recognise ourselves for what we are, to recognise, in fact, what we *want*" (p. 60).

30. MacIntyre, *Dependent Rational Animals,* 69.

31. So McCabe: "Human morality is entirely concerned with doing what I want to do, but in man too we have to reckon with several levels of wanting, and we can only truly do what we want, only truly be free, if we get the priorities right" (*What Is Ethics All About?* 45).

"Love One Another"

contemporary psychological counseling has had to make it a priority to help patients cultivate ways of reflecting on their felt wants and needs, which, for a wide variety of reasons remain unnamed. In this respect it may be appropriate to think of certain strands of psychological counseling as but the institutionalization of the recognition that because my own desires are often not transparent even to me, I will need help from others if I am to become able to deliberate about my wants and needs.

I think it is important to linger for a bit over this notion of psychotherapy as the institutionalization of the obstacles met in the everyday demand for self-transparency, self-possession, and security. Psychotherapy has often been criticized for providing nothing more than a series of techniques for "getting what I want," as a palliative that restores patients' comfort with infantile desires and dependence, or as a stimulus to egoistic development (here's a problem I'm encountering; give me the equipment to flex my psychological muscles in overcoming it). In these ways it aids and abets the cultural assumption that we should be transparent to ourselves. In another respect, however, some kinds of psychotherapy have become, since their encounter with Heidegger, important arenas for the organized frustration of infantile desire, in which the contradiction between my identification with my wants and the things that would be necessary to realize them is not ameliorated at the level of gratification. Rowan Williams, again in *Lost Icons*, comments on the therapeutic dimensions of such frustration:

> You may begin analysis assuming that what will happen is the learning of truths that already exist but are hidden (never yet brought to consciousness); and this learning is to be facilitated by a skilled professional who is able to give you an authoritative account of what you really mean, what is really going on. When "transference" occurs, when the person being analysed makes a substantial emotional investment in the analyst, this is all about the analyst's position as the person who has something I desire. But the critical importance of working through transference lies in the handling of the frustration, the sense of betrayal, experienced when the analyst refuses to tell me or give me what I want. My perspective, as the person undergoing analysis, is that . . . there is an Other in whom is the secret that will heal me or satisfy me, that will answer to my desire in such a way that I no longer feel the pain of desiring. When the analyst refuses to gratify me, to reveal (or indeed to *become*) the answer to my desire, refuses to put an end to my

pain, then and only then may I perhaps begin to understand what a self is and what it isn't.³²

The frustration that Williams identifies as involved in working through transference is, it seems to me, analogous to the dependence on others that MacIntyre thinks necessary for persons to emerge from infantile dependence into independent practical reasoners. Analogous, I say, because there is a central difference: in the psychotherapeutic relationship the otherness of the analyst characteristically disappears in the analysand's emergent awareness that the analyst represents an otherness he or she can never fully inhabit. The analyst is the "vanishing mediator" of the subject's desire, disappearing in the analysand's correction of his or her fundamental error, namely, the failure to conceive of the "self" as desire and, as such, incomplete. Sebastian Moore puts the point with lapidary economy: "A person is a relationship of which the other is infinite."³³

For the acknowledgment of virtues of dependence appropriate to MacIntyre's conception of independent practical reasoners, however, it is absolutely crucial that others persist in the particularities of their otherness. The "other" is here not the deep structure of the desiring self, but the difference of people who make demands on us. Hence, what goes understated in many accounts of psychotherapy today is the nature of appeal to authority. We are not dependent on other people simply for the naming and working through the frustration of our desires, whatever they may be. We also properly depend on others to tell us what it would be good for us to do. MacIntyre discussed the contemporary ambivalence toward authority in practical deliberation ably in *After Virtue*.³⁴ In *De-*

---

32. Williams, *Lost Icons*, 150-51.
33. Moore, *The Fire and the Rose Are One*, 51.
34. See *After Virtue*, 30-31. There, as in *Whose Justice? Which Rationality?*, MacIntyre makes the case with reference to Philip Rieff, *The Triumph of the Therapeutic: Uses of Faith After Freud* (New York: Harper & Row, 1966). MacIntyre's comments in *Whose Justice? Which Rationality?* are interesting given the difference between his stance and Williams's, which I am here attempting to draw out. MacIntyre writes:

> The problem of the self in liberal society arises from the fact that each individual is required to formulate and to express, both to him or herself and to others, an ordered schedule of preferences. Each individual is to present him- or herself as a single, well-ordered will. But what if such a form of presentation always requires that schism and conflict within the self be disguised and repressed and that a false and psychologically disabling unity of presentation is therefore required by a liberal order?
>
> Those who have most cogently identified the relevant kind of schism and conflict

pendent Rational Animals, he supplements his earlier discussion with the recognition that

> What is or would be good or best for me is something on which, apart from the fact that generally and characteristically I know more about myself than others do, I may in many and crucial respects be no more of an authority than some others and in some respects a good deal less of an authority than some others.[35]

Apart, then, from contexts of practical deliberation in which it is the naming and ordering of desires that is at stake, a second kind of unclarity can present itself in which we simply lack the relevant resources on which to draw in order to know how best to act. And our reliance on the authority of others in cases such as these is not for MacIntyre, as it was for Kant, an indication of our failure as independent practical reasoners. It is no accident that the examples MacIntyre adduces as instances of appropriate dependence on others parallel those Kant decried in the opening paragraphs of his essay, "What Is Enlightenment?": physicians and teachers (MacIntyre, conspicuously, does not name priests). Our self-knowledge, that is, "depends in key part upon what we learn about ourselves from others, and more than this, upon a confirmation of our own judgments about ourselves by others who know us well, a confirmation that only such others can provide."[36]

MacIntyre's point is that, in situations where we either don't know

---

> within the self, such as Freud and Jacques Lacan, have often not appeared to be threatening the liberal view of the self by their views, because along with diagnosis they have offered their own therapeutic remedies. And within liberalism's social and culture order there has therefore not surprisingly been a preoccupation with the therapeutic, with means of curing the divided self. (347)

In failing to note that Freud and, to an even greater degree, Lacan present the "means of curing the divided self" precisely as the recognition that subjective schism stems from the incurability of human desire, MacIntyre, to my mind, betrays a key part of his thesis concerning the importance of sociality to human moral development. That betrayal becomes apparent in *Dependent Rational Animals,* where he limits his account of the move from infantile dependence to independent rational agency to the capacities for assessing reasons for acting, on the one hand, and evaluation of the good, on the other. Yet, part of what it means to emerge from infantile dependence, and thus to learn to desire the right things rightly, is that the very fact of desiring is part of what it means for humans to flourish qua humans.

35. MacIntyre, *Dependent Rational Animals,* 71.
36. MacIntyre, *Dependent Rational Animals,* 94.

what we want or lack the relevant skills to deliberate about the good, we find ourselves paralyzed in our ability to reflect on our actions unless we depend on others to aid us in our development as independent practical reasoners. Those others enter the history of our development in various social contexts, contexts in which I am dependent on others in that they provide the resources for my emergence as an independent practical reasoner, as well as contexts where my dependence on others consists in their reliance on me as a provider of the resources they need in order to flourish as human beings. And commonly, particular others will enter into the history of my moral development as both resources and the occasion for my resourcefulness.

On MacIntyre's view, then, we realize both that our development as independent practical reasoners is something to which others make essential contributions, and that those contributions take the form of social relationships extended through time. Investigating the kinds of relationship that provide the context for both our emergence and sustenance as independent practical reasoners will be of paramount importance if human beings are to flourish in the aspects of their lives to which those relationships are addressed.

Now, what I am suggesting is that it is useful in understanding Yoder's conception of the church as a voluntary community to think about the church as that form of social dependence without which humans cannot become capable practical deliberators about the goods internal to Christianity. In particular, it helps us to understand what Yoder means when he says that

> Communities which are genuinely voluntary can affirm individual dignity (at the point of the uncoerced adherence of the member) without enshrining individualism. They can likewise realize community without authorizing lordship or establishment. The alternative to arbitrary individualism is not established authority but an authority in which the individual participates and to which he or she consents. The alternative to authoritarianism is not anarchy but freedom of confession.[37]

The deep temptation, which I noted at the beginning of this chapter, is to read this passage and others like it as advocating a contractarian conception of community, a going-together appropriate to like-minded people

---

37. Yoder, *Priestly Kingdom*, 24-25. And notice that, here, a community that is genuinely voluntary seems to mean simply one to which you do not have to belong.

who agree to cooperate instrumentally in the pursuit of some perceived good or set of goods. But just insofar as community is conceived of as an instrument, tool, or mere means of pursuing goods knowable in abstraction from the life of the community, its members will remain subject, no doubt in varying degrees, to infantile forms of dependence, not because they have no choice about which others on whom they will need to depend in order to secure the goods they pursue, but rather because they will not be able to conceive of the community as the arena in which they must be dependent on others in order to have their desires transformed so as to pursue the goods of which the community is itself the embodiment.

Notice that I am not arguing that Yoder courts this misreading because he fails to disavow contractarianism and the conception of voluntariety correlative to it. Indeed, in *Body Politics* he says precisely that the kinds of social dependence required by voluntary communities like the church translate "into social ethics, in ways that cannot be reduced either to individualism plus social contract on the one hand or to corporatism and subsidiarity on the other, although it will support some of the criticism that each of those theoretical systems directs against the others."[38] The point is rather that in a society as hypersensitized to an at least partly mythical notion of totalitarian excess as is ours, it becomes extraordinarily hard to imagine "healthy" forms of dependence that are non-individualistic. Consequently, contractarian misreadings of Yoder's ecclesiology are the most likely misreadings to emerge.

Now it is all very nice for Yoder, or me for that matter, to say that his conception of the voluntary church is non-voluntaristic, but that claim will lack legs unless we display how the church represents an alternative to individualism-plus-social contract (mis)conceptions of community. The first part of this chapter, with its excursus on MacIntyre, was meant to prepare for such a display by helping us to reflect on the extent to which independent practical reasoning and "individual dignity" require and rely on forms of social dependence that are not primarily the product of choices abstracted from the social contexts in which they arise. Moreover, MacIntyre helps us to see that we do not simply approach relationships with ready-made desires, but that relationships are also things we do in which our desires are modified, clarified, and redirected, precisely by the presence of others who trust and rely on us, and in and on whom we also learn

---

38. John Howard Yoder, *Body Politics: Five Practices of the Christian Community before the Watching World* (Nashville: Discipleship Resources, 1992), 50.

to trust and rely. Correspondingly, we also learn in relationships of interdependence to cultivate expectations of each other, which, outside contexts of mutual trust and reliance, would be inappropriate in that they would trap us in infantile forms of dependence. By attending to MacIntyre in this way, I hope we are now in a position to begin to reflect with Yoder on how participation in a particular community, the church, can not only obligate us to fulfill expectations that would otherwise be inappropriate, like Paul's expectation that we owe each other love, but also provide the conditions under which such love might take a concrete social shape.

To my mind, in Yoder's work the ecclesial practices designated as the fullness of Christ and the rule of Paul are the clearest expressions of what he and the other participants in the Concern group had come to realize in their encounter with the older generation of Mennonite leaders, particularly Harold S. Bender, namely, that questions of the shape of ecclesial authority and the very structure of the church itself are not incidental to the church's posture when faced with identifiable social ethical "issues."[39] What the fullness of Christ and the rule of Paul do in particularly visible ways is to routinize the church's acknowledgment that each of its members is accepted, given and requiring time and social space, treated not only as a potential answer to the felt wants and needs of others in the community but also as a focus for attention and fascination in his or her own right.[40] When the apostle Paul wrote in various contexts throughout the epistolary

---

39. I will not repeat Yoder's detailed accounts of either practice. Put briefly, the fullness of Christ refers to the apostolic church's practice of defining a "diversity of enablements" within its body that led to and expressed itself as a process of sharing roles in the congregation. In so doing, the church both *relativized* hierarchical patterns of leadership and *directed* the function of each member toward the good of the community as a whole. See *Body Politics*, 47-60, and the important but often misunderstood chapter of *The Politics of Jesus: Vicit Agnus Noster* (Grand Rapids: Eerdmans, 1994), "Revolutionary Subordination." The rule of Paul (1 Cor. 14) builds on the vision of the diversity of gifts attested by the church's practice of the fullness of Christ by prescribing a model for intra-ecclesial dialogue that foregrounds listening to others so as to ensure the acknowledgment of each member's gifts within the body. Both practices function on the assumption that because the Holy Spirit is present and active in the gathered community, the best way to discern the will of God is through patient attentiveness to the voice of each member. Moreover, we might consider these practices apropos of Herbert McCabe's comments concerning ethics as communicating with people: "It means being prepared to give up the security of my present self to venture into a larger context. It means a constant criticism of the identity that is offered to me by my current language and other media of communication" (*What Is Ethics All About?* 114). On the Concern group, see p. 14 above.

40. Cf. Rowan Williams, *Lost Icons*, 155, on the experience of being in love.

"Love One Another"

literature of the New Testament about the diversity of spiritual gifts within the Christian movement, he was not (only or merely) making the point made since within humanistic anthropologies that each person is unique — itself a truthful statement that is hard for many of us to hear without overly sentimentalizing it. Paul rather, says Yoder, organizes his discussion of the ecclesial recognition of each member around the diversity of gifts, not simply as an awareness of ubiquitous unique qualities, but as social functions appropriate to the body of Christ and (therefore) empowered by the Holy Spirit.[41]

---

41. A word about this "therefore." Yoder's argument runs like this: because certain roles within the life of the church "show themselves" (in the Wittgensteinian sense) as contributing to its upbuilding, we know that the capacity to fill those roles is a gift of the Holy Spirit. The claim is one about how Christians discern gifts; it is not about evacuating pneumatology either into Christology or an ungraced sociology. It is safe, I think, to say that just as Yoder had no use for a pneumatology that is not given its specific shape by the church's encounter with Jesus, so also he had no use for the notion of a sociology prior to or abstracted from grace. This is of paramount importance in two connections.

First, it is central to understanding what his deployment of the church/world dichotomy is not, for, if we fail to realize that (to use somewhat "un-Yoderian" terms) nature is always-already graced, we will not be able to make sense out of a statement like this: "Church and world are not two compartments under separate legislation or two institutions with contradictory assignments, but two levels of pertinence of the same Lordship" (*Body Politics*, ix). To put it pointedly, if nevertheless hermetically, to get Yoder wrong on spiritual gifts is to undermine his critique of sectarianism.

Secondly, Yoder has been criticized for eliminating the "vertical dimension" of the church's encounter with God by reducing to social processes the ways in which the church is incandescent to grace. He has similarly been censured for evacuating Christianity of its "existential" and "spiritual" volume. So, for instance, A. James Reimer, in "The Nature and Possibility of a Mennonite Theology," says both that the "strong urge in Yoder to *de-spiritualize* the *kerygma* and to de-emphasize the cultic and ritual (the priestly sacramental) dimension of the early Christian message and religious experience in general fails to adequately meet the crisis of the modern age in which this mystical, contemplative, sacramental quality of life has lost out to technical and historical reason" and that "Yoder's emphasis on the social-political-ethical significance of the New Testament message is rooted in a theological method that is fundamentally historical-eschatological (horizontal) in nature and entails a tacit bias against a metaphysical and ontological (vertical) understanding of the Christ event." See Reimer, *Mennonites and Classical Theology: Dogmatic Foundations for Christian Ethics* (Kitchener, ON: Pandora, 2001), 169-70. While prescinding from an evaluation of the usefulness of Reimer's categories (historical-eschatological : horizontal :: metaphysical-ontological : vertical) it does seem clear from Yoder's text that he considers the practices of the church to be pneumatologically driven in a way that is more concerned to discipline "what counts" as spirituality, existentiality, and metaphysics than it is to deny their validity as grammars Christians might use to talk about their faith. The currently renewed interest in

This, in turn, makes sense only within a context of dialogical vulnerability where the capacity for being heard is not a function of the volume of one's voice or of the insistence with which one pursues one's own desires, but is rather a function of the community's social shape in which the freedom to be heard is coupled with the freedom to hear, both of which freedoms will be derailed by contractual conceptions of voluntariety, which operates, as we have seen, in the register of filling up each other's stipulated wants and needs, and so objectifying and instrumentalizing the ways in which particular others function for us. For Yoder, the rule of Paul and the fullness of Christ inscribe into the very heart of the church practices that resist the objectification of otherness. In these practices the church "shows itself" as an exception to the objectification which elsewhere — even and perhaps especially in its own life — is always possible and sometimes desirable.[42]

By contrast, a community organized by practices that foreground dialogical vulnerability will discover a way of living together that is more than the ability to meet each other's needs. That every member of the church is specifically empowered by the Holy Spirit, and that therefore every member of the community is to be the focus for attention — in other words, is to be listened to — is to discover the kind of dependence on each other that is best described as both joyful and charitable: joyful, because, in recognizing each member's participation in its life as an ongoing and developing set of relations, the community will expect to be surprised by emergent dimensions of its life that it could not have anticipated; charitable because the expectation it cultivates for the unexpected requires the patience to relate to those within its midst, as well as to those outside it, generously.

All of this needs a good deal more unpacking, but what is clear is how difficult it would be to capture the life of the church organized by the rule of Paul and the fullness of Christ within post-Enlightenment conceptions of

---

"Chalcedonian" and "neo-Chalcedonian" Christology, and particularly that of Maximus the Confessor, is a hopeful but to my mind inadequately explored arena for helping us to see how social process and sacramental language are not two discrete terms of a zero-sum game, which I take to be Yoder's point throughout *Body Politics*. This is to say that, whereas Reimer's interest in retrieving the resources of "classical theology" for contemporary Christian ethics is one with which I am in deep sympathy, I do not think he will find there means for critiquing Yoder's theology as reductionistic.

42. Cf. Jean-Luc Marion, "The Formal Reason for the Infinite," in *The Blackwell Companion to Post-Modern Theology*, ed. Graham Ward (Oxford: Blackwell, 2001), 410-11.

voluntariety, because these practices evoke the sense of dependence on others that is beyond the sphere of mutually acknowledged needs.

The Fullness of Christ, the Rule of Paul, the Economy of the Gift, and the Image of God

By delineating various ecclesial practices that move outside the registers of contractarian voluntarism, Yoder's thought enables a set of convergences with other Christian theologians that might not at first glance be apparent. There is, I think, a certain rapprochement with those theologians who, in conversation with Continental phenomenological philosophy, have begun to investigate the intelligibility of an economy of the gift. In the remainder of this chapter, I shall discuss this convergence via a return to the theology of John Milbank, and show how these considerations elucidate in important respects how the voluntary character of the church is transfigured by the practices of dialogical vulnerability. I begin with Milbank's discussion of the economy of the gift.

Something of the language of gift has already arisen in Chapter One, where I discussed Yoder's and Milbank's common sense that salvation is to be thought about by Christians in non-individualistic ways, that is, that salvation is "only in common." In the course of that discussion, however, it became apparent that Milbank and Yoder conceive differently of the place of the church within the *via salutis*. Consequently, in Chapter One I explored the possibility that Milbank's metanarrative realism commits him to a Constantinian ecclesiology that undermines his conception of an ontology of peace. That ontology of peace, for reasons I shall elucidate shortly, is in Milbank's theology nearly synonymous with an economy of gift. Here, therefore, I want to supplement the discussion of Chapter One by further investigating how Milbank's conception of gift both enables and delimits his thought about the church.

In "The Midwinter Sacrifice" Milbank continues his ambitious project of narrating Christian theology's overcoming of secular metaphysics in its modern and postmodern guises by differentiating the Christian economy of gift from the notions of gift given currency by Jan Patočka, Jacques Derrida, and Jean-Luc Marion.[43] Milbank's thesis in this essay is that unilat-

---

43. John Milbank, "The Midwinter Sacrifice," in *The Blackwell Companion to Post-Modern Theology*, 107-30; originally published in *Christian Ethics* 10:2 (1997). Milbank's em-

eral uses of the logic of gift and donation radicalize a "sacrificial economy" of giving oneself up for the other in a way that renders ethics impossible. The logic of gift that culminates in self-sacrifice is thus immoral (because impossible) and also a deformation of the Christian gospel, in which "the ethical is only imaginable as a mutual and unending gift-exchange, construed as an absolute surrender to moral luck or absolute faith in the arrival of the divine gift, which is grace."[44] How does Milbank substantiate these claims? His argument, compressed, is as follows.

In the first place, contemporary investigations into the economy of the gift claim the concern for securing a space for the ethical found in both classical eudaimonism and Enlightenment ethics as part of their heritage. But eudaimonism always had an uneasy relationship with its stated goal, securing true happiness over the course of an entire lifetime, because fortune, or moral luck, was seen to be both a necessary condition for and the most serious threat to happiness.[45] Since fortune enjoyed this

---

ployment of the logic of the gift is not by any means limited to this essay. See also, e.g., "Can a Gift Be Given? Prolegomena to a Future Trinitarian Metaphysic," in *Rethinking Metaphysics*, ed. L. Gregory Jones and Stephen Fowl (Oxford: Blackwell, 1995), 119-61; "Can Morality Be Christian?" in *The Word Made Strange: Theology, Language, Culture* (Oxford: Blackwell, 1996), esp. 225-29; "Socialism of the Gift, Socialism of Grace," *New Blackfriars* 77:910 (1996): 532-48; "Stones of Sacrifice," *Modern Theology* 12:1 (January 1996): 27-56.

Those Milbank engages around the economy of gift include, but are not limited to, works that take flight from Emmanuel Lévinas, *Otherwise Than Being or Beyond Essence*, trans. Alphonso Lingis (Boston: Martinus Nijhoff, 1981). In particular, Milbank engages Jan Patočka, *Essais hérétiques sur la philosophie de l'histoire*, trans. E. Abrams (Paris: Verdier, 1981); Jacques Derrida, *The Gift of Death*, trans. David Willis (Chicago: University of Chicago Press, 1995); and, in a more positive, if nevertheless critical vein, Jean-Luc Marion, "Esquisse d'un Concept Phénoménologique du Don," in *Archivo di Filosofia* 62:1-3 (1994): 75-94, as well as the view taken in his books, *Reduction and Givenness: Investigations of Husserl, Heidegger and Phenomenology*, trans. Thomas A. Carlson (Evanston, IL: Northwestern University Press, 2002), and *Étant donné: Essai d'une phénoménologie de la donation* (Paris: Presses Universitaires de France, 1997).

44. Milbank, "Midwinter Sacrifice," 121.

45. In "Can Morality Be Christian?" Milbank argues that virtue is by its nature reactive, in that it always shores its practitioners up against some inceptive loss or threat of loss: "Every occasion for every 'good' act is always like this — there is always some initial evil, some deficiency, some threat, some terror, something to be warded off. This condition moreover is never simply passive, never just evil *in itself*, but also always evil towards us, even if what it threatens or disturbs is simply our peace of mind, even if what it assaults is merely our conscience. Hence virtue is paradigmatically heroism, the essence of manhood in action, *virtus*, the male force which sustains the bounds of self, or the bounds of the city. It is that which wards off external danger, so always sustaining both a *here* and an *elsewhere*"

ambivalent relationship to happiness, eudaimonism, taken to its logical outcome, deconstructs itself, and this for at least two reasons: on the one hand, because the very attempt to secure happiness erodes the space for the fortune required if happiness is to be real and not merely illusory, while, on the other, because our deaths prevent us from ever surveying the course of our entire lives in a way that we could legitimately deem ourselves happy.

When, in modernity, eudaimonism gave way to the ethics of Enlightenment, the requirement for securing a space for the ethical was not abandoned. So, paradigmatically in Kant, the ethical is seen as that act alone which is purely free: it is done for no other reason than that duty requires it and is therefore not subject to the chances of fortune. Yet this view, too, is beset by irresoluble tensions, for, as Hegel rightly saw, an act done from duty always stands the chance of being misinterpreted, the agent's intention notwithstanding. Moreover, other-regarding ethics of the Kantian variety falter to the degree that they evacuate the particularities of others into the formality of the moral law.[46] And if, as Kant himself knew, the moral law in its pure formality cannot be thought, then our attempts to maximize happiness while acting on maxims prescribed by the moral law

---

(p. 220). Two things need to be said with respect to this characterization of virtue. (1) Milbank recognizes in "The Midwinter Sacrifice" that lack and threat are not merely restraints externally imposed upon the pursuit of virtue, but are also internal requirements of *eudaimonia*. Happiness must be fragile to be happiness. Hence, the element of compromise in all eudaimonistic ethics. (2) It is unclear that Milbank's account of virtue applies to MacIntyre's supplementation of classical accounts of virtue with the virtues of acknowledged dependence, for the practice of these virtues requires the recognition that vulnerability is not only a threat but also in some respects a positive and ineliminable aspect of the conditions for human flourishing (and here we might also point the question to Aquinas's account of the theological virtues, which as infused nevertheless habitually direct humanity toward supernatural happiness — *Summa Theologiae* I-II 62). Milbank could argue that such a recognition of vulnerability merely further ensconces virtue within a reactive context, but in so doing he would fail to recognize that the interdependence for which MacIntyre's account of the virtues aims does not resist external encroachment as such, but requires that generosity be receptively modulated precisely toward the outside, not now viewed as threat, but also as possibility.

46. So also in "Can Morality Be Christian?": "To respect the other in his nonobjective subjectivity, which is the rule in Levinas as much as in Kant, means only to place first the general community, which is bound together by such respect for generalized otherness (a generality which Levinas only *purports* to overcome).... In morality there is no love for the other nor opening to the other, but always and everywhere a principle of *self-government*, whether of the soul or of the city" (p. 223).

will always be subject, in varying degrees, to the vicissitudes of chance.[47] We inevitably fall away from realizing the moral law in its austerity when we put it into practice; hence, the security sought in duty is, like eudaimonism, internally unstable.

Milbank's claim is that those thinkers whose ontology of the gift leads them to articulate an ethics of self-sacrifice secretly collude with classical eudaimonism and Enlightenment ethics precisely in seeking a way to secure the ethical against contingency and fortune. To put it in terms which Yoder was wont to use, Patočka, Derrida, and Marion are each, in different but analogous ways, committed to the search for moral scratch, a search which, precisely because it occurs in time, can never be definitively prosecuted. With eudaimonism, those who espouse an ethics of self-sacrifice will fail to secure a starting place in happiness, with Kant, they will fail to secure a starting place in duty, and, correlatively, they will fail to secure a starting place in regard for the other. This last is the case both because, in sacrificing ourselves to the other, we lose ourselves (supremely in martyrdom) and because the other whom we profess to regard is herself or himself never a finished project that we could possess in a way that would

---

47. This puts the relation between happiness and duty rather contentiously from a Kantian perspective. For Kant, happiness is both consciousness of the agreeableness of one's life as a whole and the satisfaction of a system of inclinations (*Critique of Practical Reason*, trans. and ed. Mary Gregor [Cambridge: Cambridge University Press, 1997], 20, 63, 122), but it can be in opposition to the principle of morality (pp. 32ff.) in which empirical considerations do not make the slightest difference (p. 78). Yet happiness is, Kant says, required for the determination of the highest good, although in an antinomous way (the relation between happiness and the moral law can be neither analytic nor synthetic) (pp. 92ff.). Kant's solution is to posit an intelligible author of nature who connects happiness in the sensible world with purely intellectual obedience to the moral law (p. 96; but on this point, see Lewis White Beck, "Kant's Two Conceptions of the Will in Their Political Context," in *Kant and Political Philosophy: The Contemporary Legacy,* ed. Ronald Beiner and William James Booth [New Haven: Yale University Press, 1993], 38-49, esp. 43-44; according to Beck, "Kant discovered the law as a product of pure reason and as rendered evident by 'the sole fact of pure reason,' and because he did not have to try to obtain it from the abstract concept of perfection or the concept of Wolff's 'will in general,' it was possible for him to see that the will as 'creator of the law' was an idealization of the spontaneous Willkür. Granted that, Kant did not have to look for exterior motivation for obedience to that law, *nor support it by any appeal to the authority of God or nature*"; emphasis added). Milbank's point is that if we always act toward, with and around particular others, then there can be no purely intellectual determination of the will. Hence, an ethics of duty cannot disregard happiness, or secure it through the positing of some mediating agency — to do so would be to treat happiness as a unilateral gift.

fulfill the requirements for moral scratch. The common factor in the failure of each attempt to gain an untrammeled perspective from which to deliberate morally lies in their underestimation of contingency and fortune.

But what if, Milbank asks — and this is the second point in the progression of his argument — these attempts to secure a space for the ethical fail because ethics does not consist in the search for scratch? "Suppose," he says, "it is the case that to be ethical is not to possess something, not even to possess one's own deed." He continues: "Suppose it is, from the outset, to receive the gift of the other as something that diverts one's life, and to offer one's life in such a way that you do not know in advance what it is that you will give but must reclaim it retrospectively. A total exposure to fortune, or rather to grace."[48] Then an ontology of gift that culminates in the logic of self-sacrifice, and so in an endless tragic postponement of consummation, will be replaced by an economy in which "there is no interval of debt between gift and return (which would reduce gift to a contractual economy) but rather absolute eternal coincidence of gift and exchange in the same moment which is ceaselessly perpetuated."[49] The church, Milbank argues, by participating in Christ's resurrection, practices just such an economy.

Here I think it is important to clarify what Milbank is not saying. He is not saying that Christ's resurrection is the moral scratch that secures a place for the ethical. One could argue that the hope of resurrection is made actual in Christ's resurrection (recall the power of Paul's reflection in 1 Cor. 15) and that therefore Christians need not view their deaths as an insurmountable obstacle to an ethics of self-sacrifice. But this would in a sense be merely to remythologize Christianity in a way that left the commerce between gift and sacrifice intact, to install Christian faith "as a waiting on God — in other words, as a kind of meta-ethical trust that it *will* (beyond perpetual postponement) be given to us to be ethical, given to us again to receive and again to give in such a way that a certain 'asymmetrical reciprocity' or genuine community, will ceaselessly arrive (for now in part and eschatologically without interruption)."[50] Here, the abandonment to grace would not be total, and the requirement to secure a space for the ethical would remain in effect. Or, to put it in other terms, resurrection is not the principal plus interest on a loan paid back in the world to come.

48. Milbank, "Midwinter Sacrifice," 116.
49. Milbank, "Midwinter Sacrifice," 120.
50. Milbank, "Midwinter Sacrifice," 116.

The resurrection of Christ cannot be but the promise of a gift, for if it were, Christianity would rely on the mere *possibility* of resurrection in a quasi-Kantian and thus transcendental fashion (recall Kant's postulate of the soul's immortality) and would not now resist the ontologization of violence by insisting in the life of the church that the history of loss in which we live and act is but itself a "contingent narrative upshot" that admits of the possibility of living otherwise than in accordance with its rules.[51]

Milbank's point goes beyond this installation of the resurrection as the transcendental condition of possibility for the ethical, for, on his account, the resurrection is only good news if Christians can participate in it now, and not merely possess it as a concept. What does such a participation in the economy of gift look like? In the first place, it looks remarkably like Yoder's account of the interpersonal dependencies appropriate to the church practicing the rule of Paul and the fullness of Christ. "Should our polity be restored by grace," Milbank ventures,

> Would not anxiety about our necessary preference for some not others, and our apparent sacrifice of some for others, be eased in the knowledge that we are to love our *neighbors,* because we know that others are loving theirs? In other words we would rediscover that even the conditions of *agape* can only be fulfilled in a polis where each of us exercises a particular — albeit unique and non-indentically repeated — role.... And ... if we lived in an economy of gift we would not be indifferent to the consequences of our acts, now treated like sellable products, but we would "go" with our gifts, and others in receiving them creatively would continue to care for us in this employment.[52]

This view of participating in the resurrection conceived of as an economy of gift that foregrounds reciprocity — "before a gift *can* be given, it must already have started to be received"[53] — highlights the way in which the voluntary character of the church cannot be a species of contractualism. Contracts are what we make in contexts of scarcity, where we need to secure some good against the prospect of its loss. But a "polity restored by grace" operates out of an assumption of plenitude, where the goods we pursue are not threatened and therefore do not need to be guarded or won, but rather draw us into participation in further goods we neither antici-

---

51. Cf. Milbank, "Midwinter Sacrifice," 118.
52. Milbank, "Midwinter Sacrifice," 121.
53. Milbank, "Midwinter Sacrifice," 124.

pated nor supposed we needed. Put differently, because in the life of the church "gift-giving is a mode of social being," because it is a function of time (change) and language (exchange), we are never in possession of the gifts we give in the way that would have to be the case in order to enter into voluntary agreements.[54] So to speak of an economy of gift is to speak of "the surprisingness and unpredictability of gift and counter-gift," of such an economy's "character in space as *asymmetrical reciprocity,* and . . . in time as *non-identical repetition,*" and therefore quite pointedly, "not at all . . . to surrender to the lure of contract."[55] The consequence for conceiving properly of the church is that the demands placed on others by membership in the church will not, of necessity, be inappropriate (unless they are secured by some prior agreement to treat those demands as fitting), for this would be to reduce the exchange involved in gift and counter-gift by treating it as atemporal, as if all the possible ways in which interdependence might develop were in view, needing merely to be arranged spatially vis-à-vis each other.[56]

In the second place, however, Milbank's conception of the economy of gift differs markedly from Yoder's emphasis on church practice in the degree of specificity with which it is treated. One way of putting the point is to note that in Milbank's appeal to Christianity as an economy of gift and a charismatic ethics, he does not take adequate account of the concrete shape of Paul's appeal to gifts in 1 Corinthians and elsewhere. This is the case despite Milbank's claim in "Can Morality Be Christian?" that Paul opposes "the abstract generality of law" with

> the *specificity* of divine gift which always takes the form of particular gifts in the sense of specific talents or *charismata:* these are "different gifts according to the gift given to us" (Rom. 12:6). . . . Each has his own burden to bear, yet as Paul has . . . said that we must bear each other's burdens (Gal. 6:2-4) or in other words that the gifts which are talents

---

54. Milbank, "Midwinter Sacrifice," 124.
55. Milbank, "Midwinter Sacrifice," 123.
56. Here it is perhaps important to stress that for Milbank an economy of gift is always equally an attempt to undo the ethics of self-sacrifice and to unthink the modern spatialized economics. The ethics of self-sacrifice, by installing a static logic for ethical exchange, treats all actual and potential relationships the same and so places all instances of the ethical within an abstract absolutized space, even if the "arrival" of that space is perpetually postponed. See "Midwinter Sacrifice," 126-27, and cf. "On Complex Space," in *Word Made Strange,* 268-92, esp. 277ff.

or roles must be given, passed on, exchanged for the furtherance and education of others, it is clear that there is no denying here of analogical resemblance between "gifts" (in the sense of both presents and talents), since this is the very condition of peace within the body of Christ. Each gift, each talent ("virtue") is absolutely unique, yet each repeats non-identically and so exactly the grace of God which is transcendentally, inaccessibly One.[57]

By "not taking adequate account of the concrete shape of Paul's appeal to gifts" I mean that Milbank nowhere draws attention to the extent to which Paul does not leave it entirely up to the Corinthians (or to the Romans or to the Ephesians) to decide which gifts are pneumatologically given. Paul rather says that the gifts the church should be concerned to identify and cultivate are those that contribute to its order (1 Cor. 14:40). Milbank's insistence on specificity does not take up Paul's concern to say both that everyone is empowered and that there should be decency and order, and this, I think, contributes to a certain shapelessness to Milbank's ecclesiology, noticed already in Chapter One, which is not accidental.

In pointing this out, I am aware that there is a sense in which I am making an argument from silence. That Milbank does not draw attention to Paul's lists of spiritual gifts and to the social shape they confer on the church does not necessarily mean that it is not open to Milbank to do so. Yet, as I say, I do not think his silence on this score is accidental, a product of oversight, or a recognition that Paul adequately said what needed to be said. There are, instead, currents in Milbank's thought that actively inhibit him from giving the church a concrete social shape. What are they?

When Milbank articulates what the economy of gift looks like in practice, he points, not inappropriately, to the eucharist:

> In the eucharistic liturgy, humanity enters in advance into the divine Sabbath, the eschatological banquet and cosmic nuptial, into the realm where once again we can entirely trust our *every* act as good precisely because we know that it will not merely follow our intention but be transformed and given back to us in a different and surprising mode.
>
> Here, therefore, in the Eucharist, we see the only possible paradigm for gift and therefore for ethics, not as one-way sacrifice but as a total surrender for rereception. . . . At this *symposium* and within this

---

57. Milbank, *Word Made Strange*, 227.

connubium, we give up everything, but not for the terrestrial city, and not even primarily for others: here we give up "absurdly" to God in order to confess our inherent nothingness and to receive life in the only possible genuine mode of life, as created anew. Here we hold on to nothing, here we possess nothing securely, in contrast with our exclusively ethical models which are also sacrificial. Here instead we render ourselves entirely prey to the mere good fortune that it might turn out that we have been ethical. But the name of this fortune is secretly grace, the gift or the Good; those names which convey all our Western longing.[58]

This will appear, to people schooled by Yoder, not to be saying very much. Is not the first social ethical meaning of eucharist economic sharing?[59] But to Milbank's mind, an appropriate account of the eucharist, or of any church practice, will necessarily remain underdetermined in terms of its political outworkings. For church practice to be spelled out demonstratively would be to capitulate to a spatialized economy of sacrifice, to assume that this or that practice in its specific contours need no longer be an arena for negotiation and therefore a site and product of provisional judgment. Thus, the way particular histories of church practice align with the economy of gift appears in Milbank as a happy accident and not, as for Yoder, as necessary conditions for the faithful embodiment of the gospel.[60]

In Milbank and Yoder, then, we have two differing ways, one that starts in the logic of the economy of gift and one that starts in church practice, of resisting ecclesiological positivism, that is, of resisting the urge to use the existence of the church itself as a means of getting "handles on history." The question posed by noting the similarities between Milbank's and Yoder's uncouplings of the church from sacrificial economies and contractual voluntarism is therefore not about whether ecclesiology ought to safeguard Christians against the precariousness and risks of living in time. To that question both Milbank and Yoder answer "No," and in so doing echo Edward Schillebeeckx's profound judgment that ecclesiology needs to be done "in a minor key."[61] The question rather concerns whether Milbank's

---

58. Milbank, "Midwinter Sacrifice," 127-28.

59. Yoder, *Body Politics*, 20-21.

60. See, e.g., Milbank, "Enclaves, or Where Is the Church?" *New Blackfriars* 73:861 (June 1992): 341-52, esp. 343-44.

61. Edward Schillebeeckx, *Church: The Human Story of God*, trans. John Bowden (New York: Crossroad, 1990), xix.

economy of gift is adequate to the task of resisting handles on history, or whether the tentativeness with which he approaches describing the economy of gift might not itself be a *refusal* of aspects of that economy required in order to ensure that the gift cannot be abused. That is, given that Milbank uses the economy of gift to argue on theological grounds for contingency ("an utter abandonment to grace") and concrete particularity ("asymmetrical reciprocity" and "non-identical repetition"), is it not problematic to delimit descriptions of the way the church participates in the economy of gift to an account of the eucharist in which what it might mean to "receive life anew" cannot be thematized in practices and habits like the rule of Paul and the fullness of Christ?

In his defense, it might be argued that accounts like Yoder's of the rule of Paul and the fullness of Christ are not necessarily at odds with Milbank's conception of the eucharist, in that they do not necessarily risk securing the church as its own possession. Indeed, this is what he seems to presuppose in his essay "Enclaves, or Where Is the Church?" where he argues that "[t]he Church is only the Church because it imbibes and becomes Christ's body and re-articulates his earthly performance (1 Cor. 10:16-17)."[62] Slightly later, in the context of reflecting on what it means for Christ to be the head of the church, Milbank elaborates:

> If the "head" is a self-giving body, then no-one is submitted to anyone else, but all are submitted to all. Paul may be an apostle, but the Corinthians can be kings without him and he will be happy to rule with them (4:8). The only rule of the Christian economy must be sharing for the sake of equality (2 Cor. 8:2), and in the case of sexual exchange, each spouse must give unstintingly since each "rule" over the other (1 Cor. 7:3-4).[63]

Yet, in Milbank's account, such a rule cannot be ritually given — except as an extension of the logic of gift located in eucharistic celebration — but "can only be guaranteed as an authentic repetition [re-articulation of Christ's earthly practice] if it is genuinely reflected in the improvised 'real-life' of those who transmit it and perform it."[64] And, while he does question the distinction between ritual prescription and improvisation, Milbank's eucharistic thought nonetheless operates on the basis of a

---

62. Milbank, "Enclaves," 344.
63. Milbank, "Enclaves," 345.
64. Milbank, "Enclaves," 346.

homology between ritual and formalism that has the effect of denying normativity to "real-life," such that there can be no rules given for ecclesial order in the sense that Yoder argues is attendant upon the practice of the rule of Paul and the fullness of Christ.[65] Or, to put the point differently, if the rule of Paul and the fullness of Christ, as practices that confer on the church a set of parameters concerning its social shape, were conceived as prescriptions for the practice of an economy of gift rather than fortuitous indications of that economy when it does appear, then that would be to usurp the contingency, surprisingness, and unpredictability necessary for the gift to be received as gift. And this paradoxical need to guarantee contingency sustains Milbank's hesitancy to locate the church geographically, to say, "The church is *here* rather than *there*." For Yoder, by contrast, the "real life" of the church is epistemically and axiologically prior to the deployment of formal theological grammars.

Two comments remain to be made, both of which concern how eschatology fractures Christian judgment. First, it must be said that any attempt to locate the church geographically by focusing on its practices must be provisional. And here Milbank's hesitancy is a helpful reminder that the church is never in possession of itself. Yoder's claims about the rule of Paul and the fullness of Christ do not differ from Milbank's in this respect, for they define the church as a politics constituted by dialogical vulnerability in a way that disables contractual and consensual refractions of ecclesiology. But, and this is the second point, for Milbank the church is a promissory note on the kingdom in a way that it is not for Yoder. For Milbank the church participates, and can only participate, obscurely in the economy of gift because the kingdom has not yet "arrived." Thus, ecclesiology is heavily inflected for Milbank by the grammar of hope, and here he lapses into familiar patterns of prolepsis and eschatological consummation. For Yoder, by contrast, the church is not exactly prolepsis: "The cross is not a detour or a hurdle on the way to the kingdom, nor is it even the way to the kingdom; it is the kingdom come."[66] That recognition of the "objective" once-for-all character of Christ's reconciling of the world to God enables Yoder to be less skeptical than Milbank can be about the extent to which church practice can be a faithful witness to and, as such, participation in God's redemption of creation without lapsing into an ecclesiological reduction of the economy of gift. Correlatively, Yoder is

---

65. Cf. Milbank, "Enclaves," 342, 348.
66. Yoder, *Politics of Jesus*, 51.

more hopeful than Milbank about the prospects for positively locating the church by attending to actual church practices like the rule of Paul and the fullness of Christ.

Finally, then, to take stock: Where does this discussion leave us with respect to my initial suggestion that Yoder's focus on practices that foreground dialogical vulnerability might be construed as commentary on Paul's exhortation to "owe no one anything, except to love one another"? Two points, at least, should be made.

In the first place, Milbank's reflections on the economy of gift help to clarify that love is not, in Moore's terms, a beautiful half-truth, but the product of "an utter abandonment . . . to grace." The character of obligation in an economy of gift is thus released from a contractual economy with its voluntaristic undertone — "I will act so that love might result" — and installed in a new mode of life where the expectation to love each other is not an improper one that must result in ineradicable loss. In an economy whose *telos* is not the security of self-possession we are freed from the anxieties otherwise attendant upon an obligation to love each other. And only a love free of anxiety could after all be love.

In the second place, this is not to say that a love free of anxiety is other than fragile and capable of being frustrated, as any member of a church that recognizes the diversity of gifts and practices an open meeting will tell you. There is no security in the economy of gift, and this has everything to do with the way the church is, for Yoder, voluntary at the point of uncoerced membership. No one has to give up on the project of security; no one has to stop cultivating improper expectations of others; no one has to subject his or her voice to the vulnerabilities of dialogue. And, oddly, because love can neither be coerced nor be coercive, a church practicing the rule of Paul and the fullness of Christ might have room for those voices too. We might paraphrase Yoder thus: the real issue is not whether an economy of gift can make sense in a world obsessed with security, but whether — when it meets us in our world, as it does in fact — we want to participate. We don't have to. "That we don't have to is the profoundest proof of Christ's condescension, and thereby of his glory."[67]

---

67. Yoder, *Priestly Kingdom*, 62.

CONCLUSION

The Labor of Our Redeeming

The focal argument of the preceding two chapters was that practices of patience are necessary characteristics of the church's activity if it is to foster itself as a way of being in time that can learn to envision history as praise. Throughout the entire book I have gestured toward such a learning process as what it means for the church to speak of itself as holy without severing that holiness from its actual life. The difficulty of holiness is maintained by practices of patience like repentance, forgiveness, and reconciliation, like an open meeting, or like faith in the diversity of gifts, and so on. Moreover, this focus on practice renegotiates holiness as a way of being in time. The account of holiness I have gleaned from Yoder therefore draws into coherence a number of other themes that have been adumbrated throughout this book — not only patience, but also difficulty and dispossession. In the remaining pages, I want to draw out a few of these connections.

John Webster is certainly right to insist that Christians speak of the church's holiness as ultimately an "*alien* sanctity, a nonpossessable holiness" that constitutes the church as the ceaseless and ever-new gift of God.[1] If the church's holiness is gift, then it will be difficult to live into that holiness, appropriating it *as gift* and not as a possession to be owned and therefore performed. To put it another way, perhaps equally perplexing, Christian theology will need to take pains not to account for holiness as virtue, perhaps not even as theological virtue. Safeguarding the church's holiness as *donum* is, I take it, part of the point at stake for Thomas Aquinas, who supplemented his account of habit with an account of virtue, supplemented his account of virtue with an account of the infused virtues, and

---

1. John Webster, *Holiness* (Grand Rapids: Eerdmans, 2003), 56.

supplemented his account of the infused virtues with an account of the gifts of the Holy Spirit. On the one hand, the church is drawn forward in a posture of expectation and hope toward the next gift, where it receives itself anew from the hand of God. On the other hand, it will be difficult to continue to receive what the church is given as gift when the gifts accumulate through time. The deposit of gift can form the perception or illusion of a possession, performance, or sanctity that the church can give back to God. That is one risk: it is the risk of turning a superabundance of grace into a foundation for self-assertiveness and narcissism.

Not that self-assertiveness or narcissism would be paraded as such. It is perhaps a peculiarly Protestant temptation to assume that the real risk in ecclesiology is the church's idolatrous capacity to focus solely on its life as the exclusive incarnation of divine grace in the created order, and to assume furthermore that relativizing the church's institutions will successfully correct the imbalance. The danger I have in mind is more subtextual or ideological — namely, that in its attempt to think of its character as gift, another register of the church's speech will be obscured, a register in which the ostensible object of the church's praise and gratitude is always at risk of being arrested into the church's focus on demonstrating or showing itself as *the* embodiment of praise and, concomitantly, for showing how others can be seen as reflections of *this* embodiment. For its life to be praise, the church has to cultivate resources for resisting the expatriation of others, including God, into its own performance. Rowan Williams spoke to this hazard in "Theological Integrity":

> Praise is nothing if not the struggle to voice how the directedness of my regard depends on, is moulded by, something irreducibly other than itself. It is my speech seeking to transmute into its own substance something on whose radical difference that very substance depends; so that it must on no account absorb it into itself as that would be to lose the object's generative power.[2]

Practices of patience, practices that depend on keeping open our capacity to be surprised by the *donum* as *novum*, or by the gospel as promise, practices that allow the church to focus simultaneously on the way it demarcates its borders and hopes for breaches in its walls are necessarily dispossessive traits that require the church to work toward an acknowledg-

---

2. Rowan Williams, *On Christian Theology* (Oxford: Blackwell, 2000), 9.

ment of the substantive abundance of the gift of others as difficult, as not immediately available for recognition. And this is a praxis that will be the occasion not only for growth in recognizing proximities to others but also for the misrecognition of those proximities and the others they implicate.

A second risk, on which the last paragraph touches, is that the church will come to see the opposition between possession and performance, on the one hand, and dispossession and kenosis, on the other, as easy, not itself shot through with equivocation — in other words, as unhistorical. A key interest of the preceding chapters has been to ask what it would mean to resist that opposition, or at least to inquire about history as its constitutive but unrecognized third. Consequently, I drew on the work of O'Donovan, Troeltsch, Volf, MacIntyre, and Milbank to elicit the centrality of patience for Yoder's understanding of how the church lives while awash in the flood of its historicity.

In Chapter One, I argued that Yoder's emphasis on Jesus' imitability shaped his imagination regarding the political importance of Christian eschatological convictions. In contrast to O'Donovan's totalizing picture of the New Jerusalem from heaven (and his account of the healing of creation that is logically distinct from the creation of the church), Yoder argued that salvation is the creation of a way of life among people that encounters the gospel as promise. That promise, to be led where Christ leads, is of its nature open-ended, such that Yoder did not picture eschatology as the closure of borders or, much less, the radical expansion of borders that assimilates otherness into the purity and unity of the holy city. Rather, Yoder thought eschatology demanded the continual opening of the people of God onto new horizons of encounter with otherness — imitating the fusion in the Epistle to the Hebrews of the images of city and camp in the wilderness. Eschatology funds mission, being sent out in praise and with no other purpose than to go outside the camp. Eschatology does not mean that Christians, who believe in the last things, know how to steer the course of history toward those last things.

In Chapter Two, I studied Ernst Troeltsch's historicism for a set of analogies and disanalogies with Yoder's thought about the church's historicity. Troeltsch, I argued, is more important as a source for Yoder's thought about history than he is for understanding the impulses behind Yoder's careful rejection of a typological approach to Christian ethics. In part, this is because *The Social Teaching* should be seen merely as an instance of a more general problematic that Troeltsch discerned while attempting to theorize thinking in the light of time, namely, how to cultivate a conceptually unified field of ethical vision out of the manifold of historically contingent events, while understanding the need to unify experience into a useable whole as but another set of contingencies. Troeltsch addressed the problem by positing eschatological convictions as the final cause of ethical vision. Such a final cause, however, if it was to sustain us in a sober assessment of our historicity, could not be other than purely formal, a goal discerned "in outline and general direction." And, somewhat paradoxically, the pure contentlessness of the eschatological goal stabilized the problem of history for Troeltsch in that it dampened the register of equivocation he thought necessary to a compelling account of history. For Yoder, by contrast, eschatology was not primarily a matter of the future: the entire gospel was eschatological in character. Thus, eschatology had a determinate content for Yoder and functioned as more than a purely formal source of motivation for following one's own best insights. But that very determinate content preserved for Yoder a sense of our awashness in history because it generates an ethos that disavows the mastery of time and contingency in favor of an account of the Christian life as publicity and praise and time as grace.

In Chapter Three I continued to develop an account of the church's way of being in time via Yoder's negotiation of the "Constantinian shift." There I argued that Yoder constantly invoked but rarely engaged the history of the fourth century in his account of the Constantinian captivity of the church. The effect of this was to allow him to posit Constantinianism as something of a narratological trope that disengaged him from the very restitutionist historical practice he thought necessary to the task of proclaiming the gospel faithfully. In other words, Yoder's account of Constantinianism was in some respects methodologically Constantinian. Neither was Yoder's account of Constantinianism notable chiefly for its value as history: its mythistorical character fostered blind spots in inquiries that left his doctrinal and political history in and around the fourth century deeply inadequate. But Yoder's account of Constantinianism does highlight two things. On the one hand, it foregrounds the risk that a self-consciously non-Constantinian theology or ecclesiology could lack integrity, could bolster itself against an encounter with its own outside, by refusing the task of rediscovering things from its past "whose pertinence was not seen before." On the other hand, it also presents the need, which Yoder endorsed, for dialogical practices of negotiation and patience that generate a continual reassessment of our fallible relationships to others, including to our own pasts.

Conclusion

In Chapter Four I returned to the eschatological thematic focus of Chapters One and Two, but now having tempered that set of conversations by the difficulties attendant upon Yoder's negotiation of Constantinianism. An ecclesiology capable of seeing history doxologically, I argued, will have to be repentantly conscious of its own capacity for sanitizing the past, a task that will need to involve practices of forgiveness and reconciliation. Forgiveness is, however, hard work, especially if it is to involve an appropriate response to the pain, violence, and injustice humans inflict on others and on themselves. And, from a certain perspective, an ecclesiology like Yoder's, which promotes a kenotic ethic based in discipleship to a Lord who modeled suffering servanthood, can easily function as a palliative in the face of tremendous human suffering. In order to analyze the risks attendant upon such a vision of the church, I engaged Miroslav Volf's argument that only an eschatological hope in a divinely merciful non-recollection of the past can finally redeem our histories of loss and allow victims to be reconciled with the perpetrators of injustice against them. Practices of forgiveness and reconciliation, Volf argues, are piecemeal and insecure in the here and now, because each of us is inhabited by the memories of the violence of the past that cannot be extirpated without denying our hopes for justice, which is what a kenotic ethic of suffering servanthood would amount to asking us to do. Hung between violence unredeemed and justice denied, Volf pictures salvation as involving the obliteration of at least part of our histories. But if, as I argued throughout the preceding chapters, we are awash in our historicity, it is not clear that such a conception of salvation would be saving *for us*. Consequently, I returned to Yoder, and to his conception of practices of forgiveness and reconciliation as funded by the memory of the violence at the heart of the Christian story, the cross, where Christ, as victim, relinquished control over how his life could be redeemed.

Themes of control and the management of history are the shadow side of the eschatologies deployed by O'Donovan, Troeltsch, and Volf. But the control at stake is more than a drive for intellectual tidiness in telling stories about ourselves in the world. It also has institutional parameters. The dominant sites of identity for each thinker — creation order for O'Donovan, modern society for Troeltsch, and the self for Volf — each require an oppositional relationship to the other, whose difficulty must be mastered and overcome or at least ameliorated. Outside must be converted into inside; the other is necessary in order for otherness to be annulled. Thus, O'Donovan expunges the difficulty of the other in his erasure of the walls of the eschatological city, Troeltsch by orienting the surging manifold of the past to a formal future hope, and Volf by reconciling self and other in an effacement of the history that presented itself difficultly in the first place.

In Chapters One, Two, and Four, I presented Yoder's eschatology as different from the eschatologies presented by these other voices, but in Chapter Five I turned to the institutional parameters of his rejection of the kind of control over history that O'Donovan, Troeltsch, and Volf maintain. Yoder's ecclesiology, I argued, could be portrayed in largely Weberian terms as a voluntary association of believers, or in Hobbesian contractualist terms, but in each case the kinds of dependencies that members of the church cultivate among themselves will be seen as the chosen dependencies of free, autonomous, and rationally calculating individuals. On such an understanding of the church, agreements between people will be matters of happy coincidence and self-interest, and conflict between people will be couched in terms of one person's having placed improper expectations on others. But neither felicitous agreement nor bare oppositional conflict can reflect the practices and processes of negotiation, dialogue, and learning that Yoder thought essential to a church that could genuinely proclaim the gospel while releasing its pretensions of social control within its own polity. To spell out Yoder's conception of the church's voluntariety in a way that distinguishes it from Weberian and Hobbesian refractions of liberal social theory, I examined two ecclesiological practices, the rule of Paul and the fullness of Christ, via Alasdair MacIntyre's account of the virtues of acknowledged dependence and John Milbank's reflections on an economy of gift. The church's voluntary nature, I argued, reflects a fragility and vulnerability that come from giving up handles on history and attempting to live by grace. But this does not mean that the church lacks any social form whatsoever; rather, grace is institutionalized in the church as it cultivates practices that foster dialogical vulnerability as a way of looping back to Jesus. Those practices help it to incarnate a doxological vision of history, a vision not preoccupied with overlaying social or epistemological controls on the borders between self and other, church and world, present (or future) and past.

Patience, eschatology, history, kenosis. These are the principal concepts that I have deployed throughout the preceding chapters in order to develop Yoder's enunciation of an ecclesiology that could see its primary mode of being in time as praise. Praise sounds joyful, but the blood of the martyrs is praise too, as are the banal and everyday judgments about how to live lives together that continue to embody Christ's earthly practice. It was not, therefore, an irenic picture of the church that emerged, but one that foregrounded attention to difficult labors of ecclesiological self-questioning: "Is this what the one without spot or wrinkle is really like?" Nevertheless, throughout my inquiry two criticisms of Yoder have arisen, criticisms that concern lapses in the church's capacity to engage its life as difficult. The first criticism concerned the way Yoder's non-Constantinianism covertly "Constantinianizes" his relationship to the past, just insofar as the past needs to be clear and usable *as Constantinian* in order for an ecclesiological alternative to emerge. I suggested that Yoder's own best insights into the nature of revisionist historiography as an evangelical task were eroded by his commitment to disavowing a Constantinian heritage. The second criticism concerned the way church practice capable of incarnating patience as praise can drown the cries of victims, leaving their demands for justice unrequited. Yoder's historical method and his practices of patience institutionalize responses to these criticisms that see jeopardy as theologically important. They are part of a method that acknowledges the human capacity for misrecognizing the other, or of expatriating the other onto one's own terrain, and thus for potentially damaging relations of power and knowledge. I say Yoder institutionalizes responses to these risks; they nevertheless remain real risks for a church learning to see history doxologically. Indeed, interest in being the church without risk is the threat that lies beneath any response to such criticisms that would lay them to rest.

These criticisms throw me back to the tension between holiness and difficulty, and to the way that agonism can be sublimated into an opposition between possession/performance and dispossession/kenosis. For the truth of the matter is that I long for wounds I can use. And I both hope and fear that I am not alone in this. Many of us want our wounds to have a purpose. We long for the wounds of the past to outfit us for a brighter future, and, convicted of that brighter future, we heal, mend, and transform our relationships to our wounded and wounding pasts. The insidious thing is that practices of patience can easily become ways to use our wounds, to turn dispossession into performance. In an essay on forgiveness and reconciliation, Yoder pointed to just such a possibility:

> *The real tragedy* is not that individuals within the larger society are without guidance and without forgiveness; it is that as *church* we have come to respect as a sign of maturity the willingness to live with directionlessness and with unreconciled divisions and conflicts. We reject as immature or impatient those who would argue that something definitely must or must not be done.

> We make a virtue of the "acceptance" of intolerable situations rather than of the obedience in openness and forgiveness that could transform situations. Especially we have come to "live with" a situation in which, as a defense against "defenders of the faith" whose methods in the past were less than redemptive, we are satisfied with trying to do a decent job day by day without taking responsibility for the direction in which churches and their institutions are evolving. A sense of not knowing where to turn next is pervasive among denominational leaders.[3]

When this happens, will we not be continuing to envision holiness as ownable? And how does using the practices of patience to give purpose to our wounds transform our relation to time, if not by securing for us a place above the waves of relativity after all?

Gillian Rose's haunting epigraph in *Love's Work*, "Keep your mind in hell and despair not," counsels patience on the one hand, but on the other advocates a patience we could not use.[4] For Rose human lives are broken in ways that threaten to call up inhuman responses from us, responses that would repair the breaks in our lives without leaving scars, responses that would disavow brokenness by throwing us backward toward an original purity or forward to an eschatological city whose architecture is pliant to our imaginations here and now. From her first book, *Dialectic of Nihilism*, to the posthumously published *Mourning Becomes the Law* and *Paradiso*, Rose resisted various attempts to imagine human life without risk and thus to repair the brokenness of that life.[5] In so doing she called upon the language of holiness that I have been deploying to characterize Yoder's theology into question. Holiness, in Rose's view, offers a complete solution to political problems by edifying or erasing the boundaries between self and other in a way that denies their mutual implication and the difficulty of their relation. In its interest in edifying or erasing

---

3. Yoder, *The Royal Priesthood: Essays Ecclesiological and Ecumenical*, ed. Michael G. Cartwright (Grand Rapids: Eerdmans, 1994), 350.

4. Gillian Rose, *Love's Work* (London: Chatto and Windus, 1995), 98.

5. In addition to *Love's Work*, I draw on the following titles by Rose: *The Broken Middle: Out of Our Ancient Society* (Oxford: Blackwell, 1992); *Dialectic of Nihilism: Post-Structuralism and Law* (Oxford: Basil Blackwell, 1984); *Hegel: Contra Sociology* (London: Athlone Press, 1981); *Judaism and Modernity: Philosophical Essays* (Oxford: Blackwell, 1993); *Mourning Becomes the Law: Philosophy and Representation* (Cambridge: Cambridge University Press, 1996); *Paradiso* (London: Menard Press, 1999). See also Gillian Rose, "Diremption of Spirit," in *Shadow of Spirit: Postmodernism and Religion*, ed. Philippa Berry and Andrew Wernick (London: Routledge, 1992), 45-56.

boundaries, in Rose's view, holiness bears the marks of "a trauma within reason itself," which she characterized as an opposition between old Athens and new Jerusalem:

> Suddenly, in the wake of the perceived demise of Marxism, Athens, for a long time already arid and crumbling, has become an uncannily deserted city, haunted by departed spirits. Her former inhabitants, abandoning her justice as well as her reason, have set off on a pilgrimage to an imaginary Jerusalem, in search of difference or otherness, love or community, and hoping to escape the *imperium* of reason, truth or freedom.[6]

What is at stake for Rose in this passage is a dualist logic evident in much postmodern thought that severs "existential *eros* from philosophical *logos*," and so represents the other of reason unequivocally. Yet, in so doing, this logic misrepresents both reason and its others, for their diremption "imparts a fixity to them, even if, or precisely when, they are defined as *fluid*.... Far from bringing to light what is difficult out of darkness and silence, difficulty is brought to certainty."[7]

The problem with holiness is that it brings difficulty to certainty by resisting equivocation in two related ways. For Rose, holiness can promote the trauma of reason and exalt ecstatic eros over reason, as, for instance, occurs in the nomadic a/theology of Mark Taylor. Taylor resists equivocation by asserting the claim of reason's other against the restrictions of reason, which is dominating, imperialistic, patriarchal, and so forth.[8] He builds up the bounds between self and other in order to have a relation of pure opposition between them. On the other hand, holiness can resist equivocation by denying the trauma within reason and tearing down the boundaries between reason and its others. Rose argued that this is what occurred in John Milbank's vision of a radically inclusive sociality marked by peacefully proliferating difference. In either case, the relation between reason and its other has ceased being difficult, the subject of negotiation, work, risk, and change through time. And this renders ethics impossible, because, as Rowan Williams put it, "the ethical without risk is powerless — that is, it is incapable of truthfully negotiating the otherness, the differences, that it always contains (in both senses

---

6. Rose, *Judaism and Modernity*, 1.
7. Rose, *Judaism and Modernity*, 4.
8. Rose, *Judaism and Modernity*, 3.

of the word)."⁹ Without risk, without legality, without institutions, how we peaceably "negotiate" life with others can only be posited as a non-representable holiness. Taylor's and Milbank's visions of holiness, as ecstatic eros or as the counter-politics of ontological peace, secretly collude in that they each foster a static and non-negotiable relationship to their others: the first need not talk to the other since accountable speech is no longer possible; the second need not listen to the other since his or her otherness has ceased to be risky.¹⁰

By contrast, in Rose's political imagination, ethics needs institutions that constitute the ground of relation between self and other. Politics, for Rose, did "not begin with a prerogative claim based on the suppression of the 'other,' which installs repetitive dualisms of power and otherness within the protest against power." Instead, Rose continued, "Here it takes three to make a relationship between two: the devastation between posited thought and being, between power and exclusion from power, implies the universal, the third partner, which allows us to recognize that devastation."¹¹ In keeping with her Hegelian roots, devastation for Rose implies work, endurance, and maintenance. Thus, the exploration of any politics worth the name involves the constitution of negotiable boundaries. In such a politics the political task characteristically consists in the recognition of and discernment concerning tangible edges and limits when they appear. It will consist in thinking through ("by means of" and "beyond") the tensions of our activity with others, while resisting the attractions of non-tensive forms of reconciliation, what Rose called the "holy" and Rowan Williams called "peace beyond time." Indeed, Williams argued, "Any imaginable claim for such a state will in practice be a commendation of some sort of political totalism."¹² For Rose, "Neither politics nor reason unifies or 'totalizes': they arise out of diremption, out of the diversity of peoples who come together under the aporetic law of the city, and who know that their law is different from the law of other cities."¹³ That kind of politics will be corrigible, revisable, and broken. The people who engage in

---

9. Rowan Williams, "Between Politics and Metaphysics: Reflections in the Wake of Gillian Rose," *Modern Theology* 11:1 (January 1995): 12-13.

10. In "Meaning After Babble," Yoder worked through a dynamic to the one Rose diagnosed in postmodern theopolitics. See Yoder, "Meaning After Babble: With Jeffrey Stout Beyond Relativism," *Journal of Religious Ethics* 24:1 (Spring 1996): 125-39, esp. pp. 128-29.

11. Rose, *Mourning Becomes the Law*, 9-10.

12. Williams, "Between Politics and Metaphysics," 13.

13. Rose, *Judaism and Modernity*, 50.

such a politics will make mistakes and will expect to make mistakes; but even more important, such a politics will depend on making mistakes. "Here," Rose said, "is the dubious angel — hybrid of hubris and humanity — who makes mistakes, for whom things go wrong, who constantly discovers its own faults and failings, yet who still persists in the pain of staking itself, with the courage to initiate action and the commitment to go on and on, learning from those mistakes and risking new ventures."[14]

I have read Yoder's ecclesiological resistance to structural dualisms, or to handles on history and various idioms of control, as a way to combat bringing difficulty to certainty. Yoder's ecclesiology is an attempt to envision ethics as necessarily involving corrigible institutions, and Rose's political imagination resonates powerfully with this. Yet the dualism with which I opened these chapters remained intact for Rose: difficulty or holiness. For her, the edge between the two is not habitable. But Yoder's church, through foregrounding social processes like open meeting, forgiveness, and economic sharing *as sacramental*, proves more difficult than Rose's politics: not difficulty or holiness, but holiness as difficulty. Had Yoder read Rose, he would undoubtedly have agreed with her commitment to moving past a notion of "[e]xceptional, edgeless love" that "effaces the risk of relation," that "commands the complete unveiling of the eyes, the transparency of the body," and "denies that there is no love without power; that we are at the mercy of others and that we have others in our mercy."[15] He would have shared Rose's interest in pursuing institutions and practices that reflect "a metaphysic in which difference is *neither* (at any moment) final, a matter of mutual exclusion, *nor* simply reducible, a matter of misperception to be resolved by either a return to the same or a cancellation of one term before the Other."[16] He would have respected the modesty with which she acknowledged that "to grow in love-ability is to accept the boundaries of oneself and others, while remaining vulnerable, woundable, around the bounds. Acknowledgment of conditionality is the only unconditionality of human love."[17]

---

14. Rose, *Judaism and Modernity*, 10.
15. Rose, *Love's Work*, 98.
16. Williams, "Between Politics and Metaphysics," 18. I think this conclusion has to be drawn, even though Yoder was uncomfortable with the term "metaphysics" — largely, however, because he thought the word was often deployed ideologically to coerce consent to a set of presuppositions about the way the world is without having to make those presuppositions vulnerable to one's interlocutor.
17. Rose, *Love's Work*, 98.

In all of this, Yoder and Rose shared an orientation toward the search for certainty in time. For both, the desire for certainty was homologous to the desire to regulate the moral, political, or epistemological landscape, which is what Yoder's "evangelically revisionist" assumptions about history and practices of patience were meant to guard against. But where Rose primarily addressed the brokenness of our engagements with others as an ancient predicament, a sign of our oldness, Yoder also saw brokenness as the occasion for reconciliation and therefore as the sign of promise and newness. That is what he meant in calling the creation of a community of followers of Jesus a "pulpit": "Just being, just being there as an unprecedented social phenomenon in which persons from two contrasting, even conflicting histories rejoice in their being reconciled, is the necessary but also sufficient condition of being able to invite the rest of the world into the new history."[18] The question that I do not know how to answer is whether such a community can recognize not only its capacity for error but also its dependence on continuing to encounter new brokenness, especially when the potential for being wrong and offending the other arises in connection with borders that have a tangible and immediate character, that demand a decisive yes or an equally decisive no.

It is certainly the case that quite close to the heart of Yoder's concern to cultivate practices of patience is the recognition of fallibility and even peccability as "providential occasions" to learn to encounter and work through the "violence" that is involved in the misrecognition of our relations with others and with ourselves.[19] And this is a long way toward a wisdom, as Rose said, that "works with equivocation." Yet, for Yoder there is equally a sense in which any affirmation of the equivocal, historical, and contingent — of brokenness as *both* painful *and* the potential for newness — is itself the outworking of an unequivocal proclamation, namely, that "the Lamb who was slain is worthy to receive power." That, in a word, is what it means to see history doxologically, and it is a proclamation capaciously open to abuse. This Lamb's wounds sound like wounds we could use. Well, we could: there is no way to escape confrontation with the fact that the very practices of patience and vision of history that cultivate the

---

18. Yoder, *For the Nations: Essays Public and Evangelical* (Grand Rapids: Eerdmans, 1997), 41. One way to read Rose's *Paradiso* (London: Menard Press, 1999) is as her deepening recognition that brokenness is also an occasion for newness.

19. Cf. Coles, "The Wild Patience of John Howard Yoder: 'Outsiders' and the 'Otherness of the Church,'" *Modern Theology* 18:3 (July 2002): 316; Yoder, "Meaning After Babble," 135; Williams, "Between Politics and Metaphysics," esp. 9.

Conclusion

difficulty of relation with the other are generated by a confidence in a proclamation that we do not have to accept. And yet, if Rowan Williams is correct that "the substance of the gospel has to do with God's giving up possession or control — in Paul's language, the Father giving up or giving over the Son to the cross, or Christ giving up his 'wealth,' security, life for the sake of human beings," then Yoder's doxological vision of history is bound into that same mystery of the gospel as promise: praise is inescapably mixed with the fact that the other need not respond to the proclamation I bring. This, too, is working very close to the heart of the gospel, to what the apostle Paul identified in another place as "a scandal to Jews and foolishness to the Greeks."[20]

---

20. Williams, *On Christian Theology*, 257.

Bibliography

Abrams, M. H., ed. *The Norton Anthology of English Literature.* 6th ed. Vol. 1. New York: W. W. Norton & Co., 1993.
Alison, James. *Raising Abel: The Recovery of the Eschatological Imagination.* New York: Crossroad Herder, 1996.
Aristotle. *Nicomachean Ethics.* Trans. Martin Ostwald. Upper Saddle River, NJ: Prentice Hall, 1999.
Ayres, Lewis. *Nicaea and Its Legacy: An Approach to Fourth-Century Trinitarian Theology.* Oxford: Oxford University Press, 2004.
Ayres, Lewis, and Gareth Jones, eds. *Christian Origins: Theology, Rhetoric, and Community.* New York: Routledge, 1998.
Bainton, Roland. *Christian Attitudes to War and Peace.* Nashville: Abingdon, 1960.
Balthasar, Hans Urs von. *Theologie der Geschichte: ein Grundriss.* 2 Aufl. Einsiedeln: Johannes Verlag, 1950.
———. *A Theology of History.* New York: Sheed and Ward, 1963.
Barnes, Michel R., and Daniel H. Williams, eds. *Arianism after Arius: Essays on the Development of the Fourth Century Trinitarian Conflicts.* Edinburgh: T&T Clark, 1993.
Barnes, T. D. *Constantine and Eusebius.* Cambridge, MA: Harvard University Press, 1981.
Barth, Karl. *The Church Dogmatics.* Vol. 3, Pt. 4. Ed. G. W. Bromiley and T. F. Torrance. Edinburgh: T&T Clark, 1961.
———. *The Church Dogmatics.* Vol. 4, Pt. 1. Ed. G. W. Bromiley and T. F. Torrance. Edinburgh: T&T Clark, 1954.
———. *The Humanity of God.* Richmond: John Knox Press, 1960.
Bartholomew, Craig, Jonathan Chaplin, Robert Song, and Al Wolters, eds. *A Royal Priesthood? The Use of the Bible Ethically and Politically: A Dialogue with Oliver O'Donovan.* The Scripture and Hermeneutics Series. Vol. 3. Grand Rapids: Zondervan, 2002.

Baumgartner, Walter. *Kennen Amos und Hosea eine Heils-eschatologie?* Zürich: A. Schaufelberger, 1953.

Begbie, Jeremy. *Voicing Creation's Praise.* Edinburgh: T&T Clark, 1991.

Behr, John. *The Way to Nicaea: The Formation of Christian Theology.* Vol. 1. Crestwood, NY: SVS Press, 2001.

Beiner, Ronald, and William James Booth, eds. *Kant and Political Philosophy: The Contemporary Legacy.* New Haven: Yale University Press, 1993.

Benjamin, Walter. *Illuminations: Essays and Reflections.* Ed. Hannah Arendt. New York: Schocken, 1968.

Berkhof, Hendrik. *Christ the Meaning of History.* Trans. Lambertus Buurman. London: SCM: 1966.

―――. *Die Theologie des Eusebius von Caesarea.* Amsterdam: Uitgeversmaatschappij Holland, 1939.

―――. *Kirche und Kaiser: Eine Untersuchung der Entstehung der byzantinischen und der theokratischen Staatsauffassung im vierten Jahrhundert.* Trans. Gottfried W. Locher. Zürich: Evangelischer Verlag, 1947.

Berry, Wendell. *Sex, Economy, Freedom and Community.* New York: Pantheon Books, 1992.

Beskow, Per. *Rex Gloriae: The Kingship of Christ in the Early Church.* Trans. Eric J. Sharp. Uppsala: Almqvist and Wiksells, 1962.

Bodenstein, Walter. *Neige des Historismus: Ernst Troeltschs Entwicklungsgang.* Gütersloh: Gerd Mohn, 1959.

The Book of Common Prayer. New York: Church Hymnal Corporation, 1979.

Bosse, Hans. *Marx-Weber-Troeltsch: Religionssoziologie und marxistische Ideologiekritik.* München: Christus Kaiser Verlag, 1970.

Braght, Thieleman J. van. *The Bloody Theater or Martyrs' Mirror of the Defenseless Christians Who Baptized Only Upon Confession of Faith, and Who Suffered and Died for the Testimony of Jesus, Their Saviour, From the Time of Christ to the Year A.D. 1660.* Trans. J. F. Sohm. Scottdale: Herald Press, 1938.

Brunner, Emil. *The Mediator: A Study of the Central Doctrine of the Christian Faith.* Philadelphia: Westminster, 1947.

―――. *The Theology of Crisis.* New York: Charles Scribner's Sons, 1929.

Bultmann, Rudolf. *History and Eschatology: The Gifford Lectures, 1955.* Edinburgh: Edinburgh University Press, 1957.

Burckhardt, Jakob. *The Age of Constantine the Great.* Trans. Moses Hadas. New York: Pantheon Books, 1949.

Cadoux, C. J. *The Early Church and the World.* Edinburgh: T&T Clark, 1925.

Carter, Craig A. *The Politics of the Cross: The Theology and Social Ethics of John Howard Yoder.* Grand Rapids: Brazos, 2001.

Cavell, Stanley. *The Claim of Reason: Wittgenstein, Skepticism, Morality and Tragedy.* Oxford: Clarendon, 1979.

Bibliography

Chakrabarty, Dipesh. *Provincializing Europe: Postcolonial Thought and Historical Difference*. Princeton: Princeton University Press, 2000.

Chapman, Mark D. *Ernst Troeltsch and Liberal Theology: Religion and Cultural Synthesis in Wilhelmine Germany*. Oxford: Oxford University Press, 2001.

Chestnut, Glenn F. *The First Christian Histories: Eusebius, Socrates, Sozomen, Theodoret and Evagrius*. Théologie Historique, vol. 46. Paris: Éditions Beauchesne, 1977.

Coakley, Sarah. *Christ without Absolutes: A Study of the Christology of Ernst Troeltsch*. Oxford: Clarendon, 1988.

Coles, Romand. *Rethinking Generosity: Critical Theory and the Politics of Caritas*. Ithaca, NY: Cornell University Press, 1997.

———. "The Wild Patience of John Howard Yoder: 'Outsiders' and the 'Otherness of the Church.'" *Modern Theology* 18:3 (July 2002): 305-31.

Cullmann, Oscar. *Christus und die Zeit. Die urchristliche Zeit- und Geschichtsauffassung*. Zollikon-Zürich: Evangelischer verlag a.g., 1946.

———. *Christ and Time: The Primitive Christian Conception of Time and History*. Philadelphia: Westminster, 1950.

Daniélou, Jean. *Essai sur le Mystère de l'Histoire*. Paris: Editions du Seuil, 1953.

———. *The Lord of History: Reflections on the Inner Meanings of History*. Trans. Nigel Abercrombie. London: Longmans, Green, 1958.

Derrida, Jacques. *Archive Fever: A Freudian Impression*. Trans. Eric Prenowitz. Chicago: University of Chicago Press, 1996.

———. *The Gift of Death*. Trans. David Willis. Chicago: University of Chicago Press, 1995.

Digeser, Elizabeth Depalma. *The Making of a Christian Empire: Lactantius and Rome*. Ithaca, NY: Cornell University Press, 2000.

Dodaro, Robert. "Eloquent Lies, Just Wars and the Politics of Persuasion: Reading Augustine's *City of God* in a 'Postmodern' World." *Augustinian Studies* 25 (1994): 77-138.

Drake, H. A. *Constantine and the Bishops: The Politics of Intolerance*. Baltimore: Johns Hopkins University Press, 2000.

Drescher, Hans-Georg. *Ernst Troeltsch: His Life and Work*. Minneapolis: Fortress, 1993.

Eichrodt, Walther. *Der Herr der Geschichte. Jesaja 12-23 und 28-39*. Stuttgart: Calwer Verlag, 1967.

Eller, David B., ed. *From Age to Age: Historians and the Modern Church: A Festschrift for Donald F. Durnbaugh*. Brethren Life and Thought 43:3, 4 (Summer and Fall 1997).

Farrow, Douglas. *Ascension and Ecclesia: On the Significance of the Doctrine of the Ascension for Ecclesiology and Christian Cosmology*. Grand Rapids: Eerdmans, 1999.

Fields, Lester R., Jr. *Liberty, Dominion, and the Two Swords: On the Origins of West-*

ern Political Theology (180-398). Notre Dame: University of Notre Dame Press, 1998.
Foucault, Michel. *Discipline and Punish: The Birth of the Prison.* New York: Vintage, 1979.
———. *The Order of Things: An Archaeology of the Human Sciences.* New York: Random House, 1970.
Fukuyama, Francis. *The End of History and the Last Man.* New York: Free Press, 1992.
Gadamer, Hans-Georg. *Truth and Method.* 2nd rev. ed. New York: Continuum, 1997.
Gallay, P., ed. *Grégoire de Nazianze. Lettres théologiques.* Sources chrétiennes 208. Paris: Cerf, 1974.
Grant, George. *Time as History.* Toronto: Canadian Broadcasting Corp., 1969.
Greer, Rowan A. *The Captain of Our Salvation: A Study in the Patristic Exegesis of Hebrews.* Beiträge zur Geschichte der biblischen Exegese. 15. Bd. Hrsg. Oscar Cullmann, et al. Tübingen: J. C. B. Mohr (Paul Siebeck), 1973.
Gregory of Nyssa. *De hominis opificio.* In *Patrologia graeca (PG).* Vol. 44: 123-257. Ed. J.-P. Migne. Paris: Migne, 1863.
———. *From Glory to Glory: Texts from Gregory of Nyssa's Mystical Writings.* Trans. and ed. Herbert Musurillo. New York: Scribner, 1961.
Gunton, Colin E., ed. *Trinity, Time and Church: A Response to the Theology of Robert W. Jenson.* Grand Rapids: Eerdmans, 2000.
Hanson, R. P. C. *The Search for the Christian Doctrine of God: The Arian Controversy 381-381.* Edinburgh: T&T Clark, 1988.
Hardt, Michael, and Antonio Negri. *Empire.* Cambridge, MA: Harvard University Press, 2000.
Harvey, Van A. *The Historian and the Believer: The Morality of Historical Knowledge and Christian Belief.* New York: Macmillan, 1966.
———. *The Historian and the Believer: The Morality of Historical Knowledge and Christian Belief.* 2nd ed. Urbana and Chicago: University of Illinois Press, 1996.
Hauerwas, Stanley. *The Hauerwas Reader.* Ed. John Berkman and Michael Cartwright. Durham, NC: Duke University Press, 2001.
Hauerwas, Stanley, and James Fodor. "Remaining in Babylon: Oliver O'Donovan's Defense of Christendom." *Studies in Christian Ethics* 11:2 (1998): 30-55.
Hauerwas, Stanley, Chris Huebner, Harry Huebner, and Mark T. Nation. *The Wisdom of the Cross: Essays in Honor of John Howard Yoder.* Grand Rapids: Eerdmans, 1999.
Hauerwas, Stanley, and Charles Pinches. *Christians Among the Virtues: Theological Conversations with Ancient and Modern Ethics.* Notre Dame: University of Notre Dame Press, 1997.

Hawkley, Louise, and James C. Juhnke, eds. *Nonviolent America: History through the Eyes of Peace.* Newton, KS: Mennonite Press, 1993.

Hegel, G. W. F. *The Phenomenology of Spirit.* Trans. A. V. Miller. New York: Oxford University Press, 1977.

Hodgson, Peter C. *God in History: Shapes of Freedom.* Nashville: Abingdon, 1989.

Hollerich, Michael J. *Eusebius of Caesarea's Commentary on Isaiah: Christian Exegesis in the Age of Constantine.* Oxford: Clarendon Press, 1999.

Holmes, Arthur. *War and Christian Ethics.* Grand Rapids: Baker, 1975.

Hornus, Jean-Michel. *It Is Not Lawful for Me to Fight: Early Christian Attitudes Toward War, Violence and the State.* Rev. ed. Trans. Alan Kreider and Oliver Coburn. Scottdale, PA: Herald Press, 1980.

Huebner, Chris K. "Unhandling History: Anti-Theory, Ethics and the Practice of Witness." Ph.D. diss., Duke University, 2001.

Hutterian Brethren, trans. *Das große Geschichtbuch der Hutterischen Brüder.* Rifton, NY: Plough, 1987.

Jaspers, Karl. *The Origin and Goal of History.* London: Routledge and Kegan Paul, 1953.

Jenson, Robert W. *Systematic Theology.* Vol. 1: *The Triune God.* New York: Oxford University Press, 1996.

———. *Systematic Theology.* Vol. 2: *The Works of God.* New York: Oxford University Press, 1999.

Jones, L. Gregory, and Stephen Fowl. *Rethinking Metaphysics.* Oxford: Blackwell, 1995.

Kant, Immanuel. *Critique of Pure Reason.* Ed. and trans. Paul Guyer and Allen W. Wood. Cambridge: Cambridge University Press, 1997.

———. *Critique of Practical Reason.* Trans. and ed. Mary Gregor. Cambridge: Cambridge University Press, 1997.

———. *Religion within the Boundaries of Mere Reason and Other Writings.* Ed. Allen W. Wood and George di Giovanni. Cambridge: Cambridge University Press, 1998.

Käsemann, Ernst. *The Wandering People of God: An Investigation of the Letter to the Hebrews.* Trans. Roy A. Harrisville and Irving L. Sandberg. Minneapolis: Augsburg, 1984.

Kearney, Richard, and Mark Dooley, eds. *Questioning Ethics: Contemporary Debates in Philosophy.* London: Routledge, 1999.

Kenneson, Philip D. *Beyond Sectarianism: Re-imagining Church and World.* Harrisburg, PA: Trinity Press International, 1999.

Kermode, Frank. *The Genesis of Secrecy: On the Interpretation of Narrative.* Cambridge, MA: Harvard University Press, 1979.

Kreider, Alan, ed. *The Origins of Christendom in the West.* Edinburgh: T&T Clark, 2001.

Kroeker, Travis. "Why O'Donovan's Christendom Is Not Constantinian and

Yoder's Voluntariety Is Not Hobbesian: A Debate in Theological Ethics Redefined." *Annual of the Society of Christian Ethics* 20 (2000): 41-64.

Levinas, Emmanuel. *Otherwise Than Being or Beyond Essence*. Trans. Alphonso Lingis. Boston: Martinus Nijhoff, 1981.

Lieu, Samuel N. C., and Dominic Montserrat, eds. *Constantine: History, Historiography and Legend*. New York: Routledge, 1998.

Lindars, Barnabas, SSF. *The Theology of the Letter to the Hebrews*. Cambridge: Cambridge University Press, 1991.

Long, D. Stephen. *The Goodness of God: Theology, the Church, and Social Order*. Grand Rapids: Brazos Press, 2001.

Lowe, Lisa, and David Lloyd, eds. *The Politics of Culture in the Shadow of Capital*. Durham: Duke University Press, 1997.

Luibhéid, Colm. *The Council of Nicaea*. Galway, Ireland: Galway University Press, 1982.

———. *Eusebius of Caesarea and the Arian Crisis*. Dublin: Irish Academic Press, 1981.

Lyotard, J.-F. *The Postmodern Condition: A Report on Knowledge*. Trans. Geoffrey Bennington and Brian Massumi. Minneapolis: University of Minnesota Press, 1984.

MacIntosh, Mark A. *Mystical Theology: The Integrity of Spirituality and Theology*. Malden, MA: Blackwell, 1998.

MacIntyre, Alasdair. *After Virtue: A Study in Moral Theory*. 2nd ed. Notre Dame: University of Notre Dame Press, 1984.

———. *Dependent Rational Animals: Why Human Beings Need the Virtues*. Chicago and La Salle, IL: Open Court Press, 1999.

———. *First Principles, Final Ends and Contemporary Philosophical Issues*. Milwaukee: Marquette University Press, 1990.

———. *Whose Justice? Which Rationality?* Notre Dame: University of Notre Dame Press, 1988.

MacMullen, Ramsey. *Christianizing the Roman Empire (A.D. 100-400)*. New Haven: Yale University Press, 1984.

Malpas, Jeff, Ulrich Arnswald, and Jens Kertscher, eds. *Gadamer's Century: Essays in Honor of Hans-Georg Gadamer*. Cambridge, MA: MIT Press, 2002.

Marion, Jean-Luc Marion. "Esquisse d'un Concept Phénoménologique du Don." *Archivo di Filosofia* 62:1-3 (1994): 75-94.

———. *Étant donné: Essai d'une phénoménologie de la donation*. Paris: Presses Universitaires de France, 1997.

———. *Reduction and Givenness: Investigations of Husserl, Heidegger and Phenomenology*. Trans. Thomas A. Carlson. Evanston, IL: Northwestern University Press, 2002.

Marrin, Albert. *War and the Christian Conscience: From Augustine to Martin Luther King, Jr.* Chicago: Regnery, 1971.

Bibliography

Martyn, J. Louis. *History and Theology in the Fourth Gospel.* 3rd ed. Louisville: Westminster/John Knox Press, 2003.
McCabe, Herbert. *What Is Ethics All About?* Washington/Cleveland: Corpus, 1968.
McCormack, Bruce L. *Karl Barth's Critically Realistic Dialectical Theology: Its Genesis and Development 1909-1936.* Oxford: Clarendon, 1995.
Milbank, John. "Enclaves, or Where Is the Church?" *New Blackfriars* 73:861 (June 1992): 341-52.
———. "Socialism of the Gift, Socialism of Grace." *New Blackfriars* 77:910 (1996): 532-48.
———. "Stones of Sacrifice." *Modern Theology* 12:1 (January 1996): 27-56.
———. *Theology and Social Theory: Beyond Secular Reason.* Oxford: Blackwell, 1990.
———. *The Word Made Strange: Theology, Language, Culture.* Oxford: Blackwell, 1996.
Moore, Sebastian. *The Crucified Jesus Is No Stranger.* Minneapolis: Seabury Press, 1977.
———. *The Fire and the Rose Are One.* New York: Seabury Press, 1980.
Nellas, Panayiotis. *Deification in Christ: Orthodox Perspectives on the Nature of the Human Person.* Trans. Norman Russell. Crestwood, NY: St. Vladimir's Seminary Press, 1997.
Newman, John Henry. *The Arians of the Fourth Century.* Notre Dame: University of Notre Dame Press, 2001.
Niebuhr, H. Richard. *Christ and Culture.* New York: Harper and Row, 1951.
———. "Ernst Troeltsch's Philosophy of Religion." Ph.D. diss., Yale University, 1924.
Nietzsche, Friedrich. *Thus Spoke Zarathustra.* Trans. Walter Kaufmann. New York: Penguin, 1978.
O'Donovan, Oliver. *The Desire of the Nations: Rediscovering the Roots of Political Theology.* Cambridge: Cambridge University Press, 1996.
———. "The Concept of Publicity." *Studies in Christian Ethics* 13:1 (2000): 18-32.
———. "Deliberation, History and Reading: A Response to Schweiker and Wolterstorff." *Scottish Journal of Theology* 54:1 (2001): 127-44.
———. "The Political Thought of the Book of Revelation." *Tyndale Bulletin* 37 (1986): 61-94.
———. *Resurrection and Moral Order: An Outline for Evangelical Ethics.* Grand Rapids: Eerdmans, 1986.
Origen. *In Exodum Homilia.* Die griechischen christlichen Schriftsteller der ersten drei Jahrhunderte. 6. Bd. Leipzig: J. C. Hinrichs, 1920.
Pannenberg, Wolfhart. *Ethics.* Trans. Keith Crim. Philadelphia: Westminster, 1981.
Patocka, Jan. *Essais hérétiques sur la philosophie de l'histoire.* Trans. E. Abrams. Paris: Verdier, 1981.
Peterson, Erik. *Der Monotheismus als politisches Problem: Ein Beitrag zur Geschich-

te der politischen Theologie im Imperium Romanum. Leipzig: Jakob Hegner, 1935.

Plant, Raymond. *Politics, Theology and History.* Cambridge: Cambridge University Press, 2001.

Ramsey, Paul. *Basic Christian Ethics.* New York: Charles Scribner's Sons, 1950.

———. *Speak Up for Just War or Pacifism: A Critique of the United Methodist Bishops' Pastoral Letter "In Defense of Creation: The Nuclear Crisis and a Just Peace."* University Park: Pennsylvania State University Press, 1988.

Rasmusson, Arne. *The Church as Polis: From Political Theology to Theological Politics as Exemplified by Jürgen Moltmann and Stanley Hauerwas.* Notre Dame: University of Notre Dame Press, 1995.

Reimer, James A. *Mennonites and Classical Theology: Dogmatic Foundations for Christian Ethics.* Kitchener, ON: Pandora Press, 2001.

Reist, Benjamin A. *Toward a Theology of Involvement: The Thought of Ernst Troeltsch.* Philadelphia: Westminster, 1966.

Reno, R. R. *Redemptive Change: Atonement and the Christian Cure of the Soul.* Harrisburg: Trinity Press International, 2002.

Ricoeur, Paul. *Paul Ricoeur: The Hermeneutics of Action.* Ed. Richard Kearney. London: Sage Publications, 1996.

Rieff, Philip. *The Triumph of the Therapeutic: Uses of Faith After Freud.* New York: Harper & Row, 1966.

Ringer, Fritz K. *The Decline of the German Mandarins: The German Academic Community, 1890-1933.* Hanover, NH: Wesleyan University Press, 1990.

Robinson, Marilynne. *Housekeeping.* New York: Farrar, Strauss & Giroux, 1980.

Rorty, Richard. *Philosophy and the Mirror of Nature.* Princeton: Princeton University Press, 1979.

Rose, Gillian. *The Broken Middle: Out of Our Ancient Society.* Oxford: Blackwell, 1992.

———. *Dialectic of Nihilism: Post-Structuralism and Law.* Oxford: Basil Blackwell, 1984.

———. *Hegel: Contra Sociology.* London: Athlone Press, 1981.

———. *Judaism and Modernity: Philosophical Essays.* Oxford: Blackwell, 1993.

———. *Mourning Becomes the Law: Philosophy and Representation.* Cambridge: Cambridge University Press, 1996.

———. *Paradiso.* London: Menard Press, 1999.

Schillebeeckx, Edward. *Church: The Human Story of God.* Trans. John Bowden. New York: Crossroad, 1990.

Scott, Peter, and William Cavanaugh, eds. *The Blackwell Companion to Political Theology.* Oxford: Blackwell, 2003.

Sebald, W. G. *On the Natural History of Destruction.* Trans. Anathea Bell. New York: Random House, 2003.

Bibliography

Shanks, Andrew. *Hegel's Political Theology*. Cambridge: Cambridge University Press, 1991.

Sider, J. Alexander. "To See History Doxologically: Miroslav Volf's and John Howard Yoder's Competing Conceptions of the Place of Memory in the Politics of Forgiveness." International Historic Peace Church Consultation, "Theology and Culture: Peacemaking in a Globalized World," Bienenberg Seminary, Switzerland.

Stassen, Glen, Diane Yeager, and John Howard Yoder. *Authentic Transformation: A New Vision of Christ and Culture*. Nashville: Abingdon Press, 1996.

Stern, Fritz. *The Politics of Cultural Despair: A Study in the Rise of the Germanic Ideology*. Berkeley: University of California Press, 1961.

Strauss, Leo. *Jewish Philosophy and the Crisis of Modernity: Essays and Lectures in Modern Jewish Thought*. Albany: SUNY Press, 1997.

Thompson, John W. *The Beginnings of Christian Philosophy: The Epistle to the Hebrews*. Catholic Biblical Quarterly Monograph Series, vol. 13. Washington, DC: Catholic Biblical Association of America, 1982.

Troeltsch, Ernst. *Die Absolutheit des Christentums und die Religionsgeschichte (1902/1912): mit den Thesen von 1901 und den handschriftlichen Zusätzen. Kritische Gesamtausgabe*. Bd. 5. Hrsg. Trutz Rendtorff und Stefan Pauler. Berlin: De Gruyter, 1998.

———. *The Absoluteness of Christianity and the History of Religions*. Trans. David Reid. Atlanta: John Knox Press, 1971.

———. *The Christian Faith*. Ed. Gertrud von le Fort. Trans. Garrett E. Paul. Minneapolis: Fortress, 1991.

———. *Christian Thought: Its History and Application*. Ed. Baron F. von Hügel. London: University of London Press, 1923.

———. *Der Historismus und seine Überwindung. Fünf Vorträge von Ernst Troeltsch*. Berlin: Rolf Heise, 1924.

———. *Ernst Troeltsch: Writings on Theology and Religion*. Ed. Robert Morgan and Michael Pye. Atlanta: John Knox Press, 1977.

———. "Eschatologie: IV Dogmatisch." *Religion in Geschichte und Gegenwart*. Tübingen: J. C. B. Mohr, 1910.

———. *Gesammelte Schriften*. Bd. 2: *Zur religiösen Lage, Religionsphilosophie und Ethik*. Tübingen: J. C. B. Mohr (Paul Siebeck), 1913.

———. *Gesammelte Schriften*. Bd. 3: *Der Historismus und seine Probleme. Erstes Buch: Das logische Problem der Geschichtsphilosophie*. Tübingen: J. C. B. Mohr, 1922.

———. *Religion in History*. Trans. and ed. James Luther Adams and Walter F. Bense. Minneapolis: Fortress, 1991.

———. *The Social Teaching of the Christian Churches*. 2 vols. Trans. Olive Wyon. Louisville: Westminster/John Knox Press, 1992.

Turner, Denys. *The Darkness of God: Negativity in Christian Mysticism.* New York: Cambridge University Press, 1995.
Vaihinger, Hans, and Bruno Bauch, eds. *Zu Kants Gedächtnis. Zwölf Festgaben zu seinem 100-jährigen Todestage.* Berlin: Reuther & Reichard, 1904.
Volf, Miroslav. *Exclusion and Embrace: A Theological Exploration of Identity, Otherness, and Reconciliation.* Nashville: Abingdon Press, 1996.
Wadell, Paul, CP. "Redeeming the Things We Can Never Undo: The Role of Forgiveness in Anne Tyler's *Saint Maybe*." *New Theology Review: An American Catholic Journal for Ministry* 8:2 (May 1995): 34-48.
Ward, Graham. *The Blackwell Companion to Postmodern Theology.* Oxford: Blackwell, 2001.
Weaver, J. Denny. *The Nonviolent Atonement.* Grand Rapids: Eerdmans, 2001.
Weber, Max. *The Protestant Ethic and the Spirit of Capitalism.* Trans. Talcott Parsons. New York: Charles Scribner's Sons, 1958.
Webster, John. *Word and Church: Essays in Christian Dogmatics.* Edinburgh: T&T Clark, 2001.
Wiles, Maurice, and Mark Santer, eds. *Documents in Early Christian Thought.* New York: Cambridge University Press, 1975.
Williams, Daniel H. *Retrieving the Tradition and Renewing Evangelicalism: A Primer for Suspicious Protestants.* Grand Rapids: Eerdmans, 1999.
Williams, George Huntston. "Christology and Church-State Relations in the Fourth Century." *Church History* 20:3 (September 1951): 3-33.
———. "Christology and Church-State Relations in the Fourth Century." *Church History* 20:4 (December 1951): 3-26.
Williams, Janet. "Judging Judgment: An Apophatic Approach." *Theology Today* 58:4 (January 2002): 541-53.
Williams, Rowan. *Arius: Heresy and Tradition.* Rev. ed. Grand Rapids: Eerdmans, 2001.
———. "Between Politics and Metaphysics: Reflections in the Wake of Gillian Rose." *Modern Theology* 11:1 (January 1995): 3-22.
———. *Lost Icons: Reflections on Cultural Bereavement.* Edinburgh: T&T Clark, 2000.
———. *On Christian Theology.* Oxford: Blackwell, 2000.
———. *A Ray of Darkness: Sermons and Reflections.* Boston: Cowley, 1995.
———. *Resurrection: Interpreting the Easter Gospel.* Harrisburg, PA: Morehouse Publishing, 1994.
———. *The Truce of God.* New York: Pilgrim Press, 1983.
———. *The Wound of Knowledge: Christian Spirituality from the New Testament to Luther and St. John of the Cross.* London: Darton, Longman and Todd, 1979.
Wittgenstein, Ludwig. *Philosophical Investigations.* Oxford: Blackwell, 1997.
Yasukata, Toshimasa. *Ernst Troeltsch: Systematic Theologian of Radical Historicality.* Atlanta: Scholars Press, 1986.

Bibliography

Yoder, John Howard. *Christian Attitudes to War, Peace and Revolution: A Companion to Bainton.* Elkhart, IN: Goshen Biblical Seminary, 1983.
———. *The Christian Witness to the State.* Newton, KS: Faith and Life Press, 1964.
———. *For the Nations: Essays Public and Evangelical.* Grand Rapids: Eerdmans, 1997.
———. "Historiography as a Ministry to Renewal." *Brethren Life and Thought* 43 (1997): 216-28.
———. "Meaning After Babble: With Jeffrey Stout Beyond Relativism." *Journal of Religious Ethics* 24:1 (Spring 1996): 125-39.
———. *The Original Revolution: Essays on Christian Pacifism.* Scottdale: Herald Press, 1971.
———. *The Politics of Jesus: Vicit Agnus Noster.* 2nd ed. Grand Rapids: Eerdmans, 1995.
———. *The Priestly Kingdom: Social Ethics as Gospel.* Notre Dame: University of Notre Dame Press, 1984.
———. *Preface to Theology: Christology and Theological Method.* Grand Rapids: Brazos Press, 2002.
———. "Reply." To "Christianity and Democracy, a Statement of the Institute on Religion and Democracy," by Richard John Neuhaus. *Center Journal* 1:3 (Summer 1982): 83-88.
———. *The Royal Priesthood: Essays Ecclesiological and Ecumenical.* Ed. Michael G. Cartwright. Grand Rapids: Eerdmans, 1994.
———. *To Hear the Word.* Eugene, OR: Wipf and Stock, 2001.
Žižek, Slavoj. *Tarrying with the Negative: Kant, Hegel, and the Critique of Ideology.* Durham: Duke University Press, 1993.

Index

Alison, James, 32
Anabaptist, 12-13, 57, 125
Anselm (of Canterbury), 19
Antonine Constitution, 110-12
Aristotle, 153, 169, 171-73
Athens, 203
Atonement, 18-19
Augustine (of Hippo), 2, 10-11, 18, 31, 39, 102, 108, 113, 155

Balthasar, Hans Urs von, 57, 58, 95, 97
Barnes, T. D., 99, 114, 119
Barth, Karl, 20, 48, 57-61, 65, 85, 89, 114
Bartholomew, Craig, 30
Baumgartner, Walter, 57-58
Bender, Harold S., 13, 57, 101, 180
Benjamin, Walter, 97, 98, 121, 127
Berkhof, Hendrik, 58, 115
Berry, Wendell, 4, 161, 202, 218
Beskow, Per, 115
Bultmann, Rudolf, 20, 58, 65
Burckhardt, Jacob, 105, 106, 113
Burkholder, J. Lawrence, 13

Cartwright, Michael, 48, 50, 103, 137, 164-66, 168-69, 202
Chalcedon: Council of, 119; Chalcedonian Christology, 182
Chapman, Mark D., 61, 77-80, 88
Coles, Romand, 2, 9, 53, 126, 206, 211

Constantine, 14-15, 71, 99, 104-8, 112-15, 117-18, 123, 129, 134
Constantinianism, 14-15, 48, 94, 97, 98-105, 107-9, 111-12, 116, 116, 120-24, 129-31, 163, 198-99, 201
1 Corinthians, 189-90, 192
Creed, the Nicene, 107, 116
Cullmann, Oscar, 57-58
Cyprian (of Carthage), 5-11, 109

Dali, Salvador, 2
Daniélou, Jean, 53, 58
Decius (Emperor of Rome), 110
Digeser, Elizabeth DePalma, 99, 110-11
Deleuze, Gilles, 65, 147
Derrida, Jacques, 80, 183-84, 186
Diocletian (Emperor of Rome), 110-12
Donne, John, 24, 153
Drake, Hal, 99, 106, 123-24
Drescher, Hans-Georg, 65, 66, 76, 81, 85

Ecclesiology, 3, 7-12, 28, 30, 34, 36, 47-49, 52, 61, 67, 96, 98-100, 106-7, 109, 113, 120, 132, 134, 169, 179, 183, 190-91, 195, 196, 198-200, 205, 211
Edict of Milan, 103-4
Eichrodt, Walther, 57-58
Enlightenment, the, 88, 109, 135, 143, 162, 177, 182, 184-86
Eschatology, 20, 28-29, 32, 42-49, 52-53,

INDEX

58, 61, 65, 74, 84, 88-88, 90-91, 94-96, 103, 118, 121, 127, 134, 136-37, 157, 181, 187, 192, 193, 197-200, 202
Eucharist, the, 9, 156, 190-92
Eusebius (of Caesarea), 105, 108, 113-15, 117-18

Foucault, Michel, 108, 111, 120-21, 130, 147

Gadamer, Hans-Georg, 60, 102, 129-31
Galerius (Emperor of Rome), 112-13
Greer, Rowan, 25
Gregory (of Nazianzus), 19, 153, 155-56
Gregory (of Nyssa), 19, 53, 170
Grünewald, Matthias, 2

Habermas, Jürgen, 146
Harnack, Adolf von, 70
Hays, Richard, 31
Hebrews, Letter to the, 21-29, 37, 46-47, 49, 57, 197
Hegel, G. W. F., 37, 75, 81, 143, 185, 202, 204
Heidegger, Martin, 175, 184
Hershberger, Guy F., 13
Hodgson, Peter, 65-66
Hollerich, Michael J., 114
Holocaust, the, 37
Huebner, Chris, 57, 94, 104, 165
Hügel, Friedrich von, 74-75
Hume, David, 81

Jaspers, Karl, 57-58
Jenson, Robert, 49-50, 138
John (of Patmos), 45-46

Kant, Immanuel, 11, 59, 68, 80-81, 88-90, 96, 149, 177, 185-86, 190
Käsemann, Ernst, 25-28
Kroeker, Travis, 48, 163

Leo (the Great), 155
Lessing, Gotthold Ephraim, 80-81, 85, 91-93, 128
Lindars, Barnabas, 22

Lord's Supper, the. *See* Eucharist, the
Luther, Martin, 72, 102
Lyotard, J.-F., 144-47, 154

MacIntyre, Alasdair, 130-31, 136, 163-74, 176-80, 185, 197, 202
Marion, Jean-Luc, 182-84, 186
Martyn, J. Louis, 23
Marx, Karl, 61, 138
Maximus (the Confessor), 1, 6, 182
McCabe, Herbert, 25, 173-74, 180
Mennonite(s), 12-13, 18, 19, 94, 98, 180-81
Milbank, John, 88, 127, 164, 183-94, 197, 200, 203-4
Moberly, Walter, 33
Moltmann, Jürgen, 20
Moore, Sebastian, 2, 172, 176, 194
Moses, 27, 34-35, 108
Mount Sinai, 34-35
Mount Zion, 27
Munus Triplex, the, 19, 40

Nicaea, Council of (325), 105, 107, 114, 116-20, 123, 156
Niebuhr, H. Richard, 13, 66, 141
Nietzsche, Friedrich, 59
Novatian (of Rome), 5-6

O'Donovan, Oliver, 12, 14, 17, 20-21, 29-49, 51-55, 95, 165, 197, 199-200, 209, 212-13, 215
Origen (of Alexandria), 31, 35, 109

Pacifism, 12, 17, 49-50, 94-95, 98, 103, 109, 116, 219
Pannenberg, Wolfhart, 20, 66
Patočka, Jan, 184
Paul, 15, 21, 161-64, 168, 171, 181-83, 187-90, 192-94, 200, 209
Peterson, Erik, 115, 117, 119
Plant, Raymond, 20-21

Ramsey, Paul, 39, 50-51, 110
Rauschenbusch, Walter, 95, 138
Reist, Benjamin, 61

Index

Reno, R. R., 19
Revelation, Book of, 45-46, 135, 137
Ringer, Fritz, 62-63
Robinson, Marilynne, 133
Romans, Letter to the, 161
Rose, Gillian, 1, 60, 75, 202-6, 215-16, 218

Salvation, doctrine of, 2, 7, 12, 15, 17-25, 27-29, 35, 47, 47-49, 51, 54-55, 72, 87, 98, 115, 139, 153-54, 183, 197, 199, 214
Schlabach, Gerald, 104, 124
Schleiermacher, Friedrich, 60, 67, 81
Schweiker, William, 33
Sebald, W. G., 133
Septuagint, the, 22
Shanks, Andrew, 37
Smith, Adam, 172

Taylor, Mark C., 203-4
Tertullian (of Carthage), 9, 109, 111, 112

Theodore (of Mopsuestia), 17-19
Theodosius (Emperor of Rome), 112
Troeltsch, Ernst, 3, 12-14, 21, 57, 58-77, 96, 98, 101, 114, 129, 197-200

Valerian (Emperor of Rome), 110
Volf, Miroslav, 134, 138-54, 157, 197, 199-200

Weaver, J. Denny, 19
Wannenwetsch, Bernd, 55
Weber, Max, 67, 88, 163
Webster, John, 195
Wilhelm II, 61, 114
Williams, D. H., 99, 107, 117
Williams, George Hunston, 115, 117-19
Williams, Janet, 20
Williams, Rowan, 16, 114, 118, 122, 167, 174-76, 180, 196, 205-7
Wolterstorff, Nicholas, 33